BOB TAYLOR AND THE AGRARIAN REVOLT
IN TENNESSEE

Bob Taylor and the Agrarian Revolt in Tennessee

BY

DANIEL MERRITT ROBISON

Assistant Professor of History
State Teachers College
Memphis, Tennessee

Chapel Hill
The University of North Carolina Press
1935

PRINTED IN THE UNITED STATES OF AMERICA BY THE EDWARDS & BROUGHTON
COMPANY, RALEIGH, N. C. BOUND BY L. H. JENKINS, INC., RICHMOND, VA.

PREFACE

ROBERT L. TAYLOR, affectionately known as "Our Bob" to thousands of Tennesseans, has become something of a legendary character in his native state. The personal side of his life has been treated by many of his contemporaries and those qualities which endeared him to so many have been recorded. So well has this been done, in fact, that "Bob" Taylor, popular figure and apostle of "Love, Laughter and Song," has all but obscured Robert L. Taylor, political leader, governor and United States senator. It is the latter Taylor who appears in these pages.

This study grew out of an interest in that unique political campaign, the War of the Roses, in which the brothers, Robert L. Taylor, Democrat, and Alfred A. Taylor, Republican, contested for the governorship of Tennessee. The writer has found that outside the state there is much interest in that campaign. How did it happen that the two major parties chose brothers as opposing candidates for high position? The attempt to answer that question led to a study of political alignments as well as the forces, circumstances and personalities which produced those alignments. In this, facts appeared which seemed to contain more than local or passing interest. The influence of economic and social forces which had their beginnings in frontier days, after-effects of civil war and reconstruction, political traditions coming down from Andrew Jackson, James K. Polk and Andrew Johnson, as well as from other illustrious Tennesseans of their times, all contributed to the peculiar situation which produced the War of the Roses.

Not only was the history of the state involved, but, particularly with reference to the nomination of Robert L. Taylor, there appeared indications of the great agrarian revolt which swept the country during the eighties and nineties of the past century, culminating in the Populist movement and the Bryan campaign of 1896. Through this period of transition from an agricultural to an industrial nation, Robert L. Taylor was an important political figure in his state and did much to shape the course of events in Tennessee. How far he influenced later political history in that state is a question which can be answered definitively only after further study has been made on the period since 1896.

Necessarily, a study of Tennessee politics during any period since 1870 must deal largely with the Democratic party and its activities. That party's dominant place in determining political issues and policies of the state government, rather than a desire to ignore the minority party, may explain the comparatively little space devoted to the Republicans.

The biographers of Robert L. Taylor have devoted little attention to the politics of his time. In response to requests for Taylor's private papers, members of the family replied that they have no knowledge of any. For the facts set forth in the following pages the writer has relied largely upon the newspapers of the period and on the official documents of the state of Tennessee and the *Congressional Record*. Liberal use has been made of materials in the Tennessee State Library, the Vanderbilt University Library, and the Carnegie Library, all at Nashville, and in the Lawson-McGhee Library at Knoxville. Some material from the libraries of the University of Tennessee and the George Peabody College for Teachers was found useful. Those in charge of the following libraries were uniformly courteous and helpful: Cossitt Library and Goodwin Institute Library, both at Memphis, and the public libraries at Johnson City and Greeneville.

In seeking to get the atmosphere and "feel" of Tennessee politics during the period indicated, conversations and interviews were held with many who were active participants or who were personally acquainted with the chief actors. Among the many who have contributed in this way, the following are due especial gratitude and recognition: Frank Avent, assistant to the secretary of state, Nashville, and a member of the legislature during much of the time; the late Andrew Johnson Pat-

terson of Greeneville, grandson of President Andrew Johnson
and personal friend of Robert L. Taylor; Park Marshall,
mayor of Franklin and member of the legislature during a part
of the period under study; C. C. Henderson, veteran newspaper
publisher, political leader, and historian of Murfreesboro;
Major Cy H. Lyle, adjutant of the National Soldiers' Home
at Johnson City, personal friend of Robert L. Taylor and co-
publisher with him of the *Johnson City Comet;* Judge Samuel
Cole Williams, noted Tennessee historian and jurist of Johnson City; Judge John H. DeWitt of the Tennessee Court of
Appeals, president of the Tennessee Historical Society, and a
personal acquaintance of Colonel A. S. Colyar and other important figures of the time; Judge Walter W. Faw, also of the
Tennessee Court of Appeals and personal friend of Robert L.
Taylor; the late W. A. Cathcart of Woodbury, private secretary of the late Congressman W. H. Houston and active in
politics during much of the decade from 1886 to 1896. An
anticipated interview with the venerable ex-Governor Alfred A.
Taylor, brother of Robert L. Taylor and his Republican opponent in the War of the Roses, was frustrated by the untimely
illness and lamented passing of that beloved figure in Tennessee
politics.

I wish to acknowledge a debt of gratitude to Professors Irby
R. Hudson, William C. Binkley, Frank L. Owsley, Carl S.
Driver, and D. F. Fleming, members of the faculty of History
and Political Science in Vanderbilt University. Their patient
scrutiny of content and text, their stimulating suggestions, and
their timely criticisms have proved invaluable. My colleague,
Professor Richmond C. Beatty, has read and criticized portions
of the manuscript. My wife, Dorothy Battenfield Robison, has
given cheerful assistance in the preparations for publication.
Any errors in interpretation or text are my own.

                                                D. M. R.

Memphis, Tennessee
1934

CONTENTS

BOB TAYLOR AND THE AGRARIAN REVOLT
IN TENNESSEE

CHAPTER I

PARTY DIVISIONS FROM JACKSON TO TAYLOR

On January 26, 1875, a young Republican member of the Tennessee legislature rushed from the capitol to the room of his Democratic friend in the old Maxwell House in Nashville and, with the words "Mr. Johnson, you are elected," fainted.[1] The young Republican was Alfred A. Taylor and his Democratic friend was Andrew Johnson, seventeenth President of the United States, and, at that moment, senator-elect from Tennessee. The victory which young Taylor announced had come after a long and bitter fight between three Democratic candidates. Johnson's opponents had been Neill S. Brown, former Whig governor of the state, and William B. Bate, former general in the Confederate army and idol of the secessionist wing of his party. The battle waged between the followers of these three candidates was to continue over a period of twenty years and was to exert a powerful influence on the politics of that state.

It was the irony of fate that, eleven years later, this same young Republican was to be defeated for governor by the identical forces which had elected his friend in 1875, and that at the later date these forces were to be led by his own brother, Robert L. Taylor. The background of this memorable contest of 1886, in which the brothers opposed each other as leaders, respectively, of a united Democracy and a consolidated Republican party, must be found in the influence of personal and factional issues. These were the forces which had dominated in determining the nature of party divisions and alignments in Tennessee during

---

[1] Lloyd Paul Stryker, *Andrew Johnson, A Study in Courage*, p. 807. See also George Fort Milton, *The Age of Hate, Andrew Johnson and the Radicals*, p. 668.

the preceding three-quarters of a century.

Although Tennesseans had adhered to the party of Thomas Jefferson from its formation, they soon divided into factions on local issues and personalities. John Sevier, the first outstanding political leader in the state, was identified with the large land-holders by whom the policies of the state government were deter-mined. But as settlers poured into the new country and land became more difficult to obtain, there developed a formidable group of frontiersmen who owned small farms and who resented the advantages given the holders of large tracts, many of whom were speculators. Andrew Jackson became the leader of this group and, as a result, there arose between him and Sevier a political and personal rivalry, which gave color to state and local politics in Tennessee until the latter's death in 1815. It was, however, a factional fight within Jefferson's party.[2]

With the rise of Jackson into national prominence because of his exploits in the War of 1812 and with his entry into the presidential contest of 1824, he became the dominating influence in Tennessee politics and remained so until the closing years of his second administration as President. During this time the Democratic party in the state became an efficient and militant organization, the chief strength of which consisted of the small-farmer, frontier class.

The political views of this Jacksonian Democracy in Ten-nessee are best illustrated by those of its leader who headed the revolution by which the frontier took a dominant place in the national government. This revolution contributed no new ideas to the conceptions of democracy advanced by Jefferson in 1776 and 1800. It did, however, bring about an application of those principles to a degree never before attempted and exerted a

---

[2] The rivalry between Jackson and Sevier in Tennessee politics is treated at length in Carl S. Driver, *John Sevier, A Pioneer of the Old Southwest.* Andrew Jackson's part in the formation of political groups in Tennessee has been discussed most interestingly by Thomas Perkins Abernethy, *From Frontier to Plantation in Tennessee,* pp. 227-249, 355. Professor Aber-nethy makes this part appear rather inglorious and questions Jackson's sin-cerity. It is no part of this study to pass judgment on Jackson's motives. The pertinent fact is that he did become the leader of the rural Democracy, both in the state and nation. The generally used term "Jacksonian Democ-racy" is evidence of that.

powerful influence on the practice of government and politics.[3] In the main they represented the practical reactions of the frontiersman to his environments and necessities rather than the mature thought of the political philosopher. With regard to the relative spheres of national and state government, the frontier views represented neither the extreme of Hamilton nor that of Jefferson as exemplified in the Kentucky and Virginia Resolutions. They embodied a healthy, vigorous nationalism together with a jealous concern for the rights of the state against encroachments of federal power. An excellent illustration of this frontier attitude is afforded by a comparison of Jackson's position on nullification in South Carolina and that which he took in the dispute between the national government and Georgia over the Indian question. The state could not defy the constitutional authority of the federal government; the latter must not disregard the sovereignty of the state.

In the matter of protective tariff and internal improvements the frontier Democrat likewise occupied a moderate position. Protection, according to his view, was constitutional and desirable so long as it contributed to the common good. It must not, however, be used to enrich a privileged class at the expense of the people. Internal improvements were to be fostered so long as they were national in character and were carried out by constitutional methods. Banks and financiers were objects of suspicion, monopolies were abhorrent and the Indians belonged beyond the settlements of white men. The frontier Democrat was resourceful and self-reliant but had no hesitancy in calling upon the general government when the task was beyond his power or means. In such a situation he wanted a national government that was strong enough to be feared by his enemies and with power enough to aid him in his need. Such was the political attitude of the people of Tennessee who supported Jackson and his policies.[4]

---

[3] Charles Edward Merriam, *American Political Theories,* pp. 176-202, 264-265; Raymond G. Gettell, *A History of Political Thought,* pp. 364-365; Arthur Meier Schlesinger, *New Viewpoints in American History,* pp. 200-218.

[4] For Jackson's views on the subjects mentioned as well as on other questions, see, James D. Richardson (compiler), *A Compilation of the Messages*

By 1834, however, the dominance of Jackson's party in his own state was broken. Newton Cannon, avowed enemy to the President, was elected governor. This successful challenge to the old general's power gave heart to an opposition which quickly consolidated under the leadership of John Bell, Hugh Lawson White, Cannon, David Crockett, Ephraim H. Foster and others. Such was the strength of this opposition that in 1836 it was able to defeat Jackson's favorite, Martin Van Buren, in the state. Not for twenty years was Tennessee's electoral vote again cast for a Democrat, although James K. Polk was a candidate in 1844. During this time the contests for control of the state government were bitter and close, with victory resting alternately with the Jacksonians and their enemies.

The Whig party in Tennessee, for such the opposition soon became, was a counterpart to the national organization in that it owed its existence to personal or political hostility to Jackson. For the most part, the men who organized and directed the new party had been supporters of the Jackson policies throughout the greater part of his administrations. They had resented the general's dictatorial methods and some of them had shown a disposition to question the wisdom of his program, but they had feared to test his popularity in the state by openly opposing him. The candidacy of Van Buren gave the malcontents their opportunity. Jackson's attempt to force this unpopular New Yorker upon his frontier followers, together with his apparently unfair treatment of his old friend and fellow Tennessean, Hugh Lawson White, proved an effective argument.[5] So cleverly was it used and so skillfully were the opposition forces directed that not for many years did the Democracy gain com-

---

and Papers of the Presidents. Messages and papers of Andrew Jackson, II, 435-656, III, 3-308. See also John Spencer Bassett (Ed.), Correspondence of Andrew Jackson. Particularly interesting is his letter to Van Buren at the time of the South Carolina controversy, ibid., III, 122-123.

[5] For a recent discussion of the early opposition to Jackson in Tennessee, see Powell Moore, "The Political Background of the Revolt Against Jackson in Tennessee," The East Tennessee Historical Society's Publications, No. 4 (1932), pp. 45-66. The effect of Jackson's championship of Van Buren is well put by Eugene Irving McCormac, James K. Polk, A Political Biography, pp. 62-91.

plete ascendancy in the state and by that time it was a different party in many respects.

Though the Whig party in Tennessee undoubtedly owed its birth, in a great measure, to the enmities and resentments which Jackson's dictatorial methods had created as well as to the effects of the old Jackson-Sevier feuds, there can be no question but that economic reasons existed for the formation of the new party. The frontier had passed beyond the Mississippi by the middle thirties and Jackson's own state was taking on the diversified interests of a settled community. There had grown up in such centers as Nashville, Knoxville, Jackson and Memphis a wealthy mercantile class which had little sympathy with the Democratic attitude toward banking interests and still less with that on internal improvements. It inclined more to Henry Clay's position on these subjects as well as on the tariff. There had also grown up a group of wealthy planters whose aristocratic tendencies brought them socially, if not economically, much nearer the rich merchants and bankers of the cities than to the small-farmer, frontier-minded Jacksonians. The disposition of the Whig strength in Tennessee shows an alliance between these two groups in this as in other states further to the south.[6] However true it may have been that the original leaders of the Whig movement in the state had been supporters of the Jackson policies, economic reasons and political necessity quickly forced them to embrace the principles of strong centralization and protective tariffs, as well as the financial ideas of the new national party.[7] These views became deep rooted in the years that followed.

The rivalry between Democrats and Whigs in Tennessee was accentuated by the parity of their strength and, as a result,

---

[6] For a treatment of the growth of the Whig party in Tennessee, see Thomas P. Abernethy, "Origin of the Whig Party in Tennessee," *Mississippi Valley Historical Review*, XII (1925-1926), 504-522. See also Abernethy, "The Political Geography of Southern Jacksonism," *The East Tennessee Historical Society's Publications*, No. 3 (1931), pp. 35-41; and Abernethy, *From Frontier to Plantation in Tennessee*. Of value too is Joshua W. Caldwell, "John Bell of Tennessee," *American Historical Review*, IV (1898-1899), 652-664. An important work on this subject is Arthur Charles Cole, *The Whig Party in the South*.

[7] For illustration, see McCormac, *op. cit.*, p. 205.

there developed a bitterness between the two groups which did not die with the passing of the latter party. Although the slavery controversy drove many of them into the Democratic ranks during the fifties, the great body of the Whigs became Know-Nothings[8] and in 1860 followed their old leader, John Bell, into the Constitutional Union party. Their contempt for the "black Republicans" did not lessen their hatred of the Democrats. This attitude of the old-line Whigs in the critical election of 1860 appears forcibly in a letter of Oliver P. Temple, one of their leaders, on the "relative merits of the Democratic and Republican parties." He expressed it as follows:

"How could you suppose that I had ever thought of becoming a Democrat? I can never fall so low as that. In conviction, in principle, in feeling, in taste, and in manners, I am opposed to Democracy. I am not certain whether I hate or despise or fear it most. I am sometimes tempted to think it Anti-Christ. . . . I believe the time has come when we, all the good and true, must grapple with Democracy as our greatest foe and destroy it or be devoured by it. . . . I should apprehend no danger from the temporary triumph of the Republican party. After the ranks of the Democracy were broken it would then be easy to organize a great conservative Whig Party."[9]

From this it is easy to see the difficulties which were to arise later when circumstances forced a union of Democrats and Whigs.

The years which witnessed the rise and fall of the Whig party in Tennessee saw marked changes in the character of the Democracy. After the retirement of Jackson from the presidency, James K. Polk became the titular head of his party in the state and, soon thereafter, in the nation. Although modern

[8] Robert Loren Hargis, *The Know-Nothing Party in Tennessee,* unpublished M. A. Thesis, Vanderbilt University, 1931. A careful study of the subject with valuable tabulations and maps showing strength of parties.

[9] To A. A. Doak, January 19, 1860, Temple MSS. in the University of Tennessee Library, quoted by Marguerite Bartlett Hamer, "The Presidential Campaign of 1860 in Tennessee," *East Tennessee Historical Society's Publications,* No. 3 (1931), p. 18. For a similar attitude but more violently expressed, see letter of Wm. G. ("Parson") Brownlow to Jordan Clark, quoted in W. G. Brownlow, *Sketches of the Rise, Progress and Decline of Secession,* pp. 63-64.

historians ascribe to Polk more of ability than had been the custom, his public career was overshadowed by that of his predecessor. His death in 1849, four years after that of his old chief, placed him definitely within the Jackson epoch. With the death of Polk, the leadership of the old Jacksonian Democracy in Tennessee passed to Andrew Johnson. Though Johnson differed from Jackson in numerous ways, there was a similarity in the intenseness of their personal feelings and, further, in their appeal to the common people. Johnson started his career as champion of the laboring classes and always looked upon himself as such. But this term must not be confused with present day ideas of labor. Although the state's population included many artisans and unskilled laborers, their political influence was insignificant compared to that of the great body of rural workmen, which included the owners of small farms. It was this class which gave Johnson his power as it was this class which had been the strength of Andrew Jackson. The strictures which Johnson directed against the over-privileged aristocrats of his day were designed to appeal to this group and are strongly suggestive of Jackson's denunciations of the favored financial magnates of his time. In spite of the antagonism which Johnson aroused among influential elements of his party, his following was of sufficient strength to keep him in the governor's chair from 1853 to 1857 and, immediately thereafter, to force his election to the United States senate.

Under Johnson's leadership, this section of the Tennessee Democracy retained many of the traditional views of Jackson's day. Its love of the Union was intense and it viewed with alarm the growing disunion sentiment in the South. At the same time it was no less hostile to any infringement on the rights of the states by the federal power. It held to the agrarian policies of the Democracy without endorsing the extremes of the South Carolina school. In a word, it held to the ideas of the old frontier as expressed at the time of the Jacksonian revolution.[10]

[10] A helpful discussion of Johnson's rise in Tennessee politics is found in Robert W. Winston, *Andrew Johnson, Plebeian and Patriot*, pp. 26-94. Of especial interest is his chapter entitled "Successor to Andrew Jackson," pp. 26-39. For less extensive treatment of same subject see Milton, *op. cit.*, pp. 74-97, and Stryker, *op. cit.*, pp. 5-35.

As was to have been expected, Calhoun's doctrine of state's rights and the resultant distrust of the national power gained a large following in Tennessee. This grew in strength and influence as attacks upon the South's "peculiar institution" increased. Economic and political theories of King Cotton more and more challenged the nationalism of the frontier. As early as 1831 Jackson recognized that the Calhoun influence extended into Tennessee.[11] In the revolt against Jackson these "state righters" combined with Bell and his group, but such a union was unnatural and could not last. They remained Democrats and, as time went on, became increasingly important in that party. Such was their strength that in 1857 their spokesman, Isham G. Harris, became Democratic nominee for governor and was elected. It is significant that Harris came from West Tennessee, where cotton culture predominated, while Johnson was of East Tennessee, where cotton and slaves formed a less important part of the economic structure. The change which had taken place in the political views of the cotton growing sections of Tennessee was a counterpart of that in the lower South.[12]

There was a striking difference between Andrew Johnson, plebeian hater of "aristocrats," and Isham G. Harris, no less aggressive spokesman of the great slave holders and champion of their political beliefs. Yet both were Tennessee Democrats and represented two powerful but mutually repellent wings in that party. The election of Harris to the governorship and Johnson to the senate in 1857 appears to have been a compromise, possible only because of a more intense dislike for the powerful remnants of the old-line Whigs. Between the three antagonistic political groups in Tennessee there was little difference on the subject of slavery. There was a difference, however, in their views as to the best means of protecting it. Johnson and his followers in the Democratic party were in agreement with the Whigs in the opinion that slavery could and must be protected in the Union and under the constitution. The Harris

---

[11] Letter to John C. McLemore, June 27, 1831, Bassett, *op. cit.*, IV, 305.

[12] An excellent discussion of the changing political thought in the South during this period appears in Vernon Louis Parrington, *Main Currents in American Thought*, II, 67-69.

Democrats were coming more and more to accept the logical conclusion of the Calhoun philosophy, should the constitutional rights of the slave holder be disregarded or threatened.

Such were the political alignments in Tennessee in 1861 when the states of the lower South decided to withdraw from the Union. Two of the three powerful groups in the state, the old-line Whigs and the Jacksonian Democrats under Johnson's leadership, were devoted to the Union and were determined that Tennessee should remain in it. Only the state's rights Democrats under Harris were in sympathy with secession. The first test of strength came in February, 1861, when the people were called upon to decide whether a convention should be held to consider the question of secession and also to name delegates to the convention, should it be called. The proposal for a convention met defeat by a majority of nearly 12,000, while in the election of delegates the results showed a vote of more than

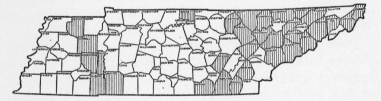

ELECTION ON SECESSION JUNE 1861
White—For Secession   Vertical—Against Secession

three to one in favor of union as against disunion. Tennessee had announced its loyalty to the Union in no uncertain terms.[13]

President Lincoln's call for troops, however, changed sentiment in the state. At an election called for the eighth of June for

[13] *Annual Cyclopaedia,* 1861, pp. 677-78. It has been asserted that "the election of February was a division along party lines. Its result was simply an indication that the Whig party of Tennessee was still opposed to the doctrine of secession." John R. Neal, *Disunion and Restoration in Tennessee,* p. 14. This statement is controverted by the fact that in the election of 1860 the total Democratic vote exceeded the Bell (Whig) vote while in the special election of the following February, the proposal to call a secession convention was defeated. Assuming the vote on the convention to be the true test of secession sentiment it would seem that Mr. Neal has ignored Andrew Johnson and his following in the state.

the purpose of voting on secession and union with the Confederacy, secession carried by a majority of 57,675 in a total vote of 152,151.[14] The division in this election was along sectional rather than party lines. Roughly speaking, East Tennessee was loyal to the Union while the middle and western portions of the state favored secession. In the latter areas, old-line Whigs who had been most opposed to separation now sided with the secessionists and became active in resisting what they considered armed invasion by the North. Democrats and Whigs of East Tennessee united to oppose secession, first at the ballot box and then in the field. For the first time in their careers, Andrew Johnson, Democrat, and "Parson" Brownlow, hater of Democrats, fought for a common cause. This election was of the greatest significance in Tennessee politics, for not only did it wipe out old political lines as they had previously existed, but it definitely determined the political map of the state down to the present time.[15]

Tennessee's location made the state the battleground of the western armies throughout most of the period from 1861-1865. As early as March 3, 1862, President Lincoln appointed Andrew Johnson military governor with instructions "to re-establish the authority of the Federal government in the state of Tennessee, and provide the means of maintaining peace and security to the loyal inhabitants of that state until they shall be able to establish a civil government."[16] Johnson, with Lincoln's encouragement, set himself to the task of reëstablishing a civil government controlled by men loyal to the Union. In spite of all his efforts he met with no success, because of frequent Confed-

---

[14] William Robertson Garrett, and Albert Virgil Goodpasture, *History of Tennessee,* p. 203. Mary Emely Robertson, *Tennessee's Attitude Toward Secession,* unpublished M. A. Thesis, Vanderbilt University, 1929. Compare chart on p. 9 with those on pp. 70, 96, 147, 175, 185, 186, 203.

[15] The vote showed isolated counties in East Tennessee which voted for secession and similar sections in Middle and West Tennessee which opposed it. The writer has seen no satisfactory explanation as to why these counties went counter to the overwhelming sentiment of their sections. It is possible that economic reasons existed, but it appears more probable that the personal influence of local leaders determined results in such instances.

[16] Johnson's commission as quoted in Clifton R. Hall, *Andrew Johnson, Military Governor of Tennessee,* pp. 32-33.

erate raids which rendered the protection of the federal power uncertain. His task was all the more difficult in view of the anomalous situation that Middle and West Tennessee, which had fallen into Federal hands, were overwhelmingly Southern in sympathy, while East Tennessee, home of the Unionists, remained in Confederate hands until the latter part of the war. Nothing resembling a *bona fide* election was held until 1864, at which time Johnson was elevated to the vice presidency.[17] On March 4, 1865, a state election was held at which William G. ("Parson") Brownlow, Johnson's old-time Whig rival and fiery Unionist, was elected governor by a vote of 23,352 to 35.[18] With Brownlow's election began reconstruction in Tennessee in the generally accepted meaning of that term. Though the full story of that epoch is not necessary in this study, it is important to understand some of its effects upon political alignments.

The end of the war found the politics of the state in a chaotic condition. The new Republican party, at that time, had few if any adherents. The old-line Whigs, who had functioned as an organized force for the last time in 1860 as the Constitutional Union party, had been hopelessly divided, and an almost similar situation existed among the Democrats. A great majority of both groups in Middle and West Tennessee were disfranchised because of participation in the "rebellion." Roughly speaking, the people were classed as loyal and disloyal, with the former in complete control of all branches of the state government as well as of the election machinery of the counties. This simple classification was not to stand, however, for as early as 1864 the loyalists had begun to be classified as radical and conservative. The story of how Andrew Johnson changed from a spokesman of the radicals to the leader of conservatives is well known. It is sufficient to say that the fight between him and the congressional radicals served to intensify the division between the groups in Tennessee. The moderates were accused of being in

---

[17] An interesting description of how conservative "loyal" men were prevented from voting in this election is found in Hall, *op. cit.,* pp. 139-155.

[18] *Ibid.,* p. 175. Compare with the total vote of 152,151 on the ordinance of secession in 1861.

sympathy with the "rebels" and their loyalty was questioned. The attitude of the extremists was pointedly expressed by Hon. L. C. Houk in a convention at Nashville in September of 1864, when he declared: "Show me a stickler for constitutions and I'll show you a man none too good a Union man."[19]

Governor Brownlow became the leader of the radicals in the state and few men were better fitted for the task either by temperament or by previous experience.[20] He held that loyal men should show no "mercy or forbearance" to leaders in the "rebellion" and as for the rank and file of those who supported it, he believed that "they should cheerfully submit to five or ten years of disenfranchisement so as to give them time to wash the blood of loyal men from their hands."[21] With such a program in mind, supported by a legislature that did his bidding, with the election machinery of the state in his hands, and backed by military power, Governor Brownlow embarked upon his administration with energy and determination. It is not surprising that such a leader, with such power, brooked no interference from the more moderate Unionists of the state.

In spite of his early opposition to Negro enfranchisement,[22] Brownlow soon accepted this along with other extreme measures emanating from Washington. The injection of this issue into politics served to intensify the opposition of many conservative Union men to the radical regime. Large numbers of them believed it unwise to grant suffrage to former slaves, and the bad feeling engendered between whites and blacks by the activities of Union League "missionaries" and carpet baggers only strengthened this belief. The hostility toward the Negro on the part of former Union men found expression in bloody race riots in Memphis in April and May of 1866. According to official reports of these riots, "very few paroled Confederates were mixed up with the rioters, . . . the larger portions being regis-

---

[19] Hall, *op. cit.*, p. 142, quoting from the *Nashville Dispatch*, September 6, 1864.

[20] For a vivid portrayal of Brownlow and his regime, see Waller Raymond Cooper, *Parson Brownlow, A Study of Reconstruction in Tennessee.*

[21] Governor's Message, *Senate Journal, General Assembly of the State of Tennessee*, Regular Session, 1865-66, pp. 1-26.

[22] *Idem.*

tered voters."[23] When it is remembered that only Union men
were registered voters at that time, it is easy to see the significance of these riots. The race question was driving large numbers of Unionists into the ranks of the conservatives.

Not the least cause of dissatisfaction among conservative men
was the alarming increase in the state debt under Brownlow's
administration. At this time some $14,500,000 in bonds were
sold, "in many instances for a few cents on the dollar," for the
"ostensible purpose of rehabilitating the various railroads."[24]

While such policies alienated large numbers of loyal men
from the Brownlow party, they deepened the resentment of disfranchised whites in Middle and West Tennessee. The result was
an alliance of conservative men of all political beliefs for the
purpose of overthrowing the radicals. They made little headway
in this until Brownlow's election to the United States senate in
1868 placed the conservative D. W. C. Senter at the head of the
state government. The latter's policy of enfranchising the
whites gave the moderates control of the government and resulted in the return of Democrats to power in 1870.[25]

As has been pointed out, political alignments in Tennessee
were chaotic at the beginning of the Brownlow régime, but by
its end party lines were being drawn which were to hold to the
present day. The fact that these lines, when consolidated, followed almost exactly those of division on secession in 1861 bears
testimony to the bitterness aroused by this and the race issue
during radical domination. Brownlow and his adherents had be-

---

[23] Report of General Stoneman, commanding Federal troops at Memphis,
to General Grant, *Annual Cyclopaedia*, 1866, pp. 730-731.

[24] Reau E. Folk, "Tennessee's Bonded Indebtedness, Retrospective and
Prospective," *An Address Before the Tennessee Bankers' Association*, Memphis, May 27, 1908, pp. 5-6.

[25] For greater details on reconstruction in Tennessee see James Walter
Fertig, *The Secession and Reconstruction of Tennessee;* Ira P. Jones, "Reconstruction in Tennessee," in *Why the Solid South; or Reconstruction and
Its Results.* The *Annual Cyclopaedia* for the years 1864-1870 gives excellent
and reliable accounts of the more important events and issues in the state.
The works by Cooper, Hall and Neal, *op. cit.,* also help to give a picture of
the period, as do Acts and Journals of the legislature, messages of Governor Brownlow, and newspaper accounts and comments. See also J. A. Sharp,
"The Downfall of the Radicals in Tennessee," *The East Tennessee Historical Society's Publications*, No. 5 (1933), pp. 105-124.

come identified with the Republican party and were in accord
with the radical wing of that organization. In areas where
Union sentiment was strong, old-line Whigs and possibly some
extremely loyal Democrats became conservative Republicans.
A notable example of this group was Nathaniel G. Taylor,
father of Alfred A. and Robert L. Taylor. These former Whigs
found it easy to espouse the protective tariff and other central-
izing policies of the Republicans. When time had allayed the
hostility aroused by Brownlow's violent measures, conservative
and radical Republicans, with their common loyalty to the
Union and inherited dislike of the Democracy, were able to
unite. They formed a party which was compact as to area and
political beliefs and which was further cemented by a long
period of continuous Federal patronage. Unlike the Republican
party in states further south, it was completely dominated by
native whites except in certain localities where the colored population was large and where little unionist sentiment had existed
during the war. In spite of the fact that native whites controlled it, the Republican organization in Tennessee championed
the rights of the blacks to the ballot as its only hope of numerical superiority. In so doing, it brought upon itself the onus of
being opposed to white supremacy. This was a tremendous
handicap in the central and western portions of the state where
the bulk of negro population was located. It consigned the Republicans permanently to the role of a strong minority party.

Though the Democrats became the majority party in 1870
and have continued so, with few interruptions, from that date,
their problem was much more complex than that which confronted the Republicans. Attention has already been directed to
the two distinct groups which existed within the Democracy
previous to secession. The state's rights Democrats entered
upon the new era all the more convinced, by the experiences of
war and reconstruction, that their views were correct. Though
forced to give up the doctrine of secession, they viewed the increasing ascendancy of federal over state sovereignty with an
apprehension deepened by the experiences through which they
had passed. To them, the prophecies of Calhoun had been fulfilled and his doctrines vindicated. With white reënfranchise-

ment and the return, soon thereafter, of their old leader, Isham G. Harris, this group occupied again a commanding position in party councils.

The other old Democratic group, the small-farmer element which had inherited the views and traditions of Jackson's frontier Democracy, had generally espoused the cause of secession when faced by President Lincoln's call for troops, though many of them had followed their old leader, Andrew Johnson, in his opposition. When Johnson, in spite of his violence against those who would overthrow the Union, saw the Federal government's encroachments upon the constitutional rights of the states, his reactions were but natural in view of his philosophy. Just as Jackson had stamped out nullification and upheld the rights of Georgia in the Indian controversy, so now Johnson became the champion of the constitutional rights of the states, without the fear and distrust of national power which characterized the Harris following. When he returned to the state after his presidential term, he found that his course at Washington had dispelled much of the bitterness which had arisen against him during the war. He was not long in consolidating his old followers for the two-fold purpose of vindicating himself and of destroying the power of the "damned brigadiers."[26]

A third distinct group was now added to the Democracy of Tennessee. The old-line Whigs of the middle and western counties had, for the most part, reluctantly followed the state into the Confederacy but, once there, had fought loyally and bravely for the Southern cause. They had felt the proscriptions of radical reconstruction and, in common with the other whites of their areas, feared negro domination in their communities if the Republican party controlled the state. Since they were, as a rule, men of property they opposed the financial policies of Brownlow and his followers which threatened excessive taxation. For these reasons they found it impossible to join with the Republicans, although they still held their old Whig views on national issues. Little stood between these old-line Whigs and the more moderate Republican party of later days except the all-important race issue. On the other hand, they had little in

---

[26] Milton, op. cit., pp. 662-666.

common with the despised Democrats, except the desire for white supremacy. They had been numerous in the area of Middle Tennessee around Nashville and of West Tennessee around Jackson and Memphis,[27] and their strength was such as to throw the state to the Republicans should they fail to find a permanent place within the Democracy.

The problem, therefore, which confronted the Democratic party in Tennessee was that of adjusting these three distinct groups which had been antagonistic and which were now held together by the fear of Negro domination. And yet this fear did not exist in the degree to which it did further south, where blacks were more numerous and where the Republican party was not controlled by native whites. The efforts of these three groups to determine policies, control party machinery, to enjoy patronage and, at the same time, to preserve the unity and supremacy of the Democratic party, play a large part in determining the course of political events in Tennessee for a quarter of a century. The scene depicted at Nashville in 1875, when Andrew Johnson won his old seat in the senate, closed one of the earlier fights in this long struggle. Here the three groups within the new Democracy had contended bitterly. William B. Bate had represented the old state's rights element, soon to be headed by Isham G. Harris. Neill S. Brown had been a Whig governor in the days before the disintegration of that party and represented those old-line Whigs who had been forced into the Democratic party. Andrew Johnson had simply consolidated his old following in the party and had again assumed its leadership. He won because the other two factions disliked each other more than they did Johnson and because a few conservative Republicans, like Alfred A. Taylor, had supported him rather than the more radical wing of their own party.[28]

Johnson's death, a few months after his victory, left that portion of the party which he had led without a spokesman and it was to remain so for a decade. It is the rise of Robert L. Taylor to the leadership of this group and, through it, to a

---

[27] See charts and maps in Hargis, *op. cit.*

[28] Milton, *op. cit.*, pp. 665-669, gives an excellent account of this contest.

commanding place in the party and in state politics that forms a major theme in this study.

During the period between Johnson and Taylor the contest for party control between the state's rights and old-line Whig elements continued without interruption. Although the former group controlled the party machinery through most of the period, the power of the latter was at all times formidable because of the possibility of its alignment with the Republicans. Henry Watterson recognized the strength of the Whig sentiment in Tennessee and predicted that the state would lead in the break-up of the Solid South as soon as the Republicans discontinued "bloody shirt" methods and removed the necessity for white solidarity in that region.[29]

The continued vitality of old Whig ideas in the state was due, in a large measure, to the policy of industrialization which came to have wide acceptance after the war. The destruction of the South's economic and social order afforded an excellent opportunity, in the eyes of many, to rebuild the section along the lines of the industrial North.[30] To attract capital and labor from the latter section became an object of prime importance, and many espoused political policies most calculated to do this. In their effort to insure the success of their program, the industrialists of the "New South" turned to the military leaders of the Confederacy to furnish prestige as well as the fruits of their experience in directing large undertakings. The outstanding example of this was the unsuccessful effort to place the name of Robert E. Lee at the head of important enterprises.[31] Others did not hesitate, however, to employ their talents and replenish

---

[29] Interview by Mr. Watterson in the *Chicago Tribune*, quoted with comments in the *Nashville Banner*, March 24, 1887 and *Nashville Union* of the same date.

[30] The break-up of the plantation system, as it took place in Georgia, is described in R. P. Brooks, *Agrarian Revolution in Georgia*. For the story of the industrial movement see Broadus Mitchell and George Sinclair Mitchell, *The Industrial Revolution in the South*, and Holland Thompson, *The New South, A Chronicle of Social and Industrial Evolution*.

[31] See letter of General Lee to General J. B. Gordon, President, Southern Life Insurance Company, Captain Robert E. Lee, *Recollections and Letters of General Robert E. Lee,* pp. 376-377. See also Gamaliel Bradford, *Lee the American,* pp. 255-256.

their fortunes as heads of business undertakings with the result
that the industrialists of the South were led by their generals,
colonels and majors. An outstanding example of military men
heading the "New South" movement is found in Georgia and
may be regarded as illustrative of the situation in other states.
General John B. Gordon, ex-Governor Joseph E. Brown, and
General Alfred H. Colquitt composed a triumvirate which practically dictated governmental and political affairs in that state
over a long period of time. Each of them was actively connected
with railroads and other industrial enterprises.[32]

Tennessee afforded an attractive field for the Southern industrialists both from the standpoint of resources and of political
conditions.[33] It is the latter which requires attention here. The
Republicans formed a strong and dependable minority. The
strong bloc of old-line Whigs in the Democratic party afforded
a weapon by which industrialist policies might be forced upon
the agricultural groups. The power and influence of this Whig-
industrialist-military group in the Tennessee Democracy is apparent. Upon its return to power in 1870 the party elected as
governor General John C. Brown, brother of the former Whig
governor, Neill S. Brown, himself a former Whig and an elector on the Bell-Everett ticket in 1860. After his two terms as
governor, Brown "became interested in the construction of railroads in the South" and, at the time of his death, was president
of the Tennessee Coal, Iron and Railroad Company.[34] Governor
Brown was succeeded by James D. Porter, a former staff officer
in the Confederate army. After two terms as governor he be-

[32] A. M. Arnett, *The Populist Movement in Georgia*, p. 22. Dr. Arnett's
work gives a valuable interpretation of the new industrialism in the South
and its political significance, especially with reference to Georgia. His desig-
nation of this new leadership as "Bourbon" gives a new meaning to that
term.

[33] A recent discussion of the efforts to attract capital and labor to Tennessee is that of W. B. Hesseltine, "Tennessee's Invitation to Carpet-Baggers," *The East Tennessee Historical Society's Publications*, No. 4 (1932),
pp. 67-101. The author uses the term "carpet-bagger" in other than the
generally accepted sense. He applies it to those who came South after the
war "to exploit the natural resources of the land" as well as to political
adventurers.

[34] John Allison, (Ed.) *Notable Men of Tennessee*, I, 102. See also Joshua
W. Caldwell, *Sketches of the Bench and Bar of Tennessee*, p. 292.

came president of the Nashville and Chattanooga Railroad in 1880.[35] General George Dibrell, Taylor's chief opponent for the Democratic gubernatorial nomination in 1886, was elected that year a director of the Southwestern Railroad and became its president three years later. He was also a director of the Bon Air Coal Company.[36]

The strength of this industrialist bloc in Tennessee can be judged from Henry Watterson's statement in 1887 that there were six important Southern newspapers which supported every Republican and opposed every Democratic policy and that the "King" of this coterie of journalists was Colonel A. S. Colyar of Nashville. Colonel Colyar was a former Whig[37] and was characterized by Watterson as "a brilliant, courageous and earnest man . . . backed by abundant capital of protected industries," who issued orders to his lieutenants in Alabama, Georgia and Louisiana.[38] It is significant in the study of the situation in Tennessee that not only did the supposed head of this newspaper group live in the state, but that three of the newspapers referred to by Mr. Watterson were published in Nashville, Memphis and Chattanooga.[39] Such were the forces within the Tennessee Democracy that kept alive the ideas and traditions of the old-line Whigs, and, by means of their strategic position within the party, sought to direct policies along lines favorable

[35] Allison, *op. cit.*, II, 87.

[36] W. S. Speer, *Sketches of Prominent Tennesseans*, p. 229. General Nathan B. Forrest was another notable example of the general turned railroad promoter. He was not successful; see Andrew Nelson Lytle, *Bedford Forrest and His Critter Company*, p. 386.

[37] John Trotwood Moore and Austin P. Foster, *Tennessee the Volunteer State*, II, 102-103.

[38] Interview of Henry Watterson, *op. cit.*

[39] *Nashville American*, May 20, 1887. According to the *American*, the papers referred to were: *Nashville Union, Memphis Avalanche, Chattanooga Times, Atlanta Constitution, Birmingham Age, New Orleans Times-Democrat*, and *Mobile Register*. About this time Colonel Colyar acquired control of the *Nashville American* and soon thereafter the *Union* was discontinued, see *Nashville American* of May 14, and *Union* of June 2, 1887. Mention must also be made of the *Nashville Banner* which claimed independence with Democratic leanings. During this period it was a strong advocate of industrial enterprises and of political policies favorable to them. Attention should be directed here to the *Atlanta Constitution*, mentioned above. Henry W. Grady, outstanding spokesman of the "New South," was its editor.

to the new industrial order which they desired to bring about. They hoped to do this in a state which has always been predominantly agricultural and in which the urban centers have been discriminated against in matters of representation.[40]

From the Democratic return to power in 1870 until 1883, the overshadowing issue in Tennessee politics was that of the state debt. Neither the details of its origins nor the incidents of the political struggle over its settlement form a part of this story. Three points are important to remember: the debt was large; the Democrats attributed it to the financial policies of the Republicans in reconstruction times; and the bulk of it had been incurred for the benefit of railroads. The question of whether the state should acknowledge the debt at its face value or should "repudiate" those portions of it which were claimed fraudulent became an issue over which the Democratic party divided. The industrialist wing favored full payment and demanded that the state's credit be maintained. Opinion among the other elements of the party varied from those who advocated repudiation of all questionable items in the debt to those who wanted an adjustment that would satisfy the bond-holders, protect the state's credit and yet lighten the burden on taxpayers. During the ten year period from 1870 to 1880 and under the successive administrations of Governors Brown, Porter and Marks, the Democrats made unsuccessful efforts to reach a satisfactory compromise. In the latter year the party split on the issue, the two factions nominated rival candidates for governor and both lost. Alvin Hawkins, the Republican nominee, was elected. Governor Hawkins met with no better success in the solution of the problem than had his Democratic predecessors.

In 1882 the Democrats appeared as hopelessly divided as in 1880. In the state convention of that year, when it seemed as if no agreement could be reached, Senator Isham G. Harris delivered a stirring appeal in which he is said to have used these words: "Fellow Democrats, I understand that the state debt is the rock on which our party is split, and now I am in

---

[40] See John Hascue Mahoney, *Apportionments and Gerrymandering in Tennessee Since 1870,* unpublished M. A. Thesis, George Peabody College for Teachers, 1930, pp. 72-75.

favor of splitting the rock."[41] Whether these were the exact
words of the senator or not, the convention acted along that
line. It was agreed "to split the difference" and General William
B. Bate, closely identified with the Harris wing, was nominated
for governor. In the campaign which followed, the personal popularity of General Bate, the normal antipathy to Republican
rule, and the predominance of moderate counsels won the day
for the Democrats. Bate was elected by a majority of nearly
30,000 over Hawkins. Supported by a friendly legislature, Governor Bate brought about a settlement along the lines of his
platform and it appeared that the last obstacle to Democratic
accord had been removed.[42]

The desired harmony did not materialize. The industrialists
denounced the settlement as repudiation while a large voiceless
element in the party, probably the old Johnson following, resented the recognition of fraudulent bonds. As a result of this
situation, Bate's majority in 1884 was reduced from nearly
30,000 to less than 7,000.[43]

An additional issue had served to alienate the industrialists
in this campaign and increased the threat to Democratic supremacy. Under the leadership of Bate and the Harris wing, a railroad commission had been established for the purpose of cor-
recting abuses suffered at the hands of the carriers. This action
was denounced by the industrialists and, as a result, a Republican railroad commission was elected in 1884 by a majority of
over 8,000.[44]

Thus it was that by 1884 the long fight between the state's
rights Democrats of the Calhoun school, led by Senator Isham
G. Harris, and the old-line Whig-industrialist faction, now

---

[41] John A. Pitts, *Personal and Professional Reminiscences of An Old
Lawyer*, p. 251.

[42] For a rather full statement of the state debt fight as it progressed from
year to year, see *Annual Cyclopaedia* for the years 1870-1885 inclusive. A
brief statement of the affair is found in Folk, *op. cit.* A concise but complete statement of the problem is found in Park Marshall, *A Life of William B. Bate,* pp. 200-221. The subject occupies much space in the governors' messages to the legislature during those years.

[43] *Election Returns,* MS. vol. in the office of the secretary of state at
Nashville.

[44] *Ibid.*

headed by Colonel A. S. Colyar, had brought the party near disruption. The other and most numerous group within the party, the rural Democracy, had been leaderless since Andrew Johnson's death, and had shown increasing tendencies to "go fishing" on election days.

CHAPTER II

DEMOCRATIC ISSUES AND CANDIDATES IN 1886

LONG rivalry between the Harris and Colyar factions, resentments over the state debt settlement, and growing apathy among the rural Democrats of the Jackson-Johnson group had brought the Democratic party to a critical condition in 1886. The defeat of the party in the state campaign of that year seemed imminent unless past differences could be forgotten, factional interests be submerged, and an enthusiasm aroused among the indifferent voters. Robert L. Taylor, recognized as an outstanding leader among the younger men in the party, expressed the true situation when he declared that the Democracy was "rent with feuds" which threatened its overthrow throughout the state. He held, along with many others, that reorganization was necessary and, with it, the substitution of harmony for discord.[1] An understanding of how this was accomplished, under Taylor's leadership, necessitates an examination of the issues, personalities, and political trends of the time, together with the steps by which the party was consolidated.

A decided tendency toward political independence had appeared among the voters of the state. One of the leading Democratic papers of Nashville had declared its freedom from party control and was urging citizens to follow its example. It asserted that men would not forever allow party loyalty to override their convictions.[2] In line with this tendency, some 580

---

[1] *Nashville Banner*, January 11, 1886. Mr. Taylor's view of the situation was expressed in a letter to friends. He said: "Our party needs reorganization. We have broken into fragments or rather factions, discordant, belligerent, and the party has been rent with feuds which have threatened its overthrow throughout the state." Similar views were expressed by the *Memphis Avalanche*, January 10, 1886.

[2] *Nashville Banner*, February 13, 15, March 8, 1886.

workingmen of Nashville had pledged themselves to forget party allegiance and to support such candidates as favored their interests, regardless of party label;[3] and in East Tennessee, laboring men were being urged to make certain demands of candidates before according them their support.[4] In this tendency toward independence there was nothing of a third party idea but rather an avowed intent to select from the nominees of the two established parties.

Democratic leaders in 1886 were disturbed, not only by the situation within their own party and the tendency toward independent voting, but by the growing strength of the Republicans in the state. Radical and conservative factions of that party, as developed during Reconstruction, had shown an increasing disposition to unite as time passed. Conservative influence had subordinated hatred of "Rebels" and demands for Negro rights as issues so that by 1886 there was not a great difference between the Republican program and that of industrialist Democrats. It is true that the Republicans of Tennessee were divided into two factions, the "ins" and the "outs," with respect to Federal patronage, but they showed that distinguishing Republican trait of fighting among themselves until election day and then casting their ballots in harmony.[5]

The Republicans were showing an increasing strength in the state. They had cast in the neighborhood of 90,000 votes for Hayes in the Presidential election of 1876 while in that of 1884 they had polled some 125,000, an increase of approximately 39 per cent. The Democratic vote was practically the same in the two contests. The Democratic majority of 43,000 in 1873 had

[3] *Ibid.*, March 16, 1886.

[4] *Sequatchie Sun,* quoted in *ibid.,* February 9, 1886.

[5] The situation within the Republican party is set forth in a petition directed to the President of the United States requesting the appointment of Hon. L. C. Houk as U. S. District Attorney for the Eastern District of Tennessee. The petition, undated, was signed by five Republican members of the Legislature and is found among the Private Papers of Hon L. C. Houk in the Lawson-McGhee Library, Knoxville, Tennessee. It goes on to say—"In East Tennessee there are two elements or factions, the 'ins' and 'outs'. . . . All the Federal offices have been monopolized, and the 'outs' who have furnished talent on the stump, labor in the field and ballots at the polls, year after year have been ignored."

been reduced to 7,000 in 1884. This increase in the Republican vote had been gradual and seemed of a permanent character.[6] The leading independent paper of the state noted that the Republican party had "gained wonderfully in substantial strength"[7] and this opinion was shared by many conservative Democrats.[8] It is not surprising that the Republican press voiced a note of confidence at this time and that the minority party, scenting victory, had girded itself for a supreme effort.[9]

Under such circumstances, many Democrats who were more interested in party than in factional success saw the necessity of harmony and, early in the year, began to work to that end. The demand that differences be buried in the interest of party success was voiced by Democratic papers in every section of the state.[10]

On January 9, control of the *Nashville American* was transferred from Major John J. Vertrees to Colonel Duncan B. Cooper. This paper was considered the organ of the Harris or "machine" group, and Major Vertrees had waged an uncompromising fight against policies favored by the Colyar faction. Though Cooper was a Harris Democrat he was regarded as more conservative than Vertrees, and this change in management was interpreted as a move toward party harmony. One editor hailed

---

[6] For results of various elections see *Election Returns* MS, vol., in the office of the secretary of state, Nashville.

[7] *Nashville Banner,* January 20, 1886.

[8] *Memphis Avalanche,* January 10, 1886, *Lebanon Register,* quoted in *Nashville Banner,* February 20, 1886.

[9] *Chattanooga Commercial; National Review* (Nashville); *Athens Athenian; Tennessee Tomahawk,* quoted in *Nashville Banner,* February 8, February 28, March 4, 1886. Republican confidence was voiced by *Philadelphia Press,* quoted in Nashville *Union,* January 28, 1886.

[10] *Nashville American,* January 24, 1886, *Nashville Union,* January 5, 12, 13, 19, 20, 24, 1886, *Memphis Avalanche,* February 22, 26, March 27, 1886, *Johnson City Comet,* early months of 1886. The attitude of the rural press may be seen from editorials or comments in *Carthage Mirror-Banner, Dresden Enterprise, Jackson Tribune-Sun, Lebanon Register, Columbia Herald, Martin Mail, Carthage Record, Cannon Courier, Winchester Home Journal, Shelbyville Gazette, Clarksville Chronicle, Smith County Record,* quoted in *Nashville Banner* February 8, 10, 15, 18, 20, 22, 23, 27, March 3, 9, 1886, *Trenton Tri-weekly Herald, Dayton Advance Gazette, Maury Democrat,* quoted in *Nashville Union,* January 20, 1886, *Athens Post, Monroe Democrat,* quoted in *Nashville American,* February 6, 1886.

it as an omen of peace since "the Vertrees school of politics will no longer dominate the party,"[11] while another looked for a cessation of the "rule or ruin" policy that had been in vogue.[12]

There were those who looked with doubt if not with cynicism upon the attempts at harmony. At Nashville the "independent hewgog"[13] twitted the dailies of the Harris and Colyar groups on their newly established amicable relations and facetiously dubbed the new arrangement "the harmonicon," a term that came into state-wide use during those months. It questioned whether true harmony could exist when the factions were at daggers point on the tariff, the Blair bill, and other questions. Yet it did applaud a disposition of party leaders to forget dead issues and to drop narrow factional policies.[14]

Conflicting ambitions of party leaders, and differences on questions of policy are the usual factors contributing to discord within political organizations, as they are the chief incentives to conflict between parties. Undoubtedly, both had contributed liberally to the plight of the Tennessee Democracy in early 1886. The success of any efforts at harmony depended upon the degree to which these factors could be minimized.

The situation in Tennessee in 1886 was extremely favorable to the movement for Democratic harmony, so far as state issues were concerned. Those of the past quarter century, centering around the Civil War and its aftermath, had been momentous but had now been settled. New ones hovered on the horizon.

Prohibition was one of the most pressing questions before the people of Tennessee at that time. They listened to heated arguments, pro and con, that sound strangely familiar to modern ears. Temperance sentiment had gained a surprising momentum in the state, particularly in rural areas and small towns. The daily papers carried frequent notices of temperance lectures,

---

[11] *Dresden Enterprise,* quoted in *Nashville Banner,* January 19, 1886.

[12] *Clarksville Tobacco Leaf,* quoted in *ibid.,* February 15, 1886.

[13] Term applied to the *Nashville Banner* by the *Dresden Enterprise,* quoted in *Banner,* February 15, 1886.

[14] *Nashville Banner,* January 20, February 24, April 21, May 7, 1886; *Clarksville Democrat,* quoted in *Nashville Banner,* February 27, 1886.

Alliance meetings and activities of various dry organizations, in every section of the state.[15]

Then, as in more recent times, a referendum was determined upon as the most suitable method of settling the question. Enthusiastic drys looked upon prohibition as a non-partisan matter and claimed leaders of both parties as their champions.[16] The State Temperance Alliance, which met in Nashville in February, sponsored a demand for a popular vote on the subject. It is not surprising that party leaders were content to let the issue remain out of politics and be settled by a special vote of the people. They ignored taunts by the independent *Nashville Banner* that both parties feared the issue and were "waiting to see how the popular cat will jump."[17] Though the election resulted in a decisive defeat of prohibition, its advocates showed unlooked for strength. They girded themselves for further struggles but, for many years, regarded the question as non-political. It did not affect the harmony program of Democratic leaders.

Another issue which had begun to receive considerable attention by 1886 concerned the abolition of the prison lease system. The growing humanitarianism rebelled against the leasing of prisoners to private interests. The belief seems to have been general that the system was wrong and this was strengthened when the warden of the state penitentiary resigned under fire. It was charged that he had been "regularly in the pay of penitentiary lessees" and that he had received a monthly salary of $100 from private concerns.[18] This opposition was reinforced

[15] The importance of the prohibition issue is indicated by the numerous editorials on the subject in *Nashville Banner* of early 1886 as well as in such papers as *Manchester Times, Hartsville Sentinel, Winchester Home Journal, McMinnville New Era, Murfreesboro Free Press, Lebanon Herald, Tullahoma Guardian, Southern Standard, Winchester News, Martin Mail, Dresden Enterprise, Clarksville Tobacco Leaf,* quoted or referred to in *Nashville Banner,* January 19, February 8, 9, 10, 15, 16, 17, 24, March 1, 2, 3, 10, 24, 27, 1886. *Nashville American,* February 24. Democratic dailies, such as *Nashville Union, Nashville American* and *Memphis Avalanche,* tended to say very little on the issue.

[16] *Dresden Enterprise,* quoted in *Nashville Banner,* February 10, 1886.

[17] *Nashville Banner,* February 23, 1886.

[18] *Ibid.,* April 22, 1886.

by that of labor groups, which naturally objected to competition with convict labor and its ruinous wage scale.[19]

Though no defense of the lease system was offered, except that of financial necessity, the people were not sufficiently aroused to demand reform. The question did become acute within a few years and some difficulties connected with its solution will appear in succeeding chapters. For the time being, at least, it was not a disrupting issue.

The year 1886 was perhaps the most turbulent one in United States history, so far as labor unrest, strikes, and violence are concerned. Disturbances were common in widely separated parts of the country. They appeared in smaller communities as well as in the great industrial centers. The daily press of that year teemed with accounts of strikes, lockouts and kindred labor troubles.[20]

Tennessee was largely unaffected by this great labor upheaval, probably because her industries had not been developed to such an extent that labor formed a major group of the population. True, the Knights of Labor met in Nashville and condemned both old political parties for not having fulfilled pledges to labor and on March 8, a Workingman's Party was organized at that place. The party made the following demands: repeal of the odious penitentiary lease; abolition of the enormous fee system attached to county offices and substitution of reasonable salaries; passage of a law to stimulate building so as to give employment to idle mechanics; and passage of a law to encour-

---

[19] For typical discussions of the prison lease system, see *Nashville Banner,* January 2, 16, 19, 23, February 6, 13, March 3, 15, 16, June 3. Aside from the *Banner,* the press of the state had little to say on the subject other than an occasional commendation of the *Banner's* position by such papers as *Lynchburg Falcon, Knoxville Journal, Roane County Republican, Memphis Scimitar, West Tennessee Whig,* quoted in *Nashville Banner,* January 25, March 2, 3, May 7, 1886.

[20] Within five days, labor trouble was reported in Cincinnati, Cleveland, St. Louis, New York, Ft. Worth, Dallas, Atchison, Kan., Sherman, Texas, Chicago, Pittsburgh, McKenney, Tex., Shreveport, Omaha, Detroit, Baltimore, Dennison and Marshall, Texas. *Nashville Banner,* March 13 to 17, 1886. For discussions of the national labor situation see Ellis Paxson Oberholtzer, *A History of the United States Since the Civil War,* IV, 415 and James Ford Rhodes, *History of the United States from the Compromise of 1850 to the McKinley-Bryan Campaign of 1896,* VIII, 269.

age the investment of capital in all legitimate enterprises.[21]

Such moderate demands appear in strong contrast to the radicalism of the Haymarket in Chicago. Yet, they probably reflected the true condition and attitude of labor in Tennessee. Under such circumstances, it is not surprising that party leaders were willing to ignore labor as an issue in the state campaign.

Tennessee did not escape the anti-railroad sentiment which became so pronounced in agricultural areas in the late seventies and eighties of the last century and which contributed so much to the Granger and Populist movements.[22] Though hostility to railroads did not reach such extremes in this state as in the West, it was based not only upon rate grievances but upon results of the state debt controversy. This bitter fight, as has been pointed out, centered largely around obligations incurred in aid of railroads. Widespread demand that these corporations be brought under stricter control resulted in the passage of an act by the legislature of 1883 providing for: regulation of railroads and of persons operating them; prevention of discrimination by railroads and for punishment of same; appointment of a railroad commission; protection to contractors and laborers for work performed and material furnished the roads.[23] The act creating the railroad commission was declared defective in Federal court. While the case was still pending before the United States Supreme Court, the legislature, in 1885, repealed the law.

The Colyar faction, regarded as representing railroad interests, was strong enough to threaten party success in 1886 should the Democrats insist on state regulation. There appeared a general disposition among party leaders who favored regulation to enter a compromise of expediency. Without "abandoning the idea of the supremacy of the state" over railroads, they realized that "practical statesmanship" did not

---

[21] *Nashville Banner*, March 8, 1886.
[22] An excellent discussion of railroad "grievances" appears in John D. Hicks, *The Populist Revolt*. A fuller treatment of the Tennessee phase of this movement is reserved for a later chapter.
[23] *Annual Cyclopaedia*, 1883, p. 757.

always require the demonstration of that supremacy.[24] There resulted a kind of "gentleman's agreement" among leaders to postpone the evil day when this issue should be fought out.[25]

With the absence of state issues, national questions naturally played a large part in the campaign of 1886. It is sufficient, here, to call to mind some of the major problems before the government at Washington. Agitation on the subject of an expanded currency and free silver was proceeding merrily and the papers of the day were filled with discussions of the Bland-Allison law. More important in the Tennessee campaign, however, were the Blair educational bill and the tariff. These issues revealed fundamental political divisions within the party. The way in which they were prevented from dividing the party affords an instructive study of Robert L. Taylor the conciliator.[26]

It can be seen that, so far as state issues are concerned, the time was most opportune for the harmony movement within the Tennessee Democracy. There were those, however, who regarded

---

[24] *Memphis Avalanche,* February 11, 1886.

[25] The moderate position is set forth by the *Memphis Avalanche,* January 22, February 11, 1886. The *Nashville Banner,* looked upon as representing railroad interests, commended the spirit manifested in the party to drop "wild railroad regulation schemes." See editorial of January 20, 1886. This attitude is set forth in repeated editorials appearing in the *Nashville Banner, Nashville Union* and *Chattanooga Times* during this period. The *Nashville American,* under control of Major Vertrees, had represented the extreme demands for railroad regulation. When that paper came under the control of Colonel Cooper it moderated its demands without changing its position. This was regarded as a concession in the interest of party harmony. The *Nashville Banner* applauded the stand of the *American* which it declared "in marked contrast with the radical views of the late management." While the *American* still stood for the principle of state regulation, declared the *Banner,* it took the considerate position that "a regard for public interests and the true welfare of the party does not demand a further agitation of the question or an insistence upon disturbing policies which have demoralized and injured the party." *Nashville Banner,* January 22, 1886.

The attitude of the rural press on the railroad compromise is difficult to determine. Liberal quotations from small town papers on other subjects appear in the *Nashville Banner.* These are conspicuously few with reference to this issue. *Winchester Times* and *Murfreesboro News* quoted in *Banner* of January 19, and February 6, 1886, show sympathy with railroads.

[26] Because of their importance in Tennessee politics of the later eighties, the Blair bill and tariff are treated in a separate chapter.

any movement in this direction as a surrender of principles or an attempt to straddle issues for mere partisan success. The chief of these critics was the independent newspaper at Nashville.[27] It admitted that the political situation in Tennessee was "peculiar" and that the "vagueness and indefiniteness of purpose" together with a "noteworthy hesitancy" on the part of leaders in both parties, indicated the "remarkable and anomalous condition of public sentiment."[28] In the face of such conditions, it warned Democratic leaders that party success depended upon meeting the issues squarely and deplored the fact that the discussion of them had reached a state of "innocuous desuetude." It favored harmony on the sound basis of "open discussion of issues" but not at the price of suppressing such discussion or of ignoring the issues altogether.[29]

The general attitude of the rural Democratic press seems to have been well expressed by one editor who declared that they who believed that the platform should be encumbered with "the extreme views" of either faction had "sadly misjudged the people."[30] An important Memphis daily appears to have sensed the true situation when it declared, "New issues are looming up which will create new discussion . . . but they are yet in nebulous form and hardly yet tangible." It described the time as "a period of plastic politics." It believed that the "chaotic" and "formulative" condition in Tennessee politics called for "harmonious discussion and reasoning together." It held that the prevailing harmony was suited to the state of politics and that those who were wise would see and adapt themselves to it.[31]

[27] *Nashville Banner.*
[28] *Ibid.,* March 24, 1886.
[29] *Ibid.,* February 26, March 23, 1886.
[30] *Cleveland Banner-News,* quoted in *Nashville Union,* May 17, 1886. See also *Jackson Forked Deer Blade,* quoted in *Nashville Banner,* April 6, 1886.
[31] *Memphis Avalanche,* February 26, 1886. Because of the light which the *Avalanche* editorial throws upon the discussion, it is quoted here at length.

"We are, in Tennessee, in the midst of a period of plastic politics where some old things have been settled, where many new things are just rising into prominence and where some steps toward settlement have been taken as to some issues, which themselves but lead to new steps.

"The state debt issue, out of which grew most of the heart-burnings and discords, belongs to the past.

Among the "nebulous" issues which were to exert a powerful
influence upon the course of Tennessee politics for the next decade were two which party leaders failed to assess at their true
value. Only those who were close to the great rural areas of the
state appreciated the fact. By 1886 the beginnings of the great
agrarian movement were apparent. The Alliance and the Wheel
had made their appearance in various sections of the South.
The day of the "Populites" was near at hand. A recent authority on Populism has held that one of the important contributions of that movement to the South was its stimulation of the
"wool hat boys" from the rural areas to an activity in political
affairs. This group, hitherto "inarticulate," sought to "obtain
weight in Southern politics."[32] The study of the campaign of
1886 in Tennessee and the rise of "Bob" Taylor to leadership
reveals the fact that the "wool hat boys" were already articulate in that state. Little as some of the old political leaders may
have realized it, the rural vote of Tennessee which had been the
support of Andrew Jackson and Andrew Johnson, was in revolt against political control by the generals, colonels and
majors of the Harris and Colyar factions. The city daily which
showed the most correct understanding of the situation warned
managers and bosses of the two factions that they had better
be "conspicuously absent" and that primaries and conventions
must be controlled by the people to "work their unfettered

"The railroad issue had been once the subject of angry dispute, ending
in an appeal to the courts and in a judicial decision and the repeal of the
commission law.

"As to the tariff question, a mighty national factional struggle has greatly
simplified the issue to a question of admission by all Democrats of the revenue principle, only modified by the necessity of conservative dealing, protection of labor and promotion of industry.

"The convict labor question and kindred labor issues are just in the for-
mulation stage. These can form no part in this year's contention between
parties or factions of parties, except as abstractions. The temperance issue,
both parties avoid and the temperance men themselves declare it out of the
pale of party contention.

"The political conditions in Tennessee are chaotic and formulative and
call for harmonious discussion and reasoning together and not for that
factional strife which is sometimes very wholesome. The prevailing harmony,
of which the *Banner* complains, precisely fits the state of politics, and those
are wise who see this and adapt themselves to it."

[32] Hicks, *op. cit.*, p. 410.

will." "The result everywhere," it declared, "must show that the people have expressed their wills."[33] Later events proved these to be prophetic words.

Another force which was to exert a tremendous influence on Democratic politics in 1886 was that of the young men's movement. Andrew Johnson had succeeded in challenging the control of the "damned brigadiers" in 1875[34] but it was only temporary. Like other states, both North and South, Tennessee was to honor its military heroes with political leadership for many years to come. Generals, colonels and majors with records of courage and sacrifice in the cause of the Confederacy had dominated the political scene long beyond the normal time of their generation. Now that old issues had been settled and new ones were on the horizon, young men were insisting upon an opportunity to deal with the problems of their day. A Republican editor at Knoxville called attention to the fierce fight being waged against General John B. Gordon in Georgia and to the "hard pulls" which a number of "old Southern war horses" were having to secure renomination to congress. This indicated, in the opinion of the editor, that "the hold of the brigadier on the Southern heart-string is weakening."[35] Another Republican paper summed up an editorial on "The Young Democracy" with this observation, "Then the brigadiers, colonels and 'majahs' are no longer the ruling factors in Tennessee politics."[36]

Such sentiments, natural to Republicans of East Tennessee, would never have been expressed by Democratic papers in the middle and western sections of the state. Nevertheless the work of the Democratic convention of 1886 led a Memphis editor to remark: "It means that shoulder straps and war memories shall not rule more."[37]

Party leaders, when they worked out their program of har-

---

[33] *Memphis Avalanche,* March 14, 1886. Similar views were expressed by *Nashville American,* January 30, 1886, *Springfield Record* quoted in *Nashville American,* January 30, 1886, *Clarksville Chronicle, Bolivar Bulletin,* quoted in *Nashville Banner,* March 10, 1886.

[34] Milton, *op. cit.,* pp. 666-668.

[35] *Knoxville Daily Chronicle,* May 26, 1886.

[36] *Knoxville Daily Journal,* August 19, 1886.

[37] *Memphis Avalanche,* August 17, 1886.

mony, little realized the force behind these movements among small farmers and young men. Yet the influence of this dissatisfaction, far from defeating the harmony program, was to insure its success.

When issues between factions had been compromised, a long step toward Democratic harmony in Tennessee had been taken. There remained, however, the difficult task of selecting a standard bearer who would be acceptable to both factions and who could arouse in Democratic voters sufficient enthusiasm to overcome a dangerous apathy prevalent among them. Leaders naturally began to scan the list of available generals, majors and colonels,[38] nor could they ignore younger men, without military titles.[39]

There appeared to be no limit to the number of men who considered themselves or were considered by their friends as suited to lead the party to victory. Before Washington's birthday was celebrated, one West Tennessee editor observed that "The number of gubernatorial boomlets that will 'die aborning' this year will be large—very large,"[40] while another from the same section noted that ". . . names are popping up all over the state for governor as fast as corn in a popper."[41] A Knoxville paper indignantly corrected a Memphis contemporary for declaring that East Tennessee was "blessed" with thirty prospective candidates. This, it declared, was an exaggeration for there were only twenty-seven.[42]

There was no alarm over scarcity of prospective candidates but there existed doubting Thomases who questioned the caliber of those mentioned. Staid editors complained that the Democracy of Tennessee was "woefully short on public leaders" and

---

[38] Among those suggested for the Democratic nomination for Governor in 1886 were, General George B. Dibrell, Colonel Robert Looney, Major T. M. McConnell, Captain Albert T. McNeal, General W. C. Whitthorne, Colonel Robert Gates, General J. B. Palmer, General Wm. B. Bate, then Governor, Colonel B. A. Enloe, Colonel W. A. Henderson, Captain Thos. L. Williams.

[39] Chief among those mentioned who held no military title were Hon. S. A. Champion, Dr. Wm. Morrow, Hon. J. C. Luttrell, Hon. R. P. Frierson and Hon. Robert L. Taylor. See newspapers of spring and summer of 1886.

[40] *Obion Democrat,* quoted in *Nashville Banner,* February 22, 1886.

[41] *Milan Exchange,* quoted in *idem.*

[42] *Knoxville Daily Journal,* quoted in *ibid.,* February 9, 1886.

that "mediocrity" had "usurped public place."[43] One of their number looked at the situation a little more philosophically. "Several of the openly announced aspirants for political honors in Tennessee," he declared, "are big men—not as big as they think they are, probably, but big enough for all practical purposes."[44] Another asked whether there ever was a time when complaints about mediocrity were not made or whether, as a matter of fact, there ever was a time when mediocrity was not actually the rule. After calling attention to the fact that Tennessee was in a transitional stage when old issues and old leaders were giving way to new, he held that the "new issues and the men who are to guide them are not yet demonstrated."[45]

Aside from the sheer number of gubernatorial aspirants, the question of sectionalism had to be considered. The belief seems to have been general that the new governor should come from East Tennessee. It had been many years since a Democrat from that section was head of the state ticket. Neither United States Senator was from that area and it seemed likely that Senator Howell E. Jackson's successor would come from Middle Tennessee. These facts led East Tennessee Democrats to insist that they were due the governorship and those from the other sections regarded the demand as reasonable.[46] The claim of East Tennessee to the gubernatorial nomination was further strengthened when the party's slate for supreme court justices failed to include a representative from that section.[47]

A summary of the situation facing the Democratic party of Tennessee in early 1886 includes the following outstanding

---

[43] *Nashville Union* and *Nashville Banner*, quoted in *Memphis Avalanche*, March 27, 1886, *Obion Democrat*, quoted in *Nashville Banner*, May 18, 1886.

[44] *Memphis Scimitar*, quoted in *Nashville Banner*, March 1, 1886.

[45] *Memphis Avalanche*, March 27, 1886.

[46] Numerous references in the press indicate the strength of the East Tennessee claim. As illustrative of this see *Nashville Banner*, January 11, February 13, May 20, *Memphis Avalanche*, January 15, also *Milan Exchange, Knoxville Daily Journal, Obion Democrat, National Review* (Nashville), *Chattanooga Commercial, Clarksville Tobacco Leaf, Sparta State and Farm, Dayton Advance Gazette*, quoted in *Nashville Banner*, January 30, February 3, 5, March 2, April 5, 19, August 5, 1886. Papers from every section of the state accepted this position.

[47] *Nashville Banner*, June 11, 1886.

facts: Leaders recognized the disrupted condition of the party and were determined to compromise on issues or to postpone their settlement. The transitional stage through which the state was passing facilitated such a program. Rural voters and young men of the party were becoming restless and were demanding a voice in the conduct of affairs. Sectionalism, which has played such an important part in Tennessee affairs, was to be considered and East Tennessee's claim to the nomination was to be given due weight. The most acceptable candidate would be he who could satisfy the rural voters, the younger generation of Democrats, East Tennessee, and who could conciliate the Harris and Colyar factions.

The bewildering number of possible candidates for the Democratic gubernatorial nomination was rapidly reduced, and by early April it was generally believed that the contest was to be among General George B. Dibrell, Colonel Robert F. Looney, Major Thos. M. McConnell, Captain Thos. L. Williams and Robert L. Taylor.[48]

General Dibrell was strongly advocated by the conservative or Colyar element of the party. In addition to his political activities, he was a director in important industrial enterprises.[49] However, this business connection was not criticized by those who did not favor General Dibrell's nomination. He seems to have commanded a respect that was state-wide and confined to no faction or party. Yet it cannot be supposed that his business interests were overlooked by the industrialists who advanced his cause. He was described by the press supporting him as a strong, dignified man who would make a desirable candidate and a good, safe governor.[50] One paper, regarded at the time as closely identified with the railroad interests, urged the General's case in these words: "What the people want is a Governor of broad mind and broad honesty and they will have it in Gen. Dibrell. If they hanker after spread-eagleism, showy and

---

[48] *Memphis Avalanche,* quoted in *Nashville Banner,* April 6, 1886; *Nashville Banner,* April 22, 29, 1886.

[49] See chapter 1, p. 19.

[50] *Dresden Enterprise, Bedford County Times,* quoted in *Nashville Banner,* August 5, 1886.

pompous or theatrical declamation, they will have to look else-where."[51] It was declared that his strength was representative of conservative thought, and one Middle Tennessee editor re-joiced that he did not play the fiddle.[52] Objections were made that General Dibrell was from Middle Tennessee and thus failed to fulfill the sectional requirement. His supporters answered this argument by pointing out that while he did live on the east-ern edge of Middle Tennessee, a majority of the counties he so long represented in congress lay in East Tennessee. General Dibrell had strong newspaper support, particularly in Middle and West Tennessee.[53]

Colonel Looney, Major McConnell and Captain Williams had purely sectional strength. The press of Memphis, Looney's home, was solidly behind him, but rural papers of West Tennes-see did not show such unanimity.[54] Colonel Looney was described as a man "particularly adapted to large enterprise," and was a pioneer in organizing, in the South, large mining corporations which operated in Mexico.[55] His prospects for the nomination were dimmed, however, by a congressional investigation into the affairs of the Pan Electric Telephone Company in which Colonel Looney had been a leading figure. The investigation involved a number of nationally prominent Southern Democrats and re-ceived wide publicity. Though nothing serious came of it and though there was considerable support for the claim that it was instigated by the Bell interests against a rival, the investigation did not help Colonel Looney's gubernatorial ambitions.

---

[51] *Nashville Banner,* August 5, 1886.

[52] *Lebanon Herald* quoted in *idem.*

[53] Among the rural papers supporting Dibrell were *Clarksville Tobacco Leaf, Sparta State and Farm, Dresden Enterprise, Bedford County Times, Lebanon Herald, Franklin County News, McMinnville New Era, Tullahoma Guardian, Humbolt Messenger, Henderson True Democrat, Savannah Cou-rier, Sparta Expositor, Brownsville State,* quoted in *Nashville Banner,* from February 11 to July 7, 1886. He likewise had the support of such city dailies as *Nashville Banner.*

[54] Colonel Looney was supported by *Memphis Avalanche, Memphis Ap-peal, Memphis Ledger.* Some smaller papers of West Tennessee, such as *Union City Anchor* and *Brownsville State and Bee,* looked with favor upon Looney although they were not vigorous in their support. See *Nashville Banner,* February 19, April 19, 1886.

[55] Speer, *op. cit.,* p. 21.

Major McConnell and Captain Williams were both East Tennesseans and their strength lay almost wholly in that area. Their importance in the pre-convention canvass was based largely on the fact that the nomination was likely to go to that section. Their activities were directed toward getting control of East Tennessee delegations.

Early in the year it became evident that Robert L. Taylor was the outstanding candidate for the nomination. His early successes in politics, together with his state-wide popularity, had established him as a rising party leader. During the first weeks of January two Democrats of Nashville wrote to Taylor, at that time pension agent at Knoxville by appointment of President Cleveland, asking him to make the race for governor. They reminded him that East Tennessee was due to furnish the candidate and that he was the most prominent Democrat of that section. They cited the small majority of Governor Bate in 1884 as proof that the Democratic party would need a popular leader and pronounced him the most available man. In his reply, Taylor let it be known that he would not refuse to run but would not stand in the way of any good Democrat who might want to make the race. After describing the dissensions which threatened the party, he added: "I am glad that, having spent my time and strength in national politics, I have never been drawn into any of our state factional fights." He had had views on these questions which he had never tried to conceal, he said, but Democrats in East Tennessee were "too few to quarrel." He concluded by saying that he would not be a candidate unless it were determined that he was the most suitable man to unite the party.[56]

---

[56] *Nashville Banner,* January 11, 1886. To quote Mr. Taylor at length:

"Our party needs reorganization. We have broken into fragments or rather factions, discordant, belligerent, and the party has been rent with feuds which have threatened its overthrow throughout the state. I am glad that, having spent my time and strength in national politics, I have never been drawn into any of our State factional fights. I have had my own views on these questions and have never concealed them but up here in the land of the 'truly loyal,' where Republicanism rides on every passing breeze and lurks in every flower, we have been too few to quarrel, too sensible to divide. . . . I am not a candidate unless it shall be determined that I can do more to unite the party than anybody else."

The rapidity with which Taylor's strength developed, in the face of difficulties, puzzled many who considered themselves politically wise. One Memphis editor, usually very astute, admitted that the Taylor boom existed but regarded it without any special foundations, and two months later he expressed surprise that there were so many Taylor "well wishers" in West Tennessee, especially since there was "no reason why he should be thought of as Governor."[57]

Of all the candidates for the nomination, Taylor was the only one who had an active opposition. This included practically every large city daily in the state as well as a large number of the smaller papers.[58] The attitude of this section of the press reflected that of party leaders. One political writer observed that the leaders were not "altogether sweet on Taylor,"[59] and a rural editor remarked that the "would-be leaders and factionists," those with "axes to grind" and with selfish purposes, were opposed to him.[60]

It must be stated that at no time was the opposition to Taylor marked with bitterness. Supporters of all candidates seemed to keep in mind the necessity of harmony. A few minor arguments against his candidacy were advanced, such as the impropriety of his seeking the governorship when he already had a

---

[57] *Memphis Avalanche*, February 21, April 24, 1886.

[58] *Nashville American*, August 12, 1886, *Jackson Dispatch*, quoted in *Nashville Banner*, July 7, 1886. Among the papers which opposed Taylor's nomination actively or passively, were, *Memphis Avalanche*, *Memphis Appeal*, *Memphis Scimitar*, *Memphis Ledger*, *Nashville Banner*, *Nashville Union*, *Nashville American*, *Chattanooga Times*, *Chattanooga Sunday Argus*, *Knoxville Tribune*, *McMinnville New Era*, *McMinnville Standard*, *Pulaski Citizen*, *Franklin County News*, *Trenton Herald*, *Dresden Enterprise*, *Lebanon Herald*, *Hartsville Sentinel*, *Jackson Blade*, *Paris Post*, *West Tennessee Whig*, *Sparta State and Farm*, *Jonesboro Herald-Tribune*, *Morristown Gazette*, *Newport Sentinel*, *Bedford County Times*, *Sparta Expositor*, *Clarksville Tobacco Leaf*, *Brownsville Democrat*, *Union City Anchor*, *Tullahoma Guardian*, *Manchester Times*, *Rhea County News*, *Bolivar Bulletin*, *Savannah Courier*, *Henderson True Democrat*, *Humbolt Messenger*, *Athens Post*, *Cleveland Banner-News*, *Brownsville State and Bee*, *Dayton Advance-Gazette*, quoted in *Nashville Banner*, February 3 to July 29, 1886, *Blount County Citizen*, *Columbia Herald*, *Shelbyville Gazette*, *McMinn Citizen*, quoted in *Nashville American*, July 7 to August 9, 1886.

[59] *Nashville Banner*, March 6, 1886, political discussion by "The Mummy."

[60] *Waverly News*, quoted in *ibid.*, February 18, 1886.

better paying position as pension agent and his seeking so important a position before he had yet "won his spurs."[61] On the whole, however, the Taylor opposition directed its activities along three lines, to show him unqualified for the office, to deprecate the spectacle of brothers engaging in an unseemly contest for office and finally, to spread propaganda designed to discourage and disintegrate the Taylor forces.

Conservative papers warned their readers that "Bob" Taylor was "remote from being fitted for the lofty post of Governor," that he was the weakest man the Democrats could name. The harmony movement within the party, it was declared, tended toward a "staid sort of conservatism" that called for a campaign of dignity and moderation. Taylor's fondness for the "fiddle" and anecdotes was the target for many an editorial dart. His skill along these lines marked the limit of his ability, they said. One paper admitted that "Bob" could make a good "whoop-em-up" speech, play the fiddle and "make the boys laugh," but held that he was deplorably lacking in "solid matter" of which statesmen were made. Supporters of other candidates rejoiced that their favorites were not "fiddlers."[62]

The Republicans nominated Alfred A. Taylor, brother of "Bob," as their candidate, seven weeks before the Democratic convention met. The selection of "Alf" seems to have been based largely on the hope that it would prevent the nomination of his brother by the Democrats.[63] At any rate, those who opposed "Bob" seized upon this as a powerful argument against him. It was unnatural, they declared, for two brothers to oppose one another in such a contest. One influential paper declared bitterly that the canvass of two brothers would present a "repulsive tableau to all who cherish the memories of childhood, home, and mother." Such a campaign, it held, would be a "contemptible farce" and would be so "unnatural and disgusting" that thou-

---

[61] *Memphis Avalanche,* February 21, April 4, 21, 1886, *Nashville Banner,* February 8, June 6, 1886, *McMinnville New Era, Murfreesboro Free Press, Franklin County News, Shelbyville Gazette,* quoted in *Nashville Banner,* February 3, 9, 22, March 5, 1886.

[62] *Memphis Avalanche,* April 24, 1886.

[63] For a more complete discussion of the Republican nomination see Chapter III.

sands of Democrats would refuse to vote. It failed to mention
the possible reaction of Republican voters. There was no state
in the Union that would tolerate a contest of this kind, it informed its readers, and in no state could there be found two
brothers "so forgetful of the mother that bore them as to enter
into such a shameful contest."[64] In a more facetious mood, this
paper suggested that the father of the "ambitious boys" be
made Prohibition candidate for governor and, to eliminate all
possible doubt as to the election of a Taylor, it thought a still
younger brother "might head the Greenback ticket." A rural
editor disagreed with this and believed the father should be the
Greenback nominee.[65] The independent editor at Nashville
warned Democrats that unless they nominated "Bob," the Taylor family, which had been "complacently contemplating the
governorship," might hold an "indignation meeting." On second
thought, however, he decided that the father might find it more
advantageous to call a "family caucus" at which the next governor of Tennessee could be selected.[66]

The favorite method of Taylor's opponents was a defeatist
propaganda that did not cease until the nomination was finally
made. City editors solemnly informed their readers that "Bob's"
strength was greatly exaggerated and his ability to carry East
Tennessee was extremely doubtful. They prophesied that he
could not command a two-thirds vote in convention and reports
that he had withdrawn from the contest were discussed.[67] Serious predictions of his defeat were enlivened by lighter observa-
tions ". . . probably Bob's boom got washed away in the big
rise," "Taylor's fiddle has snapped a string." These and many

[64] *Memphis Appeal*, July 14, August 8, 13, 1886.

[65] *Memphis Appeal*, July 14, 1886, *Hickman Pioneer*, quoted in *Nashville
Banner*, June 6, 1886. Nathaniel G. Taylor, father of the two candidates,
was offered the gubernatorial nomination by the Prohibition party but refused to accept. See James P., Alf A., and Hugh L Taylor, *Life and Career
of Senator Robert Love Taylor*, p. 179 (hereafter referred to as Taylor
Brothers).

[66] *Nashville Banner*, July 6, 17, 24, 1886.

[67] *Nashville Banner, Memphis Avalanche, Memphis Appeal*, numerous
issues of 1886.

similar expressions were used to create the impression that
Taylor was headed for defeat.[68]

From the earliest months of 1886 there was a sure and irre-
sistible movement toward Taylor among the rank and file of
Democrats in the rural areas. This movement gained strength
in spite of opposition by a large section of the press, including
all the city dailies, and by party leaders of both factions. It was
all the more remarkable because of the inactivity and apparent
indifference of Taylor. In his letter signifying his willingness
to accept the nomination he stated the conditions upon which
his name might be used. He would not fight other good Democrats who might desire the honor and he would not accept unless the party believed him the most suitable man to harmonize
discordant elements.[69] His pre-convention course proved that
he meant what he said. This letter was published on January 11,
and from that date until the convention assembled on August
11 no public utterance of his appeared. There was no reference
in the press to any speech or personal effort of any kind. This
may have been due in part to President Cleveland's strict Civil
Service regulation against Federal employees taking part in
political activities. Yet there can be no doubt as to the sincerity
of his declared unwillingness to accept the nomination at the
price of party dissension. On the second day of voting at the
convention it appeared that the opposition to him would not
yield although he had a majority of the delegates. At that time
he wired his supporters, "Don't let my friends be rash. Don't
let my candidacy interfere with good feeling and harmony. Do
not hold me on to defeat any other candidate. Tell the boys to
be cool and conservative. I do not want the nomination at the
cost of bitterness and bad blood."[70] The telegram illustrates
forcibly the whole attitude of Robert L. Taylor toward the
nomination and his course was in accordance with it. A passive
campaign of this kind would not, under ordinary circumstances,

---

[68] *Lebanon Herald, Newport Sentinel, Morristown Gazette, Chattanooga
Times, Hartsville Sentinel,* quoted in *Nashville Banner,* March 22, 24, April
5, 19, July 29, 1886, *Memphis Avalanche,* April 18, 1886.

[69] *Nashville Banner,* January 11, 1886.

[70] *Nashville American,* August 13, 1886. Telegram to J. L. Pearcy.

succeed against powerful and active opposition; yet in the face
of such disadvantages, Taylor's strength increased. Circumstances were not ordinary. Two forces had entered the campaign on which old politicians had not counted. The Democracy of Jackson and Johnson had found a leader who spoke its
language. Small farmers in the rural areas of Tennessee had
sensed the agrarian revolution that was impending. They did
not wait for a Ben Tillman, a Tom Watson or a "Sockless
Jerry" Simpson to lead them in strange paths. They preferred
that "Bob" Taylor guide them back to the agrarianism with
which they were familiar. At the same time, the youth of Tennessee had found a leader about whom it could rally. Here
was a man of its generation pitted against generals, colonels
and majors. The support of these two elements in the population was the secret of "Bob" Taylor's strength. Its concen-
tration on one man was the circumstance that was not ordinary.

City editors may not have seen the "foundations" upon which
the Taylor "boom" rested and may have been surprised that it
survived and increased in strength,[71] but not so with many of
their rural brethren. These were closer to the people and knew
what was taking place in the public mind. One Middle Tennessee weekly declared that ". . . the masses, the bone and sinew
of the party" would hail "Bob's" nomination with an enthusiasm never before witnessed in the state, and another compared
him to "the rising sun that will gladden the hearts of the Democratic hosts of Middle and West Tennessee."[72] From the rural
areas of West Tennessee came such expressions as these: "Bob
Taylor is the favorite of West Tennessee . . . certainly the
choice of the Democracy of this immediate section," "We are
for Bob as long as his hat is in the ring," "Madison and all
adjoining counties of West Tennessee are for him, first, last,
and all the time."[73] An East Tennessee observer declared him

---

[71] *Memphis Avalanche*, April 18, 1886.

[72] *Waverly News, Shelbyville Commercial,* quoted in *Nashville Banner,*
February 18, 27, 1886.

[73] *Milan Exchange, Martin Mail, Lexington Press, Jackson Dispatch,* quoted in *Nashville Banner,* July 7, February 8, 15, March 17, 1886.

the man, above all others, to be named by the convention for "he is already named by the people."[74]

Few seem to have sensed the important role that young Democrats were playing until the convention had acted. It then dawned upon the consciousness of Tennessee that the young Democracy had asserted itself. "Tennessee politics are in the hands of young men," "young men's movements," " . . . the people are disposed to be off with the old," "a shaking up of dry bones"—such editorial phrases were frequent and testify to the universal recognition of youth's revolt.[75]

Ridicule of Taylor's "fiddle" and criticism of his supposed lack of dignity made no impression on his rural supporters, one of whom declared that no man in the state, of his age, possessed such "substantial accomplishments" necessary to make a first class nominee and governor.[76] Horror of a fraternal campaign, voiced by dignified opponents, was termed "maudlin sentiment" by a small West Tennessee paper. Others failed to see the justice of denying "Bob" leadership for which he was eminently fitted because the Republicans had nominated "Alf." Perhaps the spectacle might be unusual, but such was the humor of Tennessee politics and it was well to "have a little fun as we go along." At any rate, one paper declared, "the campaign will be free from personalities and personal bitterness."[77]

The defeatist propaganda, spread by opposition papers, meant nothing to "unterrified" small town editors. "Bob Taylor will be nominated and elected by an overwhelming majority," was the retort of one and others spoke in the same vein.[78] These small town editors had read the signs correctly. In county after county of East, Middle and West Tennessee, dur-

---

[74] *Nashville Banner,* March 1, 1886.

[75] *Memphis Avalanche,* August 17, 18, September 3, 1886, *Memphis Appeal,* August 13, 1886, *Knoxville Daily Journal,* August 19, 1886, *Knoxville Tribune,* quoted in *Nashville Banner,* August 27, 1886, *Nashville American,* August 12, *Camden Herald,* quoted in *Nashville Banner,* August 27, 1886.

[76] *Martin Mail,* quoted in *Nashville Banner,* March 22, 1886.

[77] *Martin Mail, Dresden Enterprise, Waverly News, Tipton Record, Obion Democrat,* quoted in *ibid.,* June 29, July 13, 29, August 15, 1886.

[78] *Waverly News, Johnson City Comet, Shelbyville Commercial, Chester Citizen, Milan Exchange,* quoted in *ibid.,* February 11, 13, March 17, July 7, 1886.

ing the hot summer days of 1886, shirt sleeved "gallused" farmers and young Democrats went to the conventions and instructed for their own "Bob." What happened in Madison County may be taken as typical. "The result of the convention Saturday was as we predicted," ran the account. "There was a strong sentiment in the county for Taylor, and the county Democracy were on hand in good numbers. It required no leadership to rouse a strong following for Taylor. The people were for him and had been since his canvass as elector for the State on the Cleveland-Hendricks ticket. There was a respectable minority for Dibrell. . . ."[79]

When the Democratic convention met in Nashville on August 11, the chief interest of both delegates and public centered upon the gubernatorial nomination. It was realized by all that Taylor was the strongest single candidate, but he was far from having the necessary two-thirds majority. Speculation was rife as to the ability of the Taylor forces to hold together. They were from the country, young men inexperienced in convention ways, and they were without a leader. Taylor had refused to attend the convention, giving as his reason the Civil Service regulation against participation in politics by federal employees.[80] One of the first moves of the opposition was to call a caucus of East Tennessee delegates to name the man from that section on whom all would center. This, because of sectional understanding, was to be equivalent to nomination. Early in the canvass, Taylor had signified his willingness to abide the decision of such a caucus, provided it was fair and reasonable.[81] East Tennessee delegates were divided between Taylor, McConnell, Williams and Henderson, with Taylor short of a clear majority. It was so evidently a case of Taylor against the field or rather, the field against Taylor, that his friends refused to enter the caucus. McConnell was the choice of those present. As a result, the contest was between Taylor and McConnell of East Tennessee, Dibrell and Looney of Middle and West Tennessee respectively. For some reason, un-

---

[79] *Jackson Tribune-Sun,* quoted in *Nashville Banner,* August 5, 1886.
[80] *Nashville Banner,* August 11, 1886.
[81] *Nashville Banner,* August 11, 1886.

explained by the press, a convention rule prohibited nominating speeches. It is not clear who sponsored it. It may have been due to the impatience of delegates to begin voting, it may have been intended to keep down friction, it is possible that one side or another believed an advantage would be gained. At any rate, voting began soon after the platform was adopted.[82]

When the first ballot was taken Taylor led but was 119 short of a majority and some 285 short of the necessary two-thirds. The vote stood Taylor 611½, Dibrell 388½, Looney 203½, McConnell 138½. The strategy of the Taylor opponents was plain. The opposition must concentrate on one man and, at the same time, draw support from the disorganized and inexperienced Taylor forces. This plan was simplicity itself on paper but proved impossible of execution. Succeeding ballots revealed that Taylor's delegates had come to Nashville with but one object in view. They voted for "Bob" at every opportunity, with increasing noise and enthusiasm. At the same time, the opposition could not concentrate. Balloting lasted for two days with all four men before the convention. On the fourteenth ballot, toward the end of the second day, Taylor's vote had increased by 156 and Dibrell's by 20 while Looney and McConnell had lost accordingly. At this time East Tennessee delegates had decided to rally behind Taylor, for he then held four-fifths of that section's strength. On the fifteenth ballot an effort was made to withdraw Dibrell and cast his vote for McConnell in the hope that East Tennessee would desert Taylor and rally to him. But the opposition had waited too long to concentrate. The break to Taylor had come. On that ballot Taylor passed the two-thirds mark and the nomination was made unanimous.[83]

The nature of the campaign and convention fight leaves no doubt that the plans of party leaders had been upset. It is

---

[82] The platform, together with that of the Republicans, is considered in Chapter III.

[83] For accounts of the convention, see *Nashville Banner, Nashville American, Nashville Union, Memphis Avalanche,* and *Memphis Appeal,* August 11, 12, 13, 14, 1886.

difficult, however, to determine exactly what those plans were. This much is clear: the Democratic party was weakened by the feud between Harris and Colyar factions. Its defeat was imminent unless the factions effected a working arrangement. A harmony program was worked out and agreed upon. It was executed so far as the party platform was concerned. It is impossible to say definitely, on such evidence as has been examined, what the compromise was with respect to the gubernatorial nomination. This seems to have been the understanding since the Harris wing held both United States senatorships and was to continue to do so; the governorship was to go to the Colyar group. General Dibrell, a man of outstanding qualifications, was apparently agreed upon, but the entrance of Taylor into the race upset calculations. Unfortunately for the Dibrell candidacy, some one advanced the suggestion that East Tennessee should have the governorship. This was acclaimed in that section of the state and the other sections recognized the justice of it. The strategy of the pre-convention fight was to keep Taylor from getting delegates enough for nomination. Wherever possible, they were to be instructed for Dibrell. In counties where that was impossible, they were to go for a favorite son. Looney was strong in Memphis and nearby areas. In East Tennessee, McConnell, Williams and Henderson were put forward. At the proper time, in convention, the others were to throw their strength to Dibrell, but that time never came. The Taylor support was too strong, determined and enthusiastic. Delegates released by Looney and McConnell were inclined to vote for "Bob" rather than Dibrell. The opposition was prevented from concentrating until the stampede to Taylor had begun.

The strength developed by Robert L. Taylor surprised seasoned political leaders. A Nashville paper which had not supported him quickly recognized the true situation as soon as the delegates reached Nashville. It commented upon the fact that Taylor's supporters were, as a rule, the younger men and that the mass of them came from the country districts, showing, the paper said, "some strange and wonderful hold upon that element of the people." His race, it went on to say, was most remarkable, regardless of whether or not it were successful. Without leaving home, rarely ever writing a letter, with no organized plan of action and apparently indifferent to the results, Taylor had faced an opposition that included "a large and influential part of the press." The plans of all the candidates "looked toward defeating him alone." The Taylor delegates, it added, arrived in Nashville with no one to receive them, no headquarters to go to, no leaders to execute plans of organized efforts. There was no plan of action. They were "absolutely at sea" except for the one purpose "to vote for the nomination of a man whom they had never seen," and who, it might have added, was in Knoxville at the time. In such a confused condition, the paper concluded, they were confronted with "able managers" and "trained lieutenants."[84] Thus the sons of those who had fought and won for "Andy" Jackson and "Andy" Johnson, came to Nashville to fight and win for "Bob" Taylor.

---

[84] *Nashville American,* August 12, 1886.

CHAPTER III

THE WAR OF THE ROSES

THE WAR of the Roses, as the campaign between the Taylor brothers was called, has become a tradition in Tennessee. An incident which took place at Shelbyville is typical of the spirit in which it was conducted. The two candidates traveled together in their joint canvass. When they arrived at this beautiful Middle Tennessee town, says a newspaper account, "Both were conducted to the carriage of Honorable Edmund Cooper and, side by side, the two brothers rode to the elegant home of that gentleman where they had been invited to dinner. . . . Over two thousand footmen and horsemen escorted them to the residence of Col. Cooper. . . . Prominent citizens of both parties had been invited to meet the brothers and a sumptuous dinner was spread."[1]

Before proceeding further with the campaign, however, it is important to know something more of this young man from East Tennessee who had upset the calculations of seasoned politicians, and likewise to examine some of the circumstances which brought the brothers together and the issues between them.

Robert Love Taylor was of blood, distinguished in Tennessee history.[2] On the paternal side his great-grandfather was Gen-

---

[1] *Nashville American,* September 18, 1886. At the request of the Democratic State Committee, the *Nashville American* detailed its city editor, Mr. George H. Armistead, now editor-in-chief of the *Nashville Banner,* to accompany the brothers and give full reports of the debates. His contributions to his paper are invaluable to a student of the campaign.

[2] A tradition, not confined to Tennessee, has persisted that Taylor sprang from lowly mountaineer parentage. Possibly his understanding of and popularity with the common people contributed to this. This conception of Taylor was given wide circulation by a romantic sketch, "Fiddling His Way to Fame," by Will Allen Dromgoole. It was first published in the *Arena* and

eral Nathaniel Green Taylor who served with Andrew Jackson
in his Indian wars and in the War of 1812.[3] His grandfather,
James P. Taylor, was a lawyer of prominence and was the first
attorney general in the first judicial circuit of Tennessee. The
father of "Bob" and "Alf," another Nathaniel Green Taylor,
was educated in Washington College in Tennessee and at
Princeton. Though reared a Presbyterian and trained for the
law, he became a minister in the Methodist Episcopal Church.
He was honored with the degree of Doctor of Divinity and was
at one time professor of belle-letters at Athens, or Grant University, located at Athens, Tennessee. His ministerial duties did
not keep him from taking a lively interest in politics. He was a
Whig before the Civil War and, as the nominee of that party,
ran against Andrew Johnson for congress. Though Johnson
defeated him, he later served two terms in the Lower House as
representative of the first district. In 1860 "Nat" Taylor supported his old Whig leader John Bell and was presidential elector for the state-at-large on the Constitutional Union ticket.[4]
When Tennessee seceded in 1861, "Nat" Taylor, like so many
of his fellow East Tennesseans, remained loyal to the Union.
He had done his best to defeat the secession movement and, during the war, was active in helping his less fortunate neighbors.
He organized a movement in Knoxville to obtain aid in the
North for the destitute Unionists of East Tennessee. He went
North in behalf of this cause and addressed large audiences at
Cincinnati, Philadelphia, New York, Boston, and other places.[5]

When the Republicans of Tennessee divided on Reconstruction, Nathaniel G. Taylor aligned himself with the conservative
element and staunchly supported the policies of his former
political enemy, President Andrew Johnson. Taylor was elected

---

was later included in Miss Dromgoole's volume *The Heart of Old Hickory
and Other Stories of Tennessee,* pp. 39-72. In this, Governor Taylor is made
to tell the story of his life. He lapsed into the mountain dialect as he
described the mountain cabin which "faced todes the East and todes the
sunrise." The mountain "mammy" he depicts does not resemble the sister of
Landon C. Haynes, Confederate States Senator from Tennessee.

[3] Taylor Brothers, *op. cit.,* p. 18.

[4] *Ibid.,* pp. 27-33.

[5] Winston, *op. cit.,* p. 422.

to congress as a Conservative in August, 1865[6] and was among that group of representatives from Southern states denied their seats by congress. Later President Johnson appointed him commissioner of Indian affairs, which post he held until the end of the Johnson administration. The Taylor family was not to forget the favor bestowed by Johnson and this explains, partially at least, the course of Assemblyman Alfred A. Taylor in the senatorial contest of 1875, referred to in a preceding chapter. It is important to remember that the Republican members of the Taylor family were conservatives during Reconstruction. They were personal and political friends of their neighbor and fellow Unionist, Andrew Johnson. It is not surprising that the young Democratic member of the family fashioned his Democracy after the pattern set by Johnson.

On his maternal side, Robert L. Taylor was of German descent, his ancestors having come to this country soon after the American Revolution. His grandfather, David Haynes, was a prosperous farmer and successful business man of East Tennessee. He seems to have taken no active part in the controversies of the Civil War period but to have attended strictly to his farming and business interests.[7] Landon C. Haynes, son of David and an uncle of Robert L. Taylor, was an attorney of wide reputation. He cast his lot with the Confederacy and was elected as one of Tennessee's two members of the Confederate States senate, where he served until the downfall of that govern-

---

[6] Jones, *op. cit.*

[7] Taylor Brothers, *op. cit.,* p. 35. Political opponents of "Bob" Taylor, who accused him of evasiveness on certain issues, would have enjoyed the following story told on his maternal grandfather, David Haynes. The old gentleman was accosted one day by a group of Confederate cavalry which was operating in East Tennessee. He answered their inquiry by saying "I have the honor of being the father of Senator Landon C. Haynes." Satisfied of his Confederate sympathies, the troops cheered him and rode on. A band of Union cavalry was in pursuit and soon came upon the father of Senator Haynes. To similar inquiries by the Federals, he replied that he was the father of a daughter "who, gentlemen, had the extreme good sense to accept the matrimonial offer of the Hon. Nathaniel G. Taylor, late of Congress and now supporting President Lincoln and the Union." This reply had the desired effect and the grandfather of "Bob" Taylor rode on in peace. See Paul Deresco Augsburg, *Bob and Alf Taylor, Their Lives and Lectures,* pp. 22-23.

ment. Emely Haynes Taylor, sister of Senator Landon C. Haynes and wife of Nathaniel G. Taylor, was a woman of great energy. She had received, as a girl, the best education afforded by the time and place. After her marriage she devoted her life to her home and to the training of her children.

It is clear, from the above sketch, that Robert Love and Alfred Alexander Taylor were descended from families which had played an active part in the military, legal, political, religious, and business life of Tennessee. It does not appear that they had been people of great wealth, but they were families of substance, well above the average in education, and accustomed to leadership among their people. They divided on the Civil War, like so many East Tennessee families, but when the excesses of Reconstruction came, they were moderates who sought to alleviate rather than exploit the misfortunes of Tennesseans.

Robert Love Taylor was born July 31, 1850, in Happy Valley, Carter County, Tennessee. He was only eleven years old when the Civil War plunged his state and particularly his section of the state into internecine strife. The war limited his opportunities for education and a frail constitution put him to a further disadvantage. When the father was appointed commissioner of Indian affairs, the family moved North and such of the children as were of school age were entered in Pennington Seminary at Pennington, New Jersey. Here they remained until the family moved back to Tennessee where the future governor became a student at East Tennessee Wesleyan.[8] It is not recorded that "Bob," during his school days, showed any precocity in his studies. However, at Pennington and later at Wesleyan, he demonstrated a remarkable ability at humorous recitation. He, it is said, won the hearts of his fellow students and teachers with his aptness at telling anecdotes, his powers of mimicry, and with a drollness of speech that would throw his hearers into convulsions of laughter.[9] These qualities later endeared him to thousands in Tennessee and in other states. They made him popular on the lecture platform and invincible in political debates.

[8] Taylor Brothers, *op. cit.*, pp. 75-81.
[9] *Ibid.*, pp. 82-83.

Young Taylor, early in life, manifested an interest in politics. While still a boy, he espoused the cause of Democracy in spite of the fact that his father was prominent in Republican circles. This is attributed to the influence of his distinguished uncle, Landon C. Haynes, for whom the lad had profound admiration and affection.[10] Those who doubted, in 1886, whether the fraternal candidates could or would seriously debate political issues were not acquainted with the boyhood days of the Taylor brothers. While yet working on their father's farm, "Bob" and "Alf" were accustomed to engaged in numerous serious, and, at times, heated debates on questions at issue between Democratic and Republican parties. Frequently, while the boys were in the fields, some disputed question would be mentioned. They immediately laid aside their hoes, found a suitable rostrum, presumably in the shade, and the debate began. Their fellow laborers would gather about them to applaud their efforts. Such discussions may not have increased production on the Taylor farm, but they did stimulate the boys to study and research in all newspapers and political speeches that came their way.[11]

Robert L. Taylor was licensed to practice law in July, 1878, but entered politics almost immediately. His brother "Alf" had failed to capture the Republican nomination for congress in a contest with Major A. H. Pettibone. The first congressional district, in which they lived, has long been overwhelmingly Republican and, as a usual thing, a nomination by that party is equivalent to election. However, "Alf's" friends felt that Pettibone had won the nomination by unfair means and were in a mood to take revenge. Shrewd Democratic leaders, eager to nominate a man who could best capitalize on the disaffection of "Alf" Taylor's Republican friends, soon centered on his Democratic brother, "Bob." Fortunately, the latter's law business was not of such volume as to prevent his accepting the nomination. In the contest which followed, the untried boy acquitted himself with credit, though pitted against a seasoned campaigner. He used to good advantage the art of telling droll

[10] DeLong Rice, *Old Limber or the Tale of the Taylors*, p. 35.
[11] Taylor Brothers, *op. cit.*, pp. 111-112.

anecdotes which had marked his school-day orations, and demonstrated the value of the fiddle as a weapon to capture Tennessee voters.[12] The young Democrat was successful, but two years later Major Pettibone succeeded in returning him to his native mountains.

The average young congressman who spends but two years in Washington does not make a profound impression on the legislative history of the country. Taylor was no exception to the rule. He was appointed to committees on manufactures and invalid pensions.[13] Probably because of his connection with the committee on invalid pensions together with the fact that there was a large number of former Union soldiers among his constituency, he devoted his activities to pension matters and bills of like nature. His few ventures into matters of a more general character are interesting at this time because of the light they shed on his early political trend and not because of results accomplished. During his two years in congress he introduced three bills that come under this classification. One proposed to levy a tax on incomes, another to repeal the tax on tobacco in the hands of producers[14] and the third would abolish the office of assistant United States district attorney for the various districts and circuits in the United States.[15] None of the bills ever emerged from committee.

Only on two occasions did Congressman Taylor discuss bills of national interest. Speaking on an amendment to the currency bill that provided for an increased number of grains of silver

---

[12] An incident of the campaign between Taylor and Major Pettibone, which throws light on the former's method of campaigning, is told by Judge Walter W. Faw of the Tennessee Court of Appeals. Judge Faw, at the time, lived at his old home in Johnson City and was well acquainted with the men and events of the campaign. He relates that on one occasion Major Pettibone had ridiculed Taylor rather severely for his use of the fiddle in his debate. When young Taylor rose to reply to his Republican opponent he laid his fiddle upon the speaker's table and placed beside it a carpet-bag, brought for the occasion. Turning to his audience, he called upon it to choose between the fiddle and the carpet bag.

[13] *Congressional Record,* IX, 397, 46th Cong., 1st Sess., 1879.

[14] *Ibid.,* IX, 625, 46th Cong., 1st Sess., 1879, H. R. No. 668 and H. R. No. 669.

[15] *Ibid.,* p. 1057, H. R. No. 1598.

to the dollar, he bitterly assailed the gold advocates for wanting to rob the people. His reply to the argument that silver would become too plentiful was, "There is no danger of silver becoming too plentiful as long as we have four million laboring men and women among us without employment and without bread."[16] When congress voted to pay the national debt with coin rather than with greenback, Taylor protested that by such a course "millions of dollars were wrung from the suffering and sweat of the common people and given to the bondholders."[17]

The two speeches dealing with currency matters certainly show that young Congressman Taylor was looking at the question from the agrarian point of view. His plea for a more plentiful supply of money by a more liberal use of silver and his protest against contracting the currency by foregoing the use of greenback indicate the basic reasoning that prompted the Populist demands more than a decade later. It is important to note, however, that Taylor's position was much more conservative than that later taken by the Populists. Likewise, the principle of his bill taxing incomes was adopted by the People's Party in the nineties. His bills seeking to repeal the tax on tobacco in the hands of producers and to abolish the office of assistant United States district attorney were not to form a part of the announced Populist program, but both show clearly the influence of an agricultural constituency on the young congressman's views. Repeal of the tobacco tax was clearly in the interest of growers, many of whom lived in East Tennessee, and the abolishment of public offices is always agreeable to the farmer group. The most enthusiastic admirers of "Bob" Taylor, among the informed, would never have attributed to him prophetic powers or profound understanding of economic laws and such is not the purpose of these passages. It is none the less a fact that his views while in congress clearly reflected the attitude of small farmers of Tennessee. His indignation at discrimination against the working classes in favor of the moneyed groups might well have been expressed by Andrew Jackson or Andrew Johnson.

---

[16] *Ibid.*, IX, 1371, 46th Cong., 2nd Sess., 1879-80.
[17] *Ibid.*, p. 1182.

Likewise, Taylor's refusal to go to extremes corresponds to the traditions of the frontier Democracy.

The similarity of "Bob" Taylor's attitudes to those of the illustrious Democrats just named is no accident. Each had sprung from the same general section of the country and from the same general stock. Each had entered public life without training in political philosophy, but each possessed, to a marked degree, an ability to understand the thoughts of his neighbors and to interpret them in a striking manner. The technique of each was different, but each, in his way, spoke understandingly to the same constituency, the small farmer classes of Tennessee. Nor were they ignorant of this similarity. Johnson gloried in the title of Jackson's successor.[18] Taylor declared that Johnson was the truest friend the constitution and the people ever had[19] and his praise of Jackson was no less fulsome or sincere.

Although Taylor met defeat at the hands of Major Pettibone when he sought reëlection to congress in 1880, it was by a very narrow margin in a strongly Republican district. As a result of his two congressional campaigns, he became recognized as a rising young leader among the Democrats and, in January of 1881, he came within ten votes of being elected by the legislature to the United States senate. In that contest a deadlock had developed between the Harris and Colyar factions and thirty ballots were taken before Howell E. Jackson received the honor. From the twenty-fourth to the twenty-eighth ballots inclusive, Robert L. Taylor, then a young man of scarcely thirty-one years, was the leading candidate.[20] When the Democratic state convention met in June of the following year it nominated General William B. Bate as candidate for governor. Five ballots were cast before the nomination was made and, on each of them, the thirty-two year old Taylor received the second highest vote. On the third ballot, out of a total of a little over 1,300 votes, young Taylor receive 617, which was only thirty-two below that of Bate, the leading candidate.[21] During the four years

[18] Winston, op. cit., pp. 26-39.
[19] From Memphis speech, October 5, 1886, Memphis Avalanche, October 6, 1886.
[20] Senate Journal, 42nd General Assembly, Tennessee, 1881, pp. 175-235.
[21] Nashville American, June 22, 1882.

following his retirement from congress, Taylor engaged first
in the practice of law and then became publisher of the *Johnson
City Comet* but met with little financial success in either undertaking.[22] In 1884 he was elector-at-large on the Democratic
ticket and canvassed the state for Grover Cleveland. It was
during this campaign that he firmly established his popularity
among the voters of the state, for, declared one paper in discussing his gubernatorial aspirations two years later, "the people have been for him since his canvass as elector for the state
on the Cleveland-Hendricks ticket."[23] When Cleveland came into power, he appointed his Tennessee champion to the very desirable office of pension agent at Knoxville. Taylor held this position from his appointment in 1885 until after the Democratic
state convention of 1886.

The question naturally arises, in connection with the War of
the Roses, as to how it happened that two parties nominated
brothers to oppose each other for the governorship. A detailed
history of the Republican party in Tennessee is not within the
scope of this study. It is necessary, however, to review briefly
some of the events which led to the nomination of Alfred A.
Taylor.

Republican confidence of capturing Tennessee in 1886, exhibited in the early months of that year, rested largely on the
factional struggle of the Democracy. Because of its position as
a minority party and because its strength centered largely in
one section of the state, the Republican party had not divided

[22] The story of Taylor's newspaper venture was given to the writer in a
most interesting way by Major Cy H. Lyle, Adjutant of the National Soldiers' Home at Johnson City, who was associated with Taylor in the venture.
According to Major Lyle, the *Comet* was established by Charles St. John,
Nathaniel Love, and Robert L. Taylor. St. John and Love soon severed their
connection with the paper. Col. Robert Barrow and Major Lyle became
associated in the venture. Later Taylor gave his interest in the paper to
Col. Barrow and Major Lyle on the condition that they would assume the
debt which encumbered it. In general, this conforms to the account given
by Augsburg, *op. cit.*, p. 47.

[23] *Jackson Tribune-Sun,* quoted in *Nashville Banner,* August 5, 1886. *The
Memphis Avalanche,* October 7, 1886, declared that Taylor's canvass of 1884
"secured for him a firm place in the hearts of the young men of the state
and won him the admiration of the old."

to any great extent on the issues which had so nearly disrupted the Democrats. There were factions within the party, it is true, but they largely centered around questions of personal leadership and federal patronage. Such differences are usually subject to adjustment in the face of a common enemy and the Republicans of Tennessee, like those of the country generally, are adept at closing ranks in time for a fight with the opposing party. There had been a bitter division within the party during Reconstruction times. The differences between Radicals and Conservatives have already been noted. But time had softened much of the ill feeling of those days and, like the Democrats, the party was feeling the influence of the young men's movement.

The problem facing the Republican party in selecting its candidate was largely one of expediency. Who could capitalize most on Democratic discontent or best attract the growing independent vote? Very early in the year they began discussing possible candidates for governor and continued this up to convention time. Numerous names were mentioned, but no one stood out as the logical candidate. It is possible that the apparent success of the Democratic harmony movement discouraged the ambitious. There was but passing glory and much expense in leading a lost cause.[24] When the convention met in Nashville on June 18th, only two names were placed in nomination: Col. D. A. Nunn and Alfred A. Taylor. The result of the first ballot was Taylor 373, Nunn 175. Since the Republicans did not require a two-thirds majority, Taylor's nomination was made unanimous "amid the wildest excitement."[25] The reason for "Alf's" nomination has been questioned, but there seems little

---

[24] There were some twenty-one names suggested for the Republican nomination. Among them were Ex-Governor D. W. C. Senter, John J. Littleton, Col. T. A. Hamilton, Judge Frank T. Reid, Judge Edward H. East, Hon. Frank Beasley, Henry R. Gibson, General Massey, Judge Thomas Caldwell, Ex-Governor Alvin Hawkins, Judge Arch Hughes, Congressman A. H. Pettibone, Hon. Zack Taylor, Captain Warder, General Wilder, H. Clay Evans, Wm. R. Moore, Judge Randolph, Alfred A. Taylor, Col. D. A. Nunn, and G. N. Tillman. These names appeared in the *Nashville Banner* and in quotations from the state press found in that paper over a period from January 12 to June 11, 1886.

[25] *Nashville Banner*, June 18, 1886.

doubt that it was a move to prevent the nomination of "Bob" by the Democrats. Though Alfred A. Taylor had been a member of the legislature in 1875 and had been a candidate for the Republican nomination for congress against Pettibone in 1878, his name was among the very last of those mentioned for the gubernatorial nomination in 1886. Apparently, he was not considered until late in the season when it became evident that his brother was the leading contender for the Democratic nomination. A delegate from Knox County, Mr. Austin, seems to have expressed the Republican attitude when, in placing "Alf's" name before the convention, he said, ". . . the nomination of Mr. Taylor would mean the retirement of the strongest Democratic candidate—Bob Taylor."[26] Whatever may have been the reason for the nomination of "Alf" Taylor by the Republicans, it was seized upon by Democrats opposed to "Bob" as an impressive reason why he should not be nominated by their party.

A comparison of the Democratic and Republican platforms shows no striking differences so far as state issues were concerned. On the question of leasing convicts to private interests the Republicans announced their opposition to competition between convict and free labor but did favor the use of short term convicts on public roads. The Democrats opposed the farming out of convicts so as to compete with honest labor and favored terminating the system "as early as practicable." Republicans made no mention of the proposed prohibition amendment while the Democrats favored its submission to a vote of the people. In the campaign the Republicans claimed to be the champions of education because of their position on the Blair educational bill but made no mention of the subject in their platform. The Democratic party, however, pledged itself to the maintenance and improvement of public schools for the education of all classes of citizens. Republicans met certain demands of the laboring classes by declaring for the payment of wages in money rather than in scrip or merchandise and favored a bet-

---

[26] *Nashville Banner*, June 18, 1886. This view is contrary to the impression given by the Taylor brothers *op. cit.*, pp. 163-164. From this it would seem that "Bob's" nomination was for the purpose of counteracting the effective campaigning that "Alf" had done in the few weeks between the Republican convention and that of the Democrats.

ter mechanic's lien law. On these subjects the Democratic platform was silent. Finally, on the question of the ballot the parties found themselves reversed with respect to their positions during Reconstruction days. The Democrats, who then demanded a reform of election laws and machinery, were silent on the issue in 1886. Although the state had passed no discriminatory legislation against Negro voting, certain localities of the state, particularly in West Tennessee where the Negro population was greatest, were finding means to insure Democratic majorities. This fact led the Republicans to demand, in their platform, "a free ballot and a fair count." As a matter of fact, there was little difference on state issues between the two parties. Though they did not mention the subjects in their platform, Republicans favored the development of public schools, as well as the submission of the prohibition question to the people. Likewise, the Democrats were favorable to better mechanic's lien laws and opposed the hated scrip system of paying labor.

Aside from important differences on the tariff and the Blair educational bill, which will be discussed in the succeeding chapter, there was little fundamental difference in the two platforms on national issues. Democratic administrations, both state and national, were "viewed with alarm" by Republicans in the good old traditional manner while Democrats "pointed with pride." Republicans demanded a repeal of the internal revenue system while both parties gave the lion's tail a twist by expressing sympathy for Ireland and demanding home rule for that unfortunate land.[27]

Such were the platforms upon which the two sons of Nathaniel Green and Emely Haynes Taylor stood during the War of the Roses. The independent newspaper at Nashville was undoubtedly correct when it deplored the way Republicans had "bungled over" certain questions with a mere "quibble on words" and when it later pronounced the Democratic platform "vague on certain points."[28] Aside from the fact, however, that party

---

[27] For Republican platform, see *Nashville Banner,* June 18, 1886. That of the Democrats may be found in the same paper of August 12, 1886, as well as in *Nashville American* and *Nashville Union* of similar dates.

[28] *Nashville Banner,* June 18, August 12, 1886.

platforms frequently have these faults, it must be kept in mind
that the state was passing through a transitional stage. Old
issues had been settled and new ones were not clearly defined. It
is not surprising that party platforms reflected this condition.

Party managers arranged for a series of forty-one joint debates between the brothers, in which they were to visit every
section of the state. The first of these was held at Madisonville
in East Tennessee on September 9, and marked the opening of
a campaign that was to attract nation-wide attention. It became known at once as the War of the Roses in which the Democratic candidate and his followers adopted the white rose of
York while the Republican wore the red of Lancaster. The
Madisonville debate quieted the fears of those who dreaded an
unseemly or disgusting wrangle between two brothers. Succeeding debates dispelled them altogether. One editor, who confessed
to such a dread, at last commended the brothers on the delicacy
exhibited by both.[29] The critical *Nashville Banner* was relieved
that the discussions were "free from unseemly asperities" and
that the brothers "evinced a commendable regard for the pro-
prieties of the occasion."[30] As a matter of fact, the cordial and
close relationship between the candidates throughout the canvass was an outstanding feature of the campaign and has
become a fine tradition in Tennessee political history. They
traveled together, slept in the same bed and ate at the same
table. As the guests of Col. Cooper at Shelbyville, as occupants
of a single room in a Chattanooga hotel, playing their "fiddles"
together for the entertainment of enthusiastic admirers,[31] or
waiting together around railroad stations for trains that were
often late,[32] the picture is always the same. Off parade, they
were kindly, jovial brothers. Their debates were filled with
thrusts and anecdotes directed at each other but in them there
was no sting of bitterness. On one occasion only was there the
slightest display of impatience. At Franklin, after a long cam-

---

[29] *Memphis Avalanche,* October 16, 1886.

[30] *Nashville Banner,* September 10, 1886.

[31] *Nashville American,* September 14, 1886.

[32] At Athens, *Nashville American,* September 12, 1886 and at Bridgeport,
ibid., September 15, 1886.

paign had worn the nerves, there were some hasty words, but the next day the tension had passed, and for the remainder of the canvass there was not the slightest departure from a fraternal courtesy that won the admiration of all Tennesseans.

A newspaper correspondent, speaking of the brothers as they appeared in debate, described "Bob" as taller than "Alf." The Democratic candidate, with bland face, easy manner, and drollery, spoke with more ease and fluency than his Republican brother. "Bob" dealt largely in generalities while "Alf," more earnest and argumentative, had a better grasp of the subject under discussion. Both had a keen sense of humor and used a liberal supply of anecdotes. There was a difference, however, in the way they told them. "Bob" told a story as a professional and held a solemn face while "expected laughter sweeps the audience." When "Alf" told one, he seemed to enjoy it himself, "his face lights up and when he comes to the funny point, he laughs momentarily with the crowd." As between the two, according to this "unprejudiced" correspondent, "Alf gets the better of the argument."[33]

The debates were, according to some, pleasing, entertaining, and marked with dignity but were in no sense "ponderous or profound."[34] A Memphis editor, explaining the lack of directness evinced by the Democratic nominee, attributed it to the times, the platform and to "this transition stage." It was not "Bob's" fault, he declared, and "Alf" showed the same weakness. "Bob," he told his readers, showed more familiarity with political history than had been expected and if he indulged, at times, in "unpruned rhetoric," he came by it naturally, for Landon C. Haynes and Nathaniel G. Taylor, in the decade from 1850 to 1860, were outstanding orators "with a facility for a certain kind of word painting and for rhetorical effects."[35] "Bob's" former newspaper associates were more generous in their praise. According to them, his "intellectual acquirements," "fidelity to principle" and "wonderful powers on the hustings" were such as to commend him and to account for his

---

[33] *Nashville Banner,* September 16, 1886.
[34] *Idem.*
[35] *Memphis Avalanche,* September 10, 11, 16, 1886.

popularity with the masses.[36] Quite in contrast was the disgust of an East Tennessee "Democrat" at the "wheyish slop" with which "Bob" deluged his audiences. This gentleman was ashamed "even to nausea" of the "daily slush" with which a certain Nashville paper described the debates.[37] Another "citizen" of the same community believed "Bob" another "bob-tailed quarter horse" destined to reach the governorship.[38] A Middle Tennessee editor delivered a more literary thrust when he likened "Bob" to Dryden's characterization of George Villiers, second Duke of Buckingham, who

> "In one revolving moon
> Was fiddler, statesman and buffoon."[39]

As a matter of fact, the debates between the brothers were not profound and were almost devoid of serious discussion of state issues. The Memphis editor was correct in his diagnosis of the case. The vagueness of new issues and the disappearance of old ones was reflected in both party platforms and could not but influence the discussion of the candidates. One feels that a Nashville editor violated "Rule Number 5"[40] when he deplored the "musical competition" between "Rack Back Davy" and "Arkansas Traveler" while the country remained unsaved.[41]

It is refreshing to note that many editors entered into the spirit of the campaign and substituted wit, ridicule and satire for the usual campaign abuse. One Democratic editor rushed to "Alf's" defense when a New York paper dubbed "Bob" a "fiddler divine" but denied to "Alf" a "touch of lute," or "twitch of twanging wire," or "melodious squeak of horse tail hair on sweetly sounding gut." Without denying that "Bob" was unsurpassed at "Rack Back Davy," this editorial champion remembered that his brother, "with Republican looseness

[36] *Johnson City Comet,* August 19, 1886.

[37] "Democrat" of Jonesboro, *Nashville Banner,* September 18, 1886.

[38] "Citizen" of Jonesboro, *Nashville Banner,* July 27, 1886.

[39] *Lebanon Herald,* quoted in *Memphis Avalanche,* September 30, 1886.

[40] Rule Number 5, according to Tennessee tradition, goes something like this: "Don't take yourself too damned seriously."

[41] *Nashville Banner,* September 14, 1886. Though the brothers did discuss certain national issues with some ability, they did not burden the minds of their hearers unduly.

of construction," went beyond the state "to revel in Arkansas
Traveler."[42] When it was known that the debate in Memphis
took place on the same day that Mr. Barnum's circus visited the
city, there was speculation as to which entertainment would
attract the larger number. One editor was relieved when the
gubernatorial candidates kindly changed their appointment "so
that Barnum might get a crowd."[43] Home people might compare the fraternal debates to Mr. Barnum's circus, but they
took outsiders to task for belittling the contest. A Memphis
paper corrected the *New York Nation* for calling the War
of the Roses an "episode." It was an epic, this paper declared,
an "heroic poem of mixed real life and mythical life and action,
wherein giants meet, fiddlers figure, and music charms the
ear."[44]

Conservative editors and sedate citizens lifted their brows
or turned in disgust from the shallow spectacle, but not so the
"wool hat boys" from the hills, valleys, and farms of Tennessee.
Wherever the brothers appeared huge throngs greeted and
cheered them. On the day of the opening debate at Madisonville "one of the largest crowds" ever assembled in Monroe
County welcomed the candidates.[45] At Murfreesboro three thousand called on "Bob" Taylor at the hotel, an audience of eight
thousand at Franklin, a thousand horsemen met the train at
Columbia. These illustrate the newspaper reports from all sections of Tennessee during the campaign.[46] A graphic description of the interest aroused in the rural areas reads: "Curious
countrymen, eager to see the famed brothers, peered through
the car windows at every station, while the platforms at the
depots were packed with partisans who cheered their respective
candidates."[47] It was the rural areas which showed the greatest
interest and enthusiasm. In Nashville a large crowd attended
the debate but was so noisy that neither candidate could be

[42] *Memphis Avalanche,* September 16, 1886 referring to comments in
New York Sun.
[43] *Johnson City Comet,* quoted in *Nashville Banner,* September 30, 1886.
[44] *Memphis Avalanche,* September 5, 1886.
[45] *Nashville Banner,* September 10, 1886.
[46] *Memphis Avalanche,* September 21, 22, 23, 1886.
[47] *Nashville American,* September 17, 1886.

heard and each gave only a portion of his speech. A reporter, commenting on the "Bob" Taylor parade in the capital city, declared it smaller and less imposing than "any of a dozen" in some of the small towns of the state.[48]

From this picture of cheering crowds, two significant facts stand out. Robert L. Taylor was the idol of the young men and of the "wool hat" Democracy. It was generally recognized that Taylor's nomination was a victory for youth. Tennessee politics, it was declared, "are in the hands of the young men" and they were cautioned to proceed with care lest old politicians "croak at the first mistake of the young Democracy."[49] A description of the group that gathered about the nominee in Chattanooga may be taken as typical. It read "Yes, gray heads were there but that assemblage was distinctly youthful. . . . Scarcely a member had passed forty years of age, if appearances were not deceptive. It was an earnest group, hopeful, ardent. . . . It was a reflection of the sentiment of progressive Democracy which had secured for Robert L. Taylor the gubernatorial nomination."[50]

Taylor recognized the importance of the young men's movement, and, in his first speech, made an appeal to them. After reminding them that few of their number remembered the bitter experiences of war but had "happily escaped the contagion of the frenzied passions and hatreds" incident to it, he called upon them to assume the burdens and responsibilities that were falling upon them. Their fathers had fought gloriously and had accomplished wonders since the dark days of '65. They left a glorious tradition which the youth of Tennessee would sustain.[51] It is doubtful whether, in the length and breadth of the state, there was a man better suited to make such an appeal than the jovial son of Nathaniel G. Taylor, Unionist, and

---

[48] *Nashville Banner,* September 20, 1886.

[49] *Camden Herald, Knoxville Tribune,* quoted in *Nashville Banner,* August 27, September 3, 1886. See also *Memphis Avalanche,* August 18, 21, 24, September 19, 1886, *Jackson Tribune-Sun, Clarksville Tobacco Leaf,* quoted in *Memphis Avalanche,* September 2, 19, 1886.

[50] *Nashville American,* September 10, 1886.

[51] *Nashville American,* September 10, 1886. See also Knoxville speech, *Memphis Avalanche,* August 21, 1886.

nephew of Landon C. Haynes, Confederate Senator. He understood and loved the traditions of both sides in that conflict but, above all, he loved Tennessee and looked to its future.

Robert L. Taylor's "spread-eagleism" may not have impressed the more intellectual, but it suited the "wool hat boys" who crowded around him at every stop. A glimpse of two such groups is interesting: "Gathered about him was a group distinctively Democratic in the broadest sense of that word," wrote a reporter from Chattanooga, "The bar, counting room, and workshop were represented . . . and each felt himself privileged to manifest a lively interest in the man before them. There was a delicate sense of proprietorship. . . ."[52] On another occasion, when the brothers reached McMinnville, Democrats from the country round about "rushed into the cars and half overpowered him. They cheered him and patted him on the shoulder. They half pulled and half carried him out upon the platform" where a struggling mass of humanity sought to speak to him.[53] After making due allowance for reportorial enthusiasm and necessity for reader interest, one is still impressed with "Bob" Taylor's popularity with the masses in rural areas. A conservative city editor, who opposed his nomination, discovered in him "a capacity for striking the popular instincts" and an understanding of the "Democratic needs of this country and its burdened masses."[54]

In spite of "Bob" Taylor's popularity with the masses and the record-breaking attendance at the debates, the larger Democratic newspapers of the state paid very little attention to the campaign in their editorial columns after the first few discussions. The reason for this lies, to a considerable extent, in the candidate's position on the tariff and the Blair educational bill and will be discussed in connection with those issues. This, together with the fact that state issues were largely ignored by the candidates and with the additional fact that the speeches were largely repetitions, may explain editorial

---

[52] *Nashville American*, September 10, 1886.
[53] *Ibid.*, September 17, 1886.
[54] *Memphis Avalanche*, September 7, 1886.

silence on the subject. It must not be supposed, however, that the campaign has no significance in a study of the politics of the period. Political campaigns are designed to win popular support and, to the degree in which they are successful, represent the public attitude of the times. If one seeks learned discussions of important issues confronting Tennesseans or if he hopes to establish either of the candidates as a profound statesman, the campaign between Robert L. and Alfred A. Taylor is disappointing. If he seeks to obtain a true picture of the public mind at an interesting period of Tennessee political history, he cannot ignore this unique conflict.

The War of the Roses came at a transitional period in Tennessee. This fact is worthy of repetition and must be borne constantly in mind. For the preceding quarter of a century the people of the state had faced grave issues that demanded solution and entailed bitterness, whatever that solution might have been. In 1861 they faced the alternative of seceding from the Union which they loved so well or invading the land and destroying the rights of their kindred to the South. The solution of this problem left a large section of the state embittered and rebellious. There followed four years in which the state was a battleground of hostile armies and in which Tennesseans fought each other with a ferocity seldom surpassed. Next came the Reconstruction period in which the radicals in control were not "carpet baggers" from the North but were native Tennesseans, representative of the sentiment in a large section of the state. The Civil War and Reconstruction in Tennessee were fratricidal in a literal sense. Peace did not return with the passing of the Reconstruction regime in 1870. A huge public debt weighed upon the state and ruinous interest accumulations demanded a solution to the problem. For thirteen years the fight over a solution raged. Involved in the fight were distrusts and hatreds left over from war and reconstruction. Involved, likewise, was the distrust of railroads which was soon to become so pronounced in agricultural areas to the west. Finally, this state debt controversy involved that age-long hostility of the working classes against "bloated bond holders." The solution of the debt problem was no easy one. As has been pointed out, it was an issue in successive campaigns. The dominant party divided and administrations failed when attempting settlement. At last the dispute was compromised with the usual dissatisfaction attending such solutions. Finally, an attempt to regulate the politically powerful railroads was defeated after a temporary success. These were some of the problems which had faced the people of Tennessee during the two and a half decades preceding the War of the Roses. They appeared at a time when the state's economic and social structure had undergone a violent change. Their solution had left the public with a case of frayed nerves. On the horizon appeared signs of future storms. Already the farmers were organizing for the great agrarian crusade that was to culminate in the campaign of '96. Tennessee, as an agricultural state, was not to be untouched by this movement. Constant clashes between capital and labor were harbingers of the problems facing a civilization changing from an agrarian to an industrial character. An influential group was seeking to industrialize Tennessee and Tennessee politics. Abandonment of attempts at railroad regulation was a victory for this group, but few regarded the question as permanently settled. Public education in the state was far from satisfactory, and an increasing number saw that the people must make more adequate provisions for their school system. Prison reform and liquor control were other social problems that must be faced in time. Yet none of these demanded instant solution. Many of them were intangible and their full significance not understood.

The War of the Roses was a happy interlude. "Rack Back Davy" and "Arkansas Traveler" from "horse tail hair on sweetly sounding gut" may not have been instructive, but they were wonderfully relaxing. Nothing does more good for frayed nerves than genuine, hearty laughter, and this "Bob" and "Alf" provided for the people of Tennessee. Over-serious editors and citizens may have been disgusted with the shallowness of the candidates and their speeches, they may have resented "fiddling" as a substitute for discussion of "great problems of public polity,"[55] but the people were of a different mind.

---

[55] *Nashville Banner*, September 14, 1886.

One has the feeling that a rural editor voiced the sentiment of Tennessee when he asked, "Why not have a little fun as we go along?"[56] A campaign of this kind was so different from the appeals to war prejudices, which were common at the time in both North and South, that it is not surprising if people found it refreshing.

It must be remembered too that Tennessee was a rural state, and it was to the small farmer class that "Bob" Taylor made his appeal. He made it in a day when the rural population had few mental diversions. Scarcity of money and slowness of transportation tended to isolate the average farmer and to make his life drab. Public speaking still provided a free entertainment. Long sermons still appealed to the religiously inclined. Farmers would attend court and listen intently to the arguments of counsel. A campaign orator from the adjoining county could still command an attentive audience. As a rule, public speakers who addressed the countrymen were serious in their appeal. The preacher would save souls from damnation, the lawyer would rescue his client from an unjust fate, and the campaign orator would deliver his country from the hands of the Philistines, regardless of which party he represented. Into such a world, Robert L. Taylor carried his message of "Love, Laughter and Song," "Visions and Dreams," and "The Fiddle and the Bow."[57] At one moment he would hold his audience gripped with pathos and at another have it roaring with laughter. With one stroke he would paint "a great master" playing his "wondrous violin" whose "bow quivered like the wing of a bird." With another he would change the scene to the "old field school-house" where the fiddler fiddled "Old Dan Tucker" to a group of happy mountain folk. His "unpruned rhetoric" would stretch this great country "from Maine's dark pines and crags of snow to where magnolia breezes blow," but he would relieve the tension by quoting the advice of a long, lanky countryman to "let 'er stretch, durn 'er, hurrah for the Dimocratick party." There is little wonder that such

[56] *Dresden Enterprise,* quoted in *ibid.,* July 13, 1886.
[57] Titles of Taylor's popular lectures. See DeLong Rice (comp.), *Lectures and Best Literary Productions of Bob Taylor,* pp. 19-122.

a speaker, faced by a brother who was, himself, no mean campaigner, should appeal to the rural voters of Tennessee.

A modern who reads the speeches of "Bob" Taylor in the campaign of 1886 is inclined to agree with his editorial critics unless he bears in mind the character of the audience and the immediate object of the speaker. But when it is remembered that the big task of the candidate was to harmonize discordant elements in his party, and to draw the rural voters to his support, it is difficult to imagine a more suitable man or a more effective campaign technique.

Returns from the election of 1886 reveal some facts that should be noted here. The Democratic majority of 16,791 was more than double that of 1884.[58] The decreased vote given Taylor as compared to that of Bate in 1884 might tempt one to conclude that "Bob's" popularity with the masses was greatly exaggerated by the press during the campaign or that the

GOVERNOR'S ELECTION 1886
White—Democratic   Vertical—Republican

enthusiasm for their idol waned before election day. Before drawing such a conclusion, one must consider the following facts: First, the apparent certainty of Democratic victory led to overconfidence and apathy. In the second place, it was an "off-year" election in which the vote is, as a rule, comparatively small. Not only was 1884 a presidential year but it was the Democratic year which swept Grover Cleveland into

[58] *Election Returns,* MS. vol., in the office of the secretary of state, Nashville.

Gubernatorial Vote	*Year*	*Democratic*	*Republican*	*Democratic Majority*
	1884	132,201	125,276	6,925
	1886	126,628	109,837	16,791

the presidency. A conclusion drawn from a comparison of the two votes under consideration would certainly be open to question. A fairer test of Taylor's strength in Tennessee is made by comparing votes of presidential years in two of which he headed the state ticket, together with a comparison of the 1886 results with other "off-year" votes of that period.

Presidential Years	Democratic Vote for Governor	Off-Years	Democratic Vote for Governor
1876	 123,740	1878	 89,018
1880	.... 136,615[59]	1882	 118,821
1884	 132,201	*1886*	.... *126,628*
1888	.... *156,699*[60]	1890	 113,549
1892	 126,348	1894	 104,356
1896	.... *156,228*		

From a study of the above table, it would appear that Robert L. Taylor strengthened the Democratic ticket in Tennessee from between eight to twenty-four thousand votes whenever he headed it.

A further comparison of returns for the gubernatorial elections of 1884 and 1886 reveals two significant facts. Though the total Democratic vote in the "off-year" election of 1886 was 5,573 short of that in the presidential year of 1884, one-third of the rural counties in the state actually cast more votes for Taylor in 1886 than they did for the Democratic candidate in 1884.[61] The second important fact revealed by the comparison is this: of the total decrease of 5,573 votes for the entire state, 35 per cent occurred in the three counties of Knox,

---

[59] Divided between two candidates, Jno. V. Wright 79,191, and S. F. Wilson 57,424.

[60] Italics indicate years and vote when Taylor headed the state Democratic ticket. See election returns, *op. cit.*

[61] The counties in which Taylor showed this strength were

East Tennessee:—Anderson, Bledsoe, Cumberland, Hamilton, Hancock, Jefferson, Meigs, Rhea.

Middle Tennessee:—Bedford, Cannon, Hickman, Maury, Moore, Perry, Putnam, Smith, Sumner, Trousdale, Van Buren, Warren, Wayne, Williamson, Wilson.

West Tennessee:—Benton, Decatur, Dyer, Henderson, Henry, Lake, Madison, Obion, Weakley.

Davidson, and Shelby which cast only 16 per cent of the Democratic vote.[62] These facts would seem to indicate Taylor's strength in rural as compared to urban counties.

Whatever else may be deduced from the results of the War of the Roses, it is indisputable that Robert L. Taylor consolidated his party vote and overcame, for a time at least, the factional dissentions that "threatened its overthrow throughout the state." He had accepted the nomination only on condition that the party should regard him as the most suitable man to harmonize the discordant Democracy. His whole course of conduct, before, during, and after the convention, was directed toward that end. Right well had "Bob" Taylor, spokesman of the old Jackson-Johnson elements of Tennessee Democracy, begun his career as conciliator. The future was to reveal how often and successfully he would play a similar rôle.

---

[62] *Election Returns, op. cit.* These counties contain the cities of Knoxville, Nashville, and Memphis.

CHAPTER IV

THE BLAIR BILL AND THE TARIFF AS STATE ISSUES

On the night of February 27, 1887, a group of Cumberland University students assembled and, after indignant speeches, burned the effigy of Governor Robert L. Taylor.[1] Such a demonstration against the genial author of *The Fiddle and the Bow* arrests our attention and excites our curiosity.

The cause of the outburst seems inoffensive enough, a single sentence in the governor's message to the legislature delivered some two weeks before. The sentence read:

"My sense of duty to the children of the State compels me to say that if there is a surplus of money in the National Treasury, not applicable to the payment of the public debt, the appropriation of the same for this purpose [educational], stripped of the conditions of Federal supervision, would be an inestimable blessing to them."[2]

The violent action at Lebanon was no accident. It was but a youthful expression of the bitterness aroused in Tennessee by this sentence. The governor had expressed his attitude on the Blair educational bill, an important issue in his campaign the year before. This bill had also been an issue in every congressional election as well as an important factor in the choice of members of the legislature, who were to select a United States senator.[3]

The Blair bill has rested, all but forgotten, in congressional

---

[1] *Nashville Union,* March 1, 2, 3, 4, 1887.

[2] Governor's Message, *Senate Journal,* 45th General Assembly, Tennessee, 1887, p. 300.

[3] *Nashville American,* February 13, 1887.

and legislative records and musty newspaper files of the middle
eighties. Only Mr. Oberholtzer, among the general historians
of the period, has made a definite point of discussing the measure
at any length.[4] But in its time the bill was a living, vital thing,
involving policies of government which challenged the best
political thought to conflict. At intervals over a period of six
years it aroused the United States senate to spirited debate
on constitutional questions of state sovereignty and congressional power of appropriation. Its expediency occasioned ex-
haustive discussion of public education, particularly that in
the South among whites and blacks. The debates covered the
subjects of federal aid and federal control over state institutions. Introduced for the first time was the principle so
generally accepted today of matching federal dollars with state
appropriations. Men of the North warned Southerners of the
danger of federal interference in state affairs, pointing to Reconstruction in the South as the logical result of such a policy.
In the face of such warnings Southern Democrats supported a
measure sponsored by a New England Republican, involving
federal direction in state educational systems. Inseparably connected with this bill and its discussions was the subject of protective tariff. Many Southern Democrats, by their support of
this measure, gave indirect aid to the protectionists.

Possibly nowhere did the Blair bill arouse greater reactions
than in Tennessee. None of its phases were overlooked in the
heated discussions which took place in this state. Editors and
orators argued the questions of constitutionality, the advantages of federal aid and the dangers of federal interference.
The bill's relation to tariff protection was fully understood
and the alignment reveals the strength of protectionist sentiment among Democrats of Tennessee. As stated before, the
bill became an issue in contests for governor and senator while

---

[4] Oberholtzer, *op. cit.*, IV, 318, 560-563. Mr. Oberholtzer discusses the bill
almost entirely from the standpoint of social legislation and regards it as a
part of the general movement to improve education in the South. Only
indirectly does he mention its political significance and he does not connect
it with the tariff. The present study recognizes his point of view but con-
siders the bill's relation to tariff protection and the consequent political
implications as of much greater importance.

candidates for congress and state legislature were forced to declare themselves.

In order to understand the significance of the Blair bill in the Tennessee campaign, it is necessary first to sketch briefly the course of the bill in the United States senate with the idea of understanding its significance from national and sectional points of view. Alignments of the various groups in the senate will be presented with a short summary of the arguments of each. The fight in Tennessee must then be taken up in greater detail. The various major moves of the bill's friends and foes must be noted with an attempt to understand the character of the two groups. Special attention must be given to "Bob" Taylor's actions and views for, after all, it was he who determined the course and the final results of the struggle in this state.

During the seventies and eighties of the last century the United States government was troubled with an excess of revenue. The huge surplus which accumulated in the treasury greatly reduced the amount of money in circulation and, in so doing, threatened serious economic disturbances. Attempts to retire unmatured portions of the national debt proved costly because of premiums on government bonds in the open market.

Republicans were extremely embarrassed by this situation because of persistent demands that the tariff be lowered enough to cut down the constantly mounting surplus. To avoid doing this they resorted to various methods of spending the surplus and reducing the national income. In 1883 they lowered internal taxes, but the results were inadequate. Next, they advocated increased expenditures on pensions, rivers and harbors, but Democratic control of the Lower House and, later, Grover Cleveland's ready use of the veto checked their moves in this direction.

It was under such circumstances that Senator Blair of New Hampshire, Republican chairman of the committee on education and labor, introduced his bill "to aid in the establishment and temporary support of common schools."[5] It was pre-

---

[5] *Congressional Record*, XV, 36, 758, 2724—S. 398.

sented on December 3, 1883, in the opening days of the long
term, and its importance as a party measure gained it an early
hearing in the senate. While most bills lingered in committee
this one was made the chief order of business, was debated for
three weeks, and came to a vote early in April, 1884.

In the main the bill provided for the annual distribution of
certain sums to states and territories in proportion to their
illiterates over ten years of age, as determined by the secretary
of the interior. It required that certain subjects be taught and
that there be no race discrimination. In deference to the South,
separate schools for the races were not considered as discrimination so long as funds were distributed equitably. Another
important condition, and here is the first appearance of the
now well known principle of matching federal dollars, was that
states appropriate sums for education in certain specified pro-
portions to funds received. Finally, governors of states were
to report annually to the federal government on how distributed
funds were spent and whether there had been any race
discrimination.

Though the Blair bill was a Republican measure, in line
with that party's policy of spending the surplus to save the
tariff, not all Republicans favored it and many of its strongest
supporters were Southern Democrats. In their national platforms of 1884 and 1888 the Republicans endorsed the principle
of federal aid to education[6] while the Democrats, due to division
within the party, adopted planks that were extremely ambiguous.[7] The Democrats condemned excessive taxation and

[6] Kirk H. Porter, *National Party Platforms*, pp. 133-134, 150.

[7] Due to the importance of wording in Democratic platforms, they are
given in full. That of 1884 declared:

"We are opposed to all propositions which upon any pretext would con-
vert the General Government into a machine for collecting taxes to be
distributed to the states or the citizens thereof." Porter, *op. cit.,* p. 121.

That of 1888 read:

"The money now lying idle in the Federal Treasury resulting from
superfluous taxation amounts to more than $125,000,000 and the surplus
collected is now reaching the sum of more than $60,000,000 annually.

"Debauched by this immense temptation, the remedy of the Republican
party is to meet and exhaust by extravagant appropriations and expenses,
whether constitutional or not, the accumulation of extravagant taxation.

extravagant appropriations, but they did not mention the subject of federal aid. The planks were results of necessary compromise. This fact must be kept in mind when considering the arguments and votes in the senate and must be constantly remembered while studying the fight in Tennessee.

In defending the constitutionality of the bill Southern Democrats did yeoman service and none more brilliantly than Senator Howell E. Jackson of Tennessee,[8] who quoted Jefferson, Madison, Monroe, and Jackson to sustain his points. Other Democrats proved by these same patriarchs of the party that it was in violation of the constitution. It is significant that Andrew Jackson's veto message on the Maysville road bill was used with telling effect by both sides.

Arguments on the expediency of the Blair bill are most interesting. In the main, they centered around a few important questions.

Senator Blair, chairman of the committee sponsoring the bill, was the leading Republican spokesman. In an able speech, filled with a huge number of statistics, he set forth the needs of federal aid to education. His discussion centered around the themes that education was a guarantee of intelligent use of the ballot and that ignorance was a national menace, whether it be in one section of the country or another. He summed up his idea in these words:

"Considering that a majority of one in Florida or Oregon may decide the most important of national elections and determine the future history of the whole country, I for one find it impossible to sleep over this volcano."

He stated that 16 per cent of the country's potential voters were illiterate and that nearly one-third of the legal school population was not then attending school anywhere. He held that it was the nation's obligation and necessity to educate all its children regardless of state boundaries.[9]

Since the bill provided that illiteracy was to be the basis of

"The Democratic remedy is to enforce frugality in public expense and to abolish all needless taxation." Porter, *op. cit.*, p. 143.

[8] *Congressional Record*, XVII, 1468-1485.

[9] *Ibid.*, XV, 1999-2032.

distribution, it was evident that the South would get the lion's share of the money and soon the arguments revolved around that fact. The views of the bill's Northern supporters on this point were summed up as follows:

"An appropriation for education in the Southern States is not a gift of charity; it is a payment of a debt due by justice. The nation shares in the responsibility for slavery. It is wholly responsible for emancipation and enfranchisement. If the South had enfranchised the blacks, we might leave the South to educate them; but in putting the ballot in one hand we obliged ourselves to put the school-book into the other."[10]

Such liberal sentiments would not have been surprising had they come solely from idealists and educational enthusiasts but coming from very practical Republican leaders who, a decade before, had kept troops in the South to subdue and disfranchise it, such a sudden change in attitude must naturally raise a question in one's mind. When the chief proponent of such al-thruism is one whom Oberholtzer characterizes as "an acrid and supple partisan,"[11] one suspects the proverbial "nigger-in-the-wood-pile." The surplus was large but insignificant compared to the benefits of tariff protection. The South received no benefit from the tariff. National aid would be a boon to education in this impoverished region. The reasoning of the Blair bill's proponents seems to have run somewhat like this—no protection, no surplus; no surplus, no national aid to education. A dole to the South might insure the continuance of the protective system and its handsome benefits to Northern manufacturers.

Not all Republicans adopted this magnanimous attitude toward their former enemies. Senator Sherman of Ohio frankly admitted that he was unwilling to see "favoritism to the former Rebels." His objections to the bill were shared by others. They were as follows: It would distribute over eleven of the fifteen millions to the South. It was unconstitutional to appropriate money for ten years in advance. He feared that the Southern

---

[10] *Christian Union,* quoted in *New York Nation,* February 18, 1886, XLII, 142. For similar views, see *Boston Herald,* quoted in *New York Nation,* February 11, 1886, XLII, 121.

[11] Oberholtzer, *op. cit.,* IV, 560-561.

states would not be fair to all citizens. It was unfair to tax the older Northern states for the support of education in other sections.[12]

Others held that the South was not in need of federal aid. A leading magazine of the East asserted that the rural schools in the South compared favorably with those in the Northern states and denied that illiteracy was increasing in that section. Citations were made from reports of superintendents of education in every Southern state to show that attendance in the public schools was increasing each year in a most striking manner. Funds devoted to education in South Carolina had increased nearly a third in the last decade. In Georgia, Alabama and Virginia they had increased 40 per cent and in North Carolina and Florida more than 50 per cent during the same period. Messages of the governors of Mississippi and South Carolina were quoted to show that a marked progress was being made in those states toward establishing effective public school systems. There was a time, the magazine said, when appeals for federal aid might have been justified but that time had passed. The South was growing richer.[13]

It was further argued that federal aid would teach the Southern people to rely upon the national government rather than upon themselves and would thereby hurt education. Two illustrations were cited on this point. The superintendent of schools in South Carolina had testified that talk of Federal aid had revived opposition to the common school system. Woodrow Wilson of Atlanta had listened to the Georgia legislature discuss a tax for educational purposes. That body hesitated to burden the people unduly, so it defeated the tax and, instead, urged the state's congressmen to secure federal aid to education.[14]

The attitude of the Northern Democrats was best expressed by Senator Bayard of Delaware, who had been a staunch friend of the South during the dark days of Reconstruction. The devastation of war, he reminded his Southern friends, was

---

[12] *Congressional Record*, XV, 2062.
[13] *New York Nation*, March 11, 1886, XLII, 208.
[14] *Ibid.*, p. 208.

small compared to that caused by the intrusion of federal power in the management of the South's domestic affairs. He was loath to oppose a measure that would render financial aid to that section, but having seen the devastating results of federal interference there, he did not "hesitate to denounce every act of unjustified power by the Executive or by Congress." "The concession of this power," he declared, "must end in the withering of the States and the destruction of their necessary and reserved powers." He showed most clearly the close connection between the Blair bill and tariff protection and warned the South that under the protective system it contributed many times more than it received under the proposed bill. True aid, he maintained, would come from the discontinuance of this tribute paid protected interests.[15]

In the face of Senator Bayard's admonitions, a large majority of Southern senators supported the measure. Senator Jones of Florida expressed the view that it was the duty of the government to help the South educate the five million blacks whom it had made citizens.[16] Senator Wade Hampton of South Carolina stated that the Southern states were devoting every possible cent to their schools but that this was only half enough to meet the educational needs of both races.[17] Senator Pugh of Alabama supported the bill because he believed that false and foolish pride had prevented the South from grabbing its share from the national treasury while the North, amused at the stupidity of Southerners, had grown rich from a double share of federal benefits.[18]

---

[15] *Congressional Record*, XV, 2580-2585.

[16] *Ibid.*, pp. 2145-2153.

[17] *Ibid.*, p. 2331.

[18] Senator Pugh said:

"The people of the South have listened a long time to such teachings and heeded the cry that it was wrong and dangerous for them to accept Federal aid from a common treasury to which they have contributed more than their just and equal share, and that self support and self esteem were invaluable habits that would develop great qualities in the long run. They are waking up and realizing that they have had the long run, but the habits of self-support and self-reliance are not bettering their condition. They see their associates in a common government accepting and appropriating all the aid they can get from constitutional and unconstitutional legislation and

A few Southern senators opposed the measure. Isham G. Harris of Tennessee expressed their attitude most forcefully. He contended that aside from the unconstitutionality of the measure, it was objectionable on the following grounds. Protective tariff was the most uneconomical form of taxation since the government received little compared to tributes levied on the people by protected industries. It was the duty and right of every state to educate its own children without interference from other states or from the federal government. He objected to the idea of matching federal dollars, for each state knew its own needs and its ability to meet them. Finally, he was unwilling for Tennessee to assume the rôle of beggar, asking aid from those more fortunate.[19]

Reference has already been made to Woodrow Wilson's report on the action of the Georgia legislature in refusing to levy additional taxes in the hope that federal aid would provide necessary school funds. It is worth while to see Wilson's attitude toward the whole subject of federal aid at so early a period of his life. It gains added importance from the fact that he represented, as the *New York Nation* declared, "so many of the most clear sighted Southerners."[20] Mr. Wilson, at the time he heard the proceedings of the Georgia legislature, was practicing law in Atlanta, with ample time and inclination to study affairs of government. Only a short time before, he had appeared before the tariff commission, then holding hearings in Atlanta, and argued against "all protective tariff laws."[21] Some time after the event in the Georgia legislature, Mr. Wilson voiced his indignation in a letter to his friend Robert Bridges: "I heard but one speech made in opposition to this begging resolution. It was a sturdy appeal to the self-respect and independence of the majority in view of what the speaker treated as the unquestioned ability of the State to support a school

---

exacting tribute by law from every other industry except their own, and while they laugh at the self-denial of the people of the South, they are growing richer and more powerful." *Congressional Record*, XV, 2331.

[19] *Ibid.*, XVII, 1644.

[20] *New York Nation*, March 4, 1886, XIII, 184. The *Nation* quoted a letter from Wilson to the *New York Evening Post* dealing with the subject.

[21] Ray Stannard Baker, *Woodrow Wilson, Life and Letters*, I, 144-148.

6

system of any dimensions. No one seemed to regard it worth while answering the speech . . . and the resolution was carried. The whole proceeding impressed me as a shameless declaration of the determination, on the part of a well-to-do community, to enjoy the easy position of a beneficiary of the national government to the fullest possible extent."[22] Wilson believed, in the words of his biographer, that "It was another case, like that of the tariff, of running to the federal government for bounties and privileges, when the people should stand up like men and fight their own fights and pay their own bills."[23] Undoubtedly, Woodrow Wilson and Isham G. Harris spoke for a large section of Southern opinion which opposed direct federal aid, such as the Blair bill, as well as such indirect aids as tariff protection. They realized the connection between the two.

The senate vote on the measure revealed that the Republicans supported it overwhelmingly, Northern Democrats opposed it almost unanimously, and that Southern Democrats were divided with 19 supporting the bill and 9 opposing it. The bill passed the senate by a handsome majority but never reached the floor of the Democratic controlled House. In 1886 and again in 1888 Senator Blair introduced his bill and each time it passed the senate by practically the same vote. Party divisions remained very much as they had been on the first vote.[24]

In the fall of 1888 the Democrats suffered reverses and the tariff was no longer in danger. Cleveland's veto no longer prevented Republican congressmen from improving their rivers and harbors. President Harrison was in the White House and Corporal Tanner was in the pension office. The Corporal's reported exclamation of "God help the surplus" may or may not be historically correct. But regardless of what the Corporal said, the surplus did cease to be a troublesome question. Concern for Southern illiteracy no longer disturbed Republican altruists, and the Blair bill died a natural death.

The Blair bill fight became acute in Tennessee during Robert

---

[22] Quoted in *ibid.,* p. 151.
[23] *Idem.*
[24] For senate votes in the three years, see *Congressional Record,* XV, 724; XVII, 2105; XIX, 1223.

L. Taylor's rise to leadership. Though the bill had been acted
upon by the United States senate early in 1884 and had been
discussed in certain Tennessee newspapers, it was not an issue
in the state campaign of that year. Neither party platform
mentioned the subject. In the legislative session of 1885, however, the state senate, by a vote of 24 to 5, adopted a resolution
instructing the senators and requesting the representatives at
Washington to support the Blair bill.[25] The same resolution, a
week later, was lost in the lower house by one vote.[26] Thus nar-
rowly did Senator Harris escape repudiation by the legislature
of his own state. His leadership was challenged. To those familiar with the Senator's fighting qualities, it is no surprise that
the Blair bill soon became an issue in Tennessee politics. It was
essentially a fight between the "Bourbons" of Senator Harris
and the "Mugwumps" of Colonel Colyar for party control and
prestige.[27] This fact must be kept in mind while interpreting
Taylor's attitudes and statements on the measure.

The plank adopted by the state Democratic convention dealing with the Blair bill was ambiguous. Declaring it criminal to
hoard money in the treasury rather than pay it on "the matured interest-bearing" debt of the country, it demanded that
any present or future surplus be applied to the public debt and
denounced all unconstitutional appropriations by congress.[28]
Here was a plank that both pro- and anti-Blair bill Democrats
could and did claim as representing their views. The denunciation of unconstitutional appropriations meant nothing, for
the constitutionality of the bill was an important point of dispute which the platform made no attempt to decide. The statement demanding that the surplus be applied to the public debt
was also evasive since the "matured interest-bearing" obligations were already being retired and did not enter into the surplus problem. So the factions squabbled over the meaning of a
plank that was clearly and of necessity a compromise. In the

---

[25] *Senate Journal,* 44th General Assembly, Tennessee, 1885, pp. 119, 138,
162, 183.

[26] *Journal of the House of Representatives,* 44th General Assembly, Tennessee, 1885, p. 285.

[27] *Nashville American,* August 31, 1886.

[28] *Nashville American,* August 12, 1886.

meantime, each side waited impatiently for its interpretation by the young candidate for governor who had remained discreetly silent on the subject.

From the time that he was mentioned for the nomination until after the convention, Robert L. Taylor did not commit himself publicly on the Blair bill. Some two weeks after his nomination, however, he outlined his views in his letter of acceptance. He did not mention the Blair bill by name but did declare himself in favor of strict economy in expenditures, and application of the surplus to the public debt. He opposed unconstitutional appropriations. In these he simply adhered to his platform. He did declare, however, that he favored federal aid to education through the sale of the public domain. On this point he was definite and went beyond his platform. On the others he was as subject to varied interpretation as was that document.[29]

Both factions of the party claimed that he had endorsed their views, while Independents and Republicans held that he had straddled. The leading organ of the Harris wing called the letter "succinct, concise but clear and unequivocal" and held that Mr. Taylor was too good a Democrat to take any stock in such a scheme as the Blair bill.[30] Colonel Colyar's own paper believed that a reasonable construction of the letter would be— "I have not changed my views; I want Federal aid; I prefer that the money be raised by a sale of our immense domain." However, it urged the candidate to make himself clear.[31] A leading Memphis daily, which advocated the Blair bill, maintained that Mr. Taylor had squarely approved the principle of federal aid and was satisfied for, it claimed, "it is idle nonsense to quibble about the source of the aid." It warned the anti-Blair bill press that it had read into the letter sentiments that were not there.[32]

The state's leading independent paper and a staunch supporter of the bill observed that Mr. Taylor had strained himself for an expression that would antagonize neither of the op-

---

[29] *Ibid.,* August 29, 1886.
[30] *Ibid.,* September 1, 1886.
[31] *Nashville Union,* September 1, 1886.
[32] *Memphis Avalanche,* August 30, September 7, 1886.

posing elements of his party but had made a mess of it.[33] An editor from Lebanon likewise noted the double interpretation given the letter and concluded that "Robert" had dodged the issue.[34]

With the opposing factions of the Democratic party it came to be a case of whistling in the dark, each trying desperately to prove that the candidate supported its views, but each was uneasy and wanted a more definite statement. This was all the more desirable since the Republican platform had definitely endorsed the bill and its candidate, realizing his brother's embarrassing position, had evidently determined to make it a leading issue. It was believed that "Bob" Taylor would be forced to take a more definite stand when the two candidates met for their first joint debate at Madisonville on September 9th. The War of the Roses is now remembered for its picturesque and romantic character, but leaders of the two Democratic factions of that time were much more interested in their candidate's pronouncements on the tariff and the Blair bill. At this late day one can almost feel the intense expectation with which they awaited the debate.

"Bob" Taylor opened his discussion of the subject with this rather unexpected statement, "I declare to you that there is not a dollar of surplus money in the Treasury. I declare to you that there is no such thing in existence as the Blair bill." In proof of this he cited a resolution adopted by both houses of congress that year "directing the payment of the surplus in the Treasury on the public debt."[35] Since the debt far exceeded the surplus, the execution of this resolution would wipe out whatever surplus may have existed. Further, he held, when the senate passed this resolution it killed the Blair bill. On the general subject of federal aid, however, he quoted the plank in the national Democratic platform opposing "all propositions for the collection of taxes to be distributed among the states or the citizens thereof" with the assertion that both the national and state Democracy stood upon it. Then he reaffirmed his former

[33] *Nashville Banner,* August 30, September 3, 1886.
[34] *Lebanon Herald,* quoted in *ibid.,* September 16, 1886.
[35] *Congressional Record,* XVII, 1704, H. Res. 126.

position in favor of federal aid to education from proceeds of public land sales. This policy, he declared, had been instituted by a Democratic congress and approved by Jefferson, and for half a century the Democratic party had used the public lands to further the cause of education in contrast to the Republican policy of turning them over to "land grabbers, railroads and corporate monopolies." On this question, he said, he followed the plain paths of Democratic principle taught by Jefferson.[36]

It is important to fix Taylor's actual position firmly in mind, because of the controversy that later arose over his campaign views on the Blair bill. First of all, he did favor federal aid to education with funds derived from public land sales. Next, he stood on the national platform of his party which opposed the collection of taxes to be distributed among the states. In this he, like the platform, was subject to different interpretations. In respect to the existing surplus, he held that congress had disposed of it by directing its application on the public debt and that, in so doing, had killed the Blair bill. It is true that his proposal in regard to the public lands seems not to have been considered seriously by the press or by extremists in the Blair bill fight.[37] It is also true that he was accused of acting in bad faith with the public when he declared the surplus non-existent and the Blair bill dead. The resolution he referred to did pass both houses of congress just five weeks before Taylor made his speech. Congressional discussions on the measure show that it was expected to dispose of the surplus. Future developments proved the policy uneconomical and Senator Blair again intro-

---

[36] *Nashville American,* September 10, 1886.

[37] Though the city press and extremists, both for and against the Blair bill, either ignored or ridiculed Taylor's proposal respecting the public lands, it must be said that this plan had received very serious consideration. Oberholtzer refers to its popularity in congress and suggests that the reason for its not being adopted was the slowness with which funds would be secured. See Oberholtzer, *op. cit.,* IV, 559-560. It is also interesting to note that between 1880 and 1886, when Taylor made his proposal, no less than seventeen measures had been introduced in congress embodying the idea that public education be aided from proceeds of public land sales. See *Congressional Record,* Indexes to vols. X, XIII, XV, XVII. In view of these facts, it seems that Taylor's proposal deserved more consideration than it received at the hands of the extremists.

duced his bill in 1888, but it seems unjust to accuse Taylor of
bad faith because the recently adopted policy of congress did
not work.

Only one large paper expressed a sympathetic understanding
of "Bob's" predicament. It believed that he was trying to lead
the party out of "bourbonism" without abandoning old principles which were "true, genuine and essential." While it condemned his manner of dealing with questions, it admitted that
a statesman must not go too fast.[38] It further observed: "Bob
is somewhat constrained by the National platform, by the fact
that his party is in power, by his own State platform, and by
the differences within his own party, to an equivocal and non-
committal line. . . ."[39]

As a matter of fact, "Bob" Taylor pleased neither faction
with his position, and both seem to have regarded him as a hopeless case. During the remainder of the campaign he received
practically no editorial mention in the daily papers of his
party. They largely ignored his views on the Blair bill as well
as on other issues. They carried his name on the editorial page,
along with the rest of the ticket, and they printed news about
the campaign, but there was a noticeable lack of enthusiasm.
The press continued its heated discussion of the Blair bill and
Alf Taylor continued his efforts to make it the dominant issue,
but "Bob" would not be moved from his position. To the exas-
peration of the serious minded, but to the great delight of the
"wool-hat boys," he frequently dealt lightly with what he called
the "Blah" bill.

The result of the canvass has already been discussed. While
"Our Bob" had failed to please the leaders of either faction of
his party, he had pleased the voters of Tennessee.

Early in the legislative session after Taylor's election that
body expressed itself on the Blair bill and federal aid to education. By a vote of 19 to 11 the senate defeated a resolution
instructing senators and requesting representatives at Washington to support some constitutional measure granting federal
aid, which did not require states to match appropriations. This

---

[38] *Memphis Avalanche,* September 11, 1886.
[39] *Ibid.,* September 23, 1886.

latter clause clearly eliminated the Blair bill from the scope of
the resolution and for that reason all Republicans voted against
it. They were joined by eight Democrats who opposed federal
aid under any conditions. Eleven Democrats supported the
resolution.[40] In the lower house two resolutions were introduced,
the one endorsing the Blair bill specifically and the other the
principle of federal aid. These measures were tabled by a small
majority, the Democrats strongly opposing both.[41] This produced the rather interesting situation that the Democrats in
the upper house endorsed federal aid while their fellows in the
lower branch opposed it.

It was under such circumstances that Governor Taylor sent
to the legislature the message that was to arouse the students
of Cumberland University and the leaders of the Harris Democrats. To quote his exact words again:

"My sense of duty to the children of the state compels me to say
that if there is a surplus of money in the National Treasury not applicable to the payment of the National debt, the appropriation of
the same for this purpose [educational], stripped of the conditions
of Federal supervision, would be an inestimable blessing to them."[42]

Clearly, this was not an endorsement of the Blair bill, for that
measure carried much of federal supervision. On the other hand,
it was an endorsement of the principle of federal aid but this,
as we have seen, was no new position for Taylor to take. Nor
had he abandoned his belief that the surplus should be applied
to the public debt. Only in case this could not be done did he
approve federal aid. It is true, he had contended during the
campaign that no surplus existed but here he was not necessarily inconsistent for his whole position in the message was based
upon the condition: "if there is a surplus."

The only difference between Taylor's position as candidate
and governor lay in his failure to mention in his message that
aid should come from public lands. This proposal, however, had

---

[40] Senate Journal, 45th General Assembly, Tennessee, 1887, S. J. R. No. 20.

[41] House Journal, 45th General Assembly, Tennessee, H. J. R. No. 26.

[42] Governor's Message, Senate Journal, 45th General Assembly, Tennessee,
1887, p. 300.

recently been before the state senate and had met with no favor. The senate's action, rather than Taylor's acquiescence in the surplus and therefore in tariff protection, seems to have led him to abandon his demand that federal aid come from public land sales. While it is possible that his failure to insist upon this may have contributed to the dissatisfaction of the Harris wing, it seems probable that the cause was the governor's supposed acceptance of the Colyar leadership.

Whatever may have been the true reason, Taylor was repudiated by the leaders of the Harris faction. After a three-day silence, their Nashville organ spoke. Governor Taylor, it asserted, had fallen into the embraces of the little "mugwump" coterie of Nashville and had changed his views. Further, it added, "His every utterance on this subject from his letter of acceptance to his closing speech was in opposition to the Blair bill and not one single time did he ever utter or intimate such views on this question as are contained in his message."[43] The governor no longer represented the Democracy of the state, it declared, and the paper continued to maintain this position until it was bought by Colonel Colyar three months later. Such expressions were mild, however, compared to the fury of the Harris paper in Knoxville, which denounced "Bob" Taylor's "flop" and held that the governor was either a fool or else had some ulterior motives. This "mongrel administration," it declared, had betrayed the Democratic party.[44] In an editorial headed "Taylor's Treason" it claimed that forty-three party newspapers of the state had condemned the governor for his betrayal. It quoted bitter sentiments from some of these and editorial headings from many others. "Governor's Plighted Faith," "Unpardonable Perfidy," and "Contemptible Apostasy" were typical introductions to many an editorial blast.[45] This Knoxville paper

---

[43] *Nashville American,* February 13, 1887.

[44] *Knoxville Tribune,* February 26, March 10, 19, 27, 1887.

[45] *Ibid.,* April 5, 1887. The papers quoted or referred to as opposing Governor Taylor's position were: *Bristol Courier, Gallatin Tennessean, Jackson Tribune-Sun, Marshall Gazette, Dickson County Press, Martin Mail, Hartsville Sentinel, Paris Tribune, Cannon Courier, Dyer County Times, Morton's Advance, Maury Democrat, Carthage Mirror, Shelbyville Commercial, Ripley News, Clarksville Democrat, Franklin Review and Journal, Brownsville States-Democrat, Lawrence Democrat, Cleveland Banner-News, McMinn*

declared that he had fallen in with certain lobbyists at Nashville and had changed his views between the issuance of his message to the press and the time of its delivery.[46] And so for six months it raged.

The Colyar group was delighted with the message. This wing of the party had apparently become disgusted with Candidate Taylor and had rendered him only such support as regularity required. Before the message was delivered, however, it had noted certain favorable signs. The governor had appointed Professor Frank M. Smith as superintendent of public instruction. It was declared that he was "a hot high protective tariff man and a warm advocate of the Blair bill" and that his nomination had "raised the devil" in the executive session of the senate.[47] The Colyar people saw in this appointment a commendable disposition on the part of the governor to run his own administration and to accept no dictation from the machine in the matter of his appointments. In this state of mind, the Colyar press lost no time in rushing to the defense of the governor and his message when both were assailed by the hostile faction. Even the austere *Nashville Banner*, which had delighted in a campaign characterization of Bob as "the cat-gut tickler of the mountains"[48] who failed to "evince any satisfactory knowledge of the issues,"[49] now found the governor's message "an excellent document" showing a "broad minded view of State affairs."[50]

The entire Blair bill press maintained that Taylor had not changed his position on that subject, that he had favored federal aid without federal control from the very first, that he had not favored the Blair bill during his campaign and had opposed

Citizen, Trenton Herald, Chattanooga Argus, McMinnville New Era, Columbia Herald, Fayetteville Express, Clarksville Chronicle, Obion Democrat, Franklin County News, Ripley Enterprise, Athens Post, Ashland City Reporter, Union City Anchor, McNairy Review, Dayton Weekly News, Dayton Weekly Leader, Bolivar Bulletin, Monroe Democrat, Greenville Democrat, Nashville American, Knoxville Tribune.

[46] *Ibid.*, February 15, 1887.
[47] *Knoxville Tribune*, January 30, 1887.
[48] *Obion Democrat*, quoted in *Nashville Banner*, April 5, 1886.
[49] *Nashville Banner*, September 13, 1886.
[50] *Ibid.*, February 11, 1887.

it in/his message. In this it was right, but it did not explain why it had regarded his same position so coldly during the campaign and with such approval three months later. One suspects the reason when he reads further that Taylor's real offense as governor had been his refusal to place himself under the control of the machine.[51] Quotations from the forty-one papers, claimed as commending the message, carry out this theme.[52] The Lebanon editor who had been amazed at the way "Robert had dodged the issue" as candidate now opined that the "self-constituted bosses" who were trying to read the governor out of the party would regret the attempt for, it said, "Bob Taylor has the masses back of him and he can afford to laugh at the threats of the Harris henchmen."[53] Another Middle Tennessee editor said: "When the opposition to Governor Taylor is sifted down fine, the significant fact looms up that he may become a lion in Senator Harris' path. It has been decreed in words succinct that the Tennessee politician dangerous to King Isham must forthwith be beheaded."[54]

A study of editorial expression by both groups leads to the conclusion that distribution of patronage and factional prestige, rather than the governor's views on the Blair bill, were the real issues. Had his appointments been otherwise, his assailants and defenders would have taken directly opposite positions as to his message.

While the controversy over his message lasted, the governor

[51] *Nashville Banner*, February 14, 1887; *Nashville Union*, March 4, 1887.

[52] *Nashville Union*, February 21 to March 4, 1887. Papers were: *Clarksville Tobacco Leaf, Springfield Record, Memphis Ledger, Memphis Avalanche, Memphis Scimitar, Lebanon Herald, Milan Exchange, Humphreys County News, Jackson Dispatch, Sequatchie News, Martin Mail, Chattanooga Commercial, Tipton Record, Pulaski Citizen, Somerville Falcon, Camden Herald, Fayetteville Observer, Forked Deer Blade, Waverly Times-Journal, McNairy Independent, Marshall Gazette, Manchester Times, Bedford County Times, Sparta Expositor, Sparta State and Farm, Lynchburg Falcon, Union City Anchor, Dresden Enterprise, Tracy City Times, Humbolt Messenger, Pulaski Democrat, Purdy Democrat, Tullahoma Guardian, Carthage Record, Chattanooga Times, Morristown Gazette, Shelbyville Gazette, Dayton News, McMinnville New Era, Murfreesboro Times, Nashville Union.*

[53] *Lebanon Herald*, quoted in *Nashville Banner*, March 3, 1887.

[54] *Clarksville Tobacco Leaf*, quoted in *ibid.*, March 3, 1887.

maintained a complete silence. Only indirectly do we get his version at this time. The newspaper which he had jointly owned and edited before his nomination and which was still published by his friend and former partner gave this version. The message was no endorsement of the Blair bill, it held, and did not conflict with the governor's preëlection sentiment. He does not believe, it explained, that the general government has the right to collect taxes for any other purpose than the expenses of the government, economically administered. But a different principle applied to the surplus already existing, one that had governed Andrew Jackson when he disposed of an existing surplus by lending it to the states without conditions and with the general understanding that it was not to be repaid. To this principle Taylor adhered.[55]

The governor's first words on the controversy came in December, 1887, in a speech before an educational convention at Jackson, where he explained his position as follows:

". . . I am not and never have been in favor of that terrible Blair bill. . . . I said in my message . . . and I repeat it now that if, after the General government has discharged all its current obligations and met every demand, if, after this, there remains a surplus of money in the treasury not applicable to the national debt, because not yet due, then, I said, the appropriation of such a surplus for educational purposes, stripped and freed of every possible condition of Federal supervision and control, would be an inestimable blessing to the children of the State. I said in substance, and say now, that such a surplus and under such circumstances and unburdened with conditions prejudicial to the local government of the states, could not flow back to the people, to whom it belongs, through better channels than the school room.

"I want to be understood. We do not want Federal aid to education unless it be appropriated to the State of Tennessee to be used under her own laws without any Federal control whatever. We want it as we received it fifty years ago when Hickory Jackson was President. I emphasize these remarks because I have been so grievously misquoted."[56]

---

[55] *Johnson City Comet,* February 17, 1887.
[56] *Nashville Banner,* February 11, 1888.

By 1888 the Blair bill had ceased to be a topic of editorial discussion in Tennessee except in connection with Governor Taylor's renomination. It was evident early in the year that he would have strong opposition, and it was equally evident that his Blair bill position would be made the issue. That section of the party press which had been so offended at his message had not forgotten its bitterness. It was charged that the governor faced both ways and that his position one week was no indication of what it would be the next.[57] It was asserted that "Bob" was still trying to explain his attitude toward the bill but that his explanations would have to be more satisfactory than they had been if he ever got the nomination.[58] One bitter editor declared that he would support Taylor if nominated, but, he said: ". . . It will be the toughest mess of carrion crow we have ever been called upon, in our unswerving party loyalty, to partake of."[59]

Numerous candidates were brought forward in opposition but Major Tom McConnell of East Tennessee seems to have been regarded as the most logical man. Taylor's defeat was freely predicted. One Middle Tennessee paper held that anyone "with half an eye" could see that "Our Bob" would not be the nominee,[60] and a hostile Memphis editor, conceding "Bob's" defeat, speculated on what candidate his delegates would support.[61] That this was largely defeatist propaganda is evident from a remark in the latter paper a month before. It stated: "there are three newspapers in East Tennessee for Bob and thirteen against him and yet he has managed to carry every county convention so far held."[62]

Though none of the large city dailies were active in the governor's behalf, a considerable number of small town weeklies were loyal to him. These scouted the idea that he would not receive the nomination. One regarded it "a bit of grim humor" to

---

[57] *Dresden Enterprise* and *Forked Deer Blade*, quoted in *Nashville Banner* of January 1 and February 6, 1888.

[58] *Union City Advance*, quoted in *ibid.*, January 28, 1888.

[59] *Obion Democrat*, quoted in *ibid.*, February 23, 1888.

[60] *Bellbuckle Star*, quoted in *ibid.*, January 28, 1888.

[61] *Memphis Appeal*, May 7, 1888.

[62] *Memphis Appeal*, April 2, 1888.

talk of ousting "Bob" because, it asserted: "He is today nearer the great heart of the people than any other public man in Tennessee."[63] Another warned the Democratic "sore heads and malcontents" to call off their "dogs of war" for, it said, resorting to the mock scriptural: ". . . it is written that neither death nor life, nor principalities nor powers, nor things present nor things to come, nor height nor depth, nor Tom McConnell nor Tom Williams, nor any other Tom, shall be able to separate Our Bob from the people."[64]

During the pre-convention fight the governor's opponents claimed that he was supported only by the "pie eaters," while his friends were equally positive that the opposition consisted entirely of those who had been disappointed and who longed for a place at the counter. Whether or not it was merely a "pie eaters' war," certainly the Blair bill was not an issue of future policy.

The Democratic state convention, which met in May of 1888, revealed the depth of the bitterness still existing. The party platform contained the same plank on federal aid as that of 1886. It endorsed President Cleveland's administration and praised him for his leadership of the party, but it studiously refrained from mentioning the name of the Democratic governor. It was satisfied with the "successful management" of state affairs for the past two years "by the Democratic party" but, contrary to precedent, accorded the governor no praise for his part in it.[65]

On the first ballot Governor Taylor received a majority but was 230 short of the necessary two-thirds.[66] The long stubborn fight began. Ballot after ballot followed with the Taylor forces unable to reach the required number. The opposition was equally unable to break the governor's ranks. It centered on one candidate after another but the Taylor line held fast. By midnight of Saturday the thirtieth ballot had been taken and, though Taylor had gained in strength, he still lacked 75 votes

---

[63] *Jackson Whig*, quoted in *Nashville Banner*, February 7, 1888.

[64] *Rogersville Democrat*, quoted in *ibid.*, February 23, 1888.

[65] *Nashville Banner*, May 11, 1888.

[66] *Nashville American*, May 15, 1888.

of reaching the goal. In the meantime, a meeting of Democrats was held at Tullahoma and this message was wired to their delegates at Nashville: "Continue steadfast in Bob's behalf until the fodder is pulled or the pumpkins get ripe." On Saturday a mass meeting at Columbia voiced the same sentiments.[67] In fact, during these days a flood of telegrams and letters from the people back home urged many a wavering delegate that "Our Bob" deserved another term.

A Sabbath's rest and meditation failed to heal the breach, and on Monday the deadlock continued. Following the thirty-seventh ballot Major John J. Vertrees, leader of the opposition, voiced the sentiments of his followers. He pointed to the deep seated opposition existing and declared that the governor's utterances on certain public questions did not agree with the platform. His group was willing to take any man "whose record is consistent and who can stand on the platform." "We are not asking for any man," he pleaded, "but we are asking you to give us a man we are not constantly having to defend."[68] The plea fell on deaf ears and on Tuesday, after six long, bitter days and nights, Major Vertrees read the following statement to the convention: "The delegates in opposition to Governor Robert L. Taylor have decided to no longer oppose his renomination. We now permit him to be renominated by the delegates supporting him. We will not vote when the roll is called so that he may receive all the votes that may be cast."[69] On the fortieth ballot, after organized opposition had ceased, Bob Taylor was renominated but without the votes of the "bitter enders." This action of the convention closed the Blair bill fight in Tennessee only a few months before Republican successes in the national elections removed the necessity of concessions to the South by the beneficiaries of protection.

The campaign which followed lacked the color of the War of the Roses and soon became overshadowed by the national contest of that year. In spite of the fact that a general reaction against the Cleveland administration resulted in Harrison's election to the presidency, Robert L. Taylor polled the largest

---

[67] *Ibid.*, May 15, 1888.   [68] *Ibid.*, May 15, 1888.   [69] *Ibid.*

vote that had been cast for a gubernatorial candidate in Tennessee since the Civil War. Thus again he demonstrated his ability to consolidate the strength of his party in the state.

The relationship between the Blair bill and tariff protection has been noted. However, the importance of the tariff as an issue in the Tennessee gubernatorial campaign of 1886 necessitates special attention to that subject.

The national Democracy, during the middle eighties, found itself divided on the tariff. This was apparent when, in 1884, the Morrison bill for tariff reduction was defeated in the Democratic controlled House. More than a fourth of the Democrats joined with the Republicans to kill the bill which called for a downward revision of duties. In 1886 the vote on the same measure showed 26 Democratic members out of 169 opposing

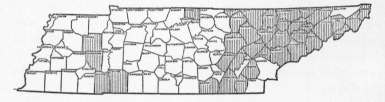

GOVERNOR'S ELECTION 1888
White—Democratic   Vertical—Republican

tariff reduction. The low tariff wing was headed by Representative William R. Morrison of Illinois while Samuel J. Randall of Pennsylvania led protectionist Democrats.[70]

This division of sentiment within the party influenced the wording of the Democratic national platform of 1884 as well as the attitude of its successful candidate for the presidency, Grover Cleveland. After denouncing Republican abuse of the tariff, the party pledged itself to "reduce taxation," and to "revise the tariff" in a spirit of fairness to all interests, having due regard for the protection of American labor against foreign competition as well as for American industries dependent upon

---

[70] F. W. Taussig, *The Tariff History of the United States*, pp. 253-254. Rhodes, *op. cit.*, VIII, 234.

protection for their "successful continuance."[71] This was described by one Tennessee editor to mean "both tweedledum and tweedledee, either, or neither, according to the predilections of any faction or voter in the party."[72] It was clearly a compromise between the Morrison and Randall followers. Grover Cleveland, usually so outspoken on his views, was not uninfluenced by this party division. In his inaugural address, he recommended adjustment of taxation so as to give relief to the people, "having due regard to the interests of capital invested and workingmen employed in American industries." He reaffirmed this position in his first message to congress.[73] When Morrison introduced his bill again in 1886, President Cleveland gave it no support sufficient to force Randall Democrats into line.[74]

In Tennessee, as has been pointed out, the strong Colyar wing of the Democratic party supported the Randall policy of protection. Its members had little patience with the "fossilized ideas" of certain "ante-bellum, free-trade doctrinaires" who opposed everything the "Yankees" favored.[75] This group of industrialists and old-line Whigs looked upon the Chicago platform as an endorsement of protectionist principles. Pointing to the clauses on protection of American labor and on "due regard" for American industries, they maintained their party orthodoxy and sought to force state organization and candidates to accept their views.[76]

The Harris wing of the Tennessee Democracy championed the traditional party views on the tariff. Its leaders pointed to the Chicago platform's denunciation of the Republican tariff and its promise to "reduce taxation" and "revise the tariff." They charged the Colyar industrialists with being Republican in principle and with attempting to impose those principles on the party in Tennessee.[77] Editorial discussion of the tariff by

[71] Porter, *op. cit.*, p. 119.
[72] *Nashville Banner*, September 21, 1886.
[73] Richardson, *op. cit.*, VIII, 302, 341.
[74] Oberholtzer, *op. cit.*, IV, 379.
[75] *Nashville Union*, July 14, 1886.
[76] See *Nashville Union, Memphis Avalanche*, and also the independent *Nashville Banner*, of early 1886.
[77] See *Nashville American* and *Memphis Appeal*, of early 1886.

7

the two factions convinces one that "Alf" Taylor was not far wrong when he declared that the tariff views of the two Democratic factions differed "as widely as from pole to pole."[78]

When it faced the alternatives of harmonizing or losing to the Republicans, the Democratic state convention "straddled" the tariff issue as it did the Blair bill. Its platform endorsed the efforts of the Cleveland administration "to reform the existing tariff," it endorsed the national platform of 1884, known as the Chicago platform, and, finally, endorsed the efforts of Tennessee congressmen "to redeem party pledges made at Chicago by attempting to secure a reformation of the tariff."[79] Both wings of the party claimed the platform a victory for its views. Colonel Colyar's own paper at Nashville expressed its satisfaction with the action of the convention by declaring that it had been a matter of uncertainty, until that body met, whether the party in Tennessee had "passed out of ante-bellum ways" but the endorsement of the Chicago platform had demonstrated its progressive attitude.[80] The Harris press, on the other hand, professed equal satisfaction with the convention's action. It pointed again to the clauses in the Chicago platform demanding reform and reduction of the tariff and was satisfied that the state Democracy had these in mind when it endorsed the Chicago position. It further pointed to the endorsement of Tennessee's Democratic congressmen, all of whom had supported the Morrison bill and tariff reduction.[81] The *Nashville Banner*, independent, declared that the state platform was not "a clear pronouncement on the tariff" and compared the Tennessee Democracy to the man who posted the Lord's prayer on his bed-post and shortened his evening's devotion by informing the Lord of his endorsement of the sentiments contained therein.[82] Another Middle Tennessee editor described the state platform

---

[78] *Nashville Banner*, September 10, 1886.

[79] *Nashville Banner*, August 12, 1886.

[80] *Nashville Union*, August 14, 1886.

[81] The attitude of this faction is fully and repeatedly expressed in the *Nashville American* of August and September, 1886.

[82] *Nashville Banner*, August 12, 1886.

as "a sort of Miss Nancy document that was meant to mean nothing."[83]

Such was the situation within the Democratic party, state and national, when Robert L. Taylor was nominated for governor in 1886. The alignment on the tariff issue in Tennessee was identical with that on the Blair bill and the tactics of the two factions, as well as those of Candidate Taylor, were similar on both issues. As a matter of fact, the two questions were so closely related that it becomes difficult at times to distinguish between the Blair bill and tariff fights. Taylor did not mention the tariff during the pre-convention campaign and was silent on the subject in his letter of acceptance. It was not until the first debate, at Madisonville on September 9th, that he expressed himself. For some reason, the reports of the discussion contained in the leading Harris and Colyar papers were identical. They read, "Here Col. Taylor explained at some length the Democratic idea of the tariff and read the Chicago plank."[84] Another account stated that he took his position on the Chicago platform but condemned a protective tariff, "calling it a Chinese wall which shuts out our trade and causes stagnation of business." According to this account, he sided with the "revenue only" plan.[85] Apparently this version was correct, for Colonel Colyar's organ expressed its dissatisfaction in these words: "Candor prompts an explicit dissent from his construction of the platform" on the tariff and "we have no choice but to differ with our candidate on the construction."[86] This "dissent" on the part of the powerful Colyar group evidently caused Candidate Taylor to modify or, at least, explain his position more fully. Two days later, "after his position had been criticized," the nominee stated his "deliberate position" which was reported as follows:

"Now, so far as I am concerned, I am not a free trader and never was. The Democratic party is not a free trade party but we are for

[83] *Clarksville Democrat,* quoted in *Nashville Banner,* August 20, 1886.

[84] *Nashville Union* and *Nashville American,* September 10, 1886.

[85] *Nashville Banner,* September 10, 1886.

[86] *Nashville Union,* September 10, 1886.

a tariff necessary for revenue, to meet the expenses of government, pay interest on the public debt and at the same time, give protection to the laborer and our industries. . . . A tariff sufficient to meet the expenses of the government economically administered and to cover the difference between the price of American labor and foreign labor."[87]

The *Union* expressed satisfaction with this declaration and placed it at the head of its editorial page, where it remained until after the election. On the day between the above pronouncement and that of his first speech, Taylor is reported to have declared, after reviewing tariff abuses, "I am for a tariff but the proper sort of tariff. I am not for the Republican tariff which lays a tax of 43 per cent on over 3,000 articles of common use."[88]

It has been pointed out, in connection with the Blair bill fight, how editors soon became weary of trying to describe and defend Taylor's positions and subjected him to an editorial boycott. The debates, however, could not be ignored in the news columns. Through these, political reporters sought to present his views in a light most favorable to the policies of their papers. Probably the best illustration of this appears in reports of the debate at Shelbyville. According to the low-tariff press, Taylor "strongly assailed the existing war tariff and the Blair bill."[89] Colonel Colyar's reporter saw the speech in an entirely different light and declared it "satisfactory to all Democrats who want a fair thing." Taylor did attack the war tariff, he admitted, but the "pith" of the speech was his assertion that reform and protection went together. The candidate took particular pains, declared this report, to emphasize the feature of the platform calling for the protection of labor.[90]

As the campaign progressed, Taylor seemed to lean more and more to the low-tariff wing but never enough to alienate the Colyar group. The press of this faction ceased to mention the candidate's tariff views, while the Harris papers praised his "su-

[87] *Ibid.*, September 12, 1886.
[88] *Nashville American,* September 10, 1886.
[89] *Ibid.*, September 18, 1886.
[90] *Nashville Union,* September 18, 1886.

perb . . . logic and invective."[91] Independents and Republicans were amused at the efforts of the two Democratic factions to prove that their candidate favored their particular tariff views. A facetious editor suggested that Taylor's position might be made "luminously clear" by applying a simple philosophical key given to the world by "one of the Concord erudites." This simple key to the mystery read: "There are many; there is one; and their unity by the oneness of the many enables us to grasp the manyness of the one in the threefoldness of its totality."[92]

The position of Robert L. Taylor on the tariff, during the campaign of 1886, was indisputably a compromise. However little it pleased the extremists on both sides of the controversy and however justly he may have been charged with "straddling," his position was in accord with both the state and the national platform of his party, and he unquestionably followed the example of President Grover Cleveland in dealing with the issue. When it is remembered that his chief object was to harmonize the discordant elements of his party and that the tariff could little affect the administration of state affairs, there appears to be some justification for his course. Viewed either from his own or his party's standpoint, there was nothing to gain and much to lose by a decided agreement with either wing. Both Taylor's political situation and his position on the tariff are strongly suggestive of Andrew Jackson's campaign of 1828. Jackson's success in pleasing the protectionists of Pennsylvania and the low-tariff Democrats of the South has long been the subject of historical comment.[93] The Tennessee President's declaration to congress that tariff changes should be gradual, that duties be first removed on necessities not produced in the United States, and his warning that the subject should be approached with "the spirit of equity, caution, and compromise" might well have been substituted for Taylor's declarations.[94] "Old Hickory's" avowal that so long as encouragement of

---

[91] *Nashville Union* and *Nashville American*, September 20 to October 3, 1886, and *Nashville Banner*, September 23, 1886.

[92] *Nashville Banner*, September 23, 1886.

[93] For example, Edward Channing, *A History of the United States*, V, 371.

[94] See Jackson's messages to congress, Richardson, *op. cit.*, II, 437, 449-451.

manufactures was directed toward national ends, it would receive his "temperate but steady support"[95] was probably as unsatisfactory to the ultras of his day as Taylor's views were to their successors in 1886. The similarity of Jackson's and Taylor's positions on the tariff, together with their popularity with the same elements in their state, suggests that each may have interpreted the tariff views of rural Tennessee better than the extremists of their times.

---

[95] Maysville Road veto, Richardson, *op. cit.*, II, 483-493.

CHAPTER V

TAYLOR AS GOVERNOR

"OUR BOB," the candidate, and Robert L. Taylor, the governor of Tennessee, present an interesting contrast. As candidate, he dealt largely in "unpruned rhetoric," made free use of his "fiddle" and "Rack Back Davy." He used to the utmost his ability to amuse his audiences with a droll humor that has seldom been surpassed in the public life of Tennessee. These tactics endeared him to the rural Democracy of his state and go far to explain his early popularity with the masses. Yet it seems necessary to look for other qualities in order to explain the public confidence he enjoyed over a period of some thirty years. A clown may win favor with the public and may gain high public honors, but when he holds the sustained confidence of an intelligent electorate, one suspects that there must be something solid back of the clownish exterior. This seems particularly true when that leadership was gained and held without the aid of party press or leaders and often in the face of their active opposition. Then too, it has been pointed out that Taylor represented, in 1886, the young, rural Democracy of his state. He was the direct successor of Andrew Jackson and Andrew Johnson in the leadership of that element in Tennessee's population, and he held this position for many years. What were his policies as governor? For, after all, he must have fulfilled, to a degree at least, the expectations of the "common people" who elected him repeatedly. These questions regarding Taylor's strong hold upon the majority of his state call for a review of the main features of his administrations as governor. This is neither a defense nor a criticism of Taylor the man or governor but an attempt to understand his policies as chief executive of Tennessee and to interpret them and him in the light of his times. It must be kept in mind that the old state issues had been settled by 1886 and that new problems were vague and not pressing. The harmony program of the party had called for their subordination until after the election. Candidate Taylor had undoubtedly "straddled" on the Blair bill and tariff, questions which had formed such a large part of the campaign discussions, but these were largely national issues and the party, both state and national, was vague as to its position on them. It was under such circumstances that Robert L. Taylor was inaugurated governor of Tennessee and announced his policies to the legislature.

In his inaugural speech, Taylor "addressed himself to the future," declared one editor, and his remarks were "full of the spirit of progress and showed true comprehension of the present needs and future possibilities of the state."[1] The *Nashville Banner*, which had criticized him for "straddling" during the campaign and had regarded him as a mere "fiddler," changed its tone when he sent his first message to the legislature. It commented upon the "conciseness" and "clearness" of the document. The new governor, it stated, presented some positive recommendations "firmly and squarely" which deserved the "special and favorable consideration of the legislature."[2] The leading Republican organ at Knoxville went so far as to admit that Taylor, in his message, presented subjects in which the people were interested "with clearness and directness, free from ambiguity." It saw in the message more to approve than to criticize.[3] Colonel Colyar's paper, commenting on the new governor, declared that all who met and talked with him were thoroughly impressed that he was "the man for the times." It described him further in these words: "afraid of nobody but fighting no battles, and determined to discharge his duty to all the people of the state and strengthen the party by making friends, recognizing all who are democrats as such, and having

---

[1] *Nashville American,* January 19, 1887.
[2] *Nashville Banner,* February 11, 1887.
[3] *Knoxville Daily Journal,* February 11, 1887.

no sympathy with the factional interests."[4] It must be remembered, however, that much of this praise came after the governor's pronouncement on the Blair bill.

Although Robert L. Taylor was the representative and leader of Tennessee's rural Democracy, his inaugural address clearly showed his sympathy for and interest in the development of all resources. The state's growth and prosperity, he declared, required extension and improvement of transportation as well as the fullest development of her agriculture, mines, and manufactures. He suggested that the state enact such laws and adopt such policies as would encourage immigration of sturdy laboring classes and attract capital from other sections. There was a need, he held, for an extended system of railroads and macadamized pikes. It was imperative that the state have a free school system "under which every child of the state could be educated." Tennessee needed "more wealth, more taxable property, more revenues and lighter burdens of taxation." All this was to be had through the development of all resources. He believed that material prosperity made for a happy and contented people. It improved social conditions, dignified labor, promoted refinement and culture, stimulated respect for property rights and stricter obedience of the law.

Taylor was the spokesman of rural Tennessee, to be sure, but he was not warped in his views. His attitude was in striking contrast to that of the radicals who were presently to lead the agrarian revolt in other sections of the country. Instead of hatred for railroads, he would encourage them as an asset to the state. Far from distrusting capital, he would welcome it as a means of raising the economic level of the people. On the other hand, Taylor was not an industrialist in the usual sense of that term. There was nothing in his suggestions that indicated a belief that capital or industry should enjoy special privileges from the state. Their encouragement was not to benefit or enrich certain individuals but to lighten the burdens of taxpayers, chiefly farmers, who then paid most of the taxes. Such development of wealth, he declared, would increase revenue, lighten

---

[4] *Nashville Union,* February 20, 1887.

taxation, meet interest without strain, pay the public debt when due, and finally, would establish and maintain a splendid system of free schools.[5] This view of industrial development strongly resembles that of Andrew Jackson, who, on repeated occasions, maintained that the national government should only encourage those industries "which served national ends." Such ends, Jackson believed, demanded equal encouragement of agriculture, commerce, and manufactures, yet it was principally as the two latter tended "to increase the value of agricultural production" and extended "their application to the wants and comforts of society" that they deserved "the fostering care of Government."[6] Taylor's attitude is also suggestive of Andrew Johnson who, as governor of Tennessee in 1853, had advocated and signed bills establishing a bureau of agriculture and increasing state aid to railroad construction.[7] Tennessee agrarian leaders, such as Jackson, Johnson, and Taylor, were never able to adopt the extreme views of either populism or industrialism.

In his inaugural address, Taylor also set forth his philosophy of state and national government. The federal government, he declared, rested upon the states as its foundation. The "strength and perpetuity" of the national government, he held, depended upon the "solidity and soundness" of the states. "Should it ever fall or degenerate into centralization and imperialism, it will be through their weakness and decay."[8] Compare this with the view of Jackson, who believed that the Union would find its "strength and glory" in the faithful discharge of a few plain and simple duties.[9] In his farewell address, Jackson warned of the impending dangers to the Union arising from attempts to extend the powers of the general government over matters of local interest and summed up his views in these words: "Every friend of our free institutions should always be prepared to maintain unimpaired and in full vigor the rights

---

[5] Inaugural address, *Senate Journal*, 45th General Assembly, Tennessee, 1887, pp. 182-185.

[6] Jackson's Messages, Richardson, *op. cit.*, II, 483-493, 437, 449-451.

[7] Milton, *op. cit.*, p. 87.

[8] Inaugural address, *Senate Journal*, 45th General Assembly, *op. cit.*, pp. 182-185.

[9] Richardson, *op. cit.*, II, 545-546, 606.

and sovereignty of the states and to confine the action of the General Government strictly to the sphere of its appropriate duties."[10] Compare, likewise, Taylor's views with those of Andrew Johnson, expressed in his first message to congress, when he declared: "The perpetuity of the Constitution brings with it the perpetuity of the States . . . so long as the Constitution of the United States endures, the States will endure. The destruction of the one is the destruction of the other; the preservation of the one is the preservation of the other."[11] Johnson's memorable fight to preserve the rights of the states against the Radical majority in congress is an outstanding chapter in American political history. These three leaders of rural Tennessee were alike in their love for the Union. They desired to see it perpetuated and strengthened, but they believed that this could only be accomplished by a strict regard for the rights, powers, and interests of the several states.

Probably no feature of Governor Taylor's administration was more criticized or made a more lasting impression upon the public mind than his liberal use of the pardoning power. The tradition still lives in Tennessee that "Bob" Taylor was the "Pardoning" governor. His friends sought to defend him by talking of his "big heart" and his inability to resist the pleas of unfortunates. Indeed, Taylor himself gave wide circulation to this idea. In scores of public lectures after his term of office had expired, he delighted to play upon the emotions and sympathies of his audience by describing the supplications for mercy and how they were received. One of the best known of these came from "a poor miserable wretch" who was without attorney or influential friends to intercede for him. In the few moments allowed him for rest from the daily drudgery of prison toil he had carved a rude fiddle with his penknife. This he sent to the governor with the request that on Christmas eve, "when his Excellency sat by his happy fireside" surrounded by his happy children, he play one tune on this rude fiddle "and think of a cabin far away in the mountains whose hearthstone is cold and desolate and surrounded by

[10] *Ibid.,* III, 298-301.
[11] *Ibid.,* VI, 356.

a family of poor little wretched, ragged children, crying for bread and waiting and watching for the footsteps of their convict father." The ex-governor would then relieve the suspense of his audience by describing how on Christmas eve the governor did take down the rough fiddle and play a tune upon it but "The hearthstone of the cabin in the mountains was bright and warm; a pardoned prisoner sat with his baby on his knee. . . ."[12] Then the speaker would laud the beauty of mercy and defy his political critics. There is small wonder that, what with political criticism and Taylor's own lectures, the tradition of his pardoning excesses became established in Tennessee. What are the facts that the records reveal?

Governor Taylor did pardon, during his first four years in office, nearly three times as many convicts as his predecessor, Governor Bate, had done in a corresponding period but not nearly so many as did his successors, Governors Buchanan and Turney. The following table is illuminating.[13] By comparison

Governor	Years	Average Number Pardons Per Year
John C. Brown.............	1871-1875	62
James D. Porter...........	1875-1879	33½
Albert S. Marks...........	1879-1881	34
Alvin Hawkins	1881-1883	49
William B. Bate...........	1883-1887	34¼
Robert L. Taylor..........	*1887-1891*	*91¾*
John P. Buchanan..........	1891-1893	113
Peter Turney..............	1893-1897	131½
Robert L. Taylor..........	*1897-1899*	*96*
Benton McMillin...........	1899-1903	47½

[12] "The Fiddle and the Bow," see Rice, *Lectures*, p. 25.

[13] A complete list of pardons granted, with name of convict pardoned, his color, home, length of sentence, date of pardon, etc., is given in each biennial report of the Superintendent and wardens of the prisons. With few exceptions, these reports are included in the *Appendix* of the House or Senate Journal of the General Assemblies of Tennessee. The reports not included in the appendixes may be found in the State Library, Nashville. Definite figures could not be obtained for the first 10½ months of Governor Jno. C. Brown's administrations and on the last 1½ months of Governor McMillin's administration. The yearly averages for these two administrations were based upon the monthly averages available. While not absolutely correct they are believed to be approximately so.

with the governors who preceded him, Taylor deserved the title of the pardoning governor, but by comparison with those who came between his second and third administrations the term is misleading.

The marked increase in pardons between the years 1887-1899 requires a study of the prison problem. The fact that Governors Buchanan and Turney exercised executive clemency much more freely than did Taylor dispels the myth that the latter was "chicken-hearted" and allowed sympathy to be the sole dictator in his use of this important power. As a matter of fact, the question of prison policies was an important state issue during this time. Only ten years before Taylor was inaugurated governor, the Michigan legislature had passed the indeterminate sentence law and the first reformatory had been established at Elmira, New York. The effects of these new ideas were, in the words of one writer, ". . . to radically change men's habits of thought concerning crime and the attitude of society toward criminals, to rewrite from end to end every penal code in Christendom. . . ."[14] Along with this change in society's attitude toward criminals, there grew up a demand for improvement of prison conditions that found much support in Tennessee. It has already been pointed out how agitation against leasing convicts to private concerns had grown up in the state. Humanitarians were supported in this demand by labor organizations which opposed competition between free and convict labor. The Democratic state platform of 1886 had declared against the lease system, but the party's harmony program kept the issue in the background.

Nothing illustrates the changing attitude toward penal problems in Tennessee better than a comparison of reports of the prison department submitted in 1886 and those of 1888. Inspectors, appointed during the administration of Governor Bate, reported finding "the conditions of the main and branch prisons fully up to the requirements of the law" and they were fully satisfied that the convicts were treated kindly and humanely

---

[14] Z. R. Brockway, "Beginning of Prison Reform in America," *Charities*, XIII (1905), 437-444. This may also be found in Corrinne Bacon (comp.), *Prison Reform*, White Plains, N. Y., 1917.

and that food and clothing were provided, "in all respects as the law requires."[15] It is true that the warden mentioned the dilapidated condition of two wings of the prison, which rendered the place uncomfortable in cold weather, "besides largely increasing the chances of escape." The superintendent called attention to certain reforms he had instituted in the convict mining camp at Tracy City. He had caused the lessees to provide each convict with a change of clothing and required "a thorough bathing and change of clothing each week." Because of the coal dust, incident to work in the mines, he had caused the convicts to be provided with sleeping garments and required their use. Furthermore, he had stopped the custom "of cooking the food of the convicts one day for their use the next day" and had directed that they be served two warm meals daily. In addition, he had instituted improvements in the poor ventilating, heating, and bathing facilities. The prison surgeon at the main prison at Nashville required the convicts to take a bath once each week and substituted iron night-buckets for the old wooden ones, "thus getting rid of the offensive odor that by absorption will attach itself to a wooden vessel." He declared that a new penitentiary building was imperative since parts of the present one were begun in 1828 "when little was known about hygienic conditions." The chaplain called attention to the fact that one-fourth the entire number in the penitentiary were twenty-one years old or under and urged that these "little boys, whose reformation is comparatively so easy," be separated from more hardened criminals.[16] He also urged appropriations for a full-time chaplain. Except for the surgeon and chaplain, others responsible for prison administration seemed satisfied with the reforms they had instituted. Certainly they showed no great desire for drastic changes and appeared to agree with the inspectors that conditions were "fully up to the requirements of the law."

This is in striking contrast to reports made two years later

[15] "Report of the Inspectors, Warden, Superintendent, Physician and Chaplain of the Tennessee Penitentiary to the 45th General Assembly of the State of Tennessee, December 1886"; contained in the *Appendix to the Senate Journal*, 45th General Assembly, Tennessee, 1887, pp. 3-4.

[16] *Ibid.*, pp. 5-137.

by prison officials appointed by Governor Taylor. In 1888 the warden declared that in the main prison there had been "a wonderful disregard of the laws of hygiene and sanitation" in the construction of the buildings and that "humanity demands a radical reform in this respect." He urged that the old prison be abandoned and a new one be constructed. He deplored the fact that the prison laws showed no motive to reform convicts, recommended a system of rewards for good conduct, and suggested that "common decency" demanded that the management of female convicts be committed to female employees. The prison surgeon joined in the demand for a new penitentiary, calling attention to the fact that the space allotted to a man in a cell did not "exceed that of an ordinary grave" which made it quite natural that "men confined in such a place, breathing the exhalations of the body, should manifest a constant deterioration of health." Conditions in prison camps, at which leased convicts mined coal for private corporations, were indeed deplorable, if the report of the superintendent of prisons may be believed. At two of them he found that female convicts were confined in out buildings within the general stockade in which it was necessary "to keep them locked up almost all the time, day and night." He thought they should be removed to the main prison at Nashville and that decency demanded a matron to look after them. He described the hospital at one camp as "a small, low, log hut" with scarcely any ventilation. In this building "the sick would swelter in the summer and freeze in the winter." During the past, convicts working in the mines had not been provided with socks. He had required that lessees furnish them with socks "for winter weather." He complained that lessees had not coöperated in improving conditions.[17] Two years later, the warden renewed his plea for better treatment of convicts with these words, "The time has come when Tennessee must begin reforms in prison management that are now being inaugurated all over the country."[18]

---

[17] "Report of the Warden, Superintendent, Physician, etc.," *Appendix to House Journal,* 46th General Assembly, Tennessee, 1st Session, 1889, pp. 3-17.

[18] "Report of Warden, Superintendent, etc.," *Appendix to House Journal,* 47th General Assembly, Tennessee, 1st Session, 1891.

The messages of Governor Taylor to the legislature show that he was in sympathy with his prison officials in their demand for reform. That of 1889, at the beginning of his second term, called attention to the deplorable lack of sanitary arrangements at the main prison and recommended the construction of a new one. In case this were impossible, he said, "common humanity" demanded a complete remodeling of portions of the old one. He admitted that there were grounds for criticizing the lease system but believed it should be continued until a "fair and intelligent consideration" could be given to the whole question. He also recommended the creation of a pardon board "to investigate petitions and advise the Executive."[19] Two years later, in the final message of his two terms as governor, he reminded the legislature of the need for a new penitentiary and declared that the financial condition of the state had become such as to warrant its construction.[20] When Taylor became governor again in 1897, the state had begun construction of its present penitentiary. However, he urged the institution of a system of graduated punishments, rewards, paroles, "so successful in other states," and that prison management in Tennessee be made "in conformity with modern ideas."[21] By the time he retired from office in 1899, the new penitentiary had been occupied, the legislature had enacted a law in line with certain recommendations he had made[22] and he could congratulate the state on having solved its prison problem.

The slowness of the legislature in providing for a new penitentiary, for abolishment of the lease system, and for other reforms which would bring the state abreast of the times in penal matters must be viewed in the light of Tennessee's financial difficulties. The devastation of the war period, the huge debt of Reconstruction days and finally, the unsatisfactory condition of agriculture during the eighties and nineties, all dictated a policy of economy in state expenditures. This fact Taylor fully recognized and when his suggestions for reforms were not com-

---

[19] *Appendix to the House Journal,* 46th General Assembly, 1889, pp. 5-7.

[20] *Appendix to the House Journal,* 47th General Assembly, 1891, pp. 5-7.

[21] Governor's Message, *Appendix to the House Journal,* 50th General Assembly, Tennessee, 1st Session, 1897, pp. 96-99.

[22] *Acts,* 50th General Assembly, Tennessee, 1897, Chapter 125.

plied with, he sought to improve conditions as much as possible through prison management. In view of this fact, it is worth while to note that, during his second administration, deaths among convicts reached the lowest figure between 1880 and the occupation of the new penitentiary, during which time the prison population remained comparatively constant.[23] It is not unlikely that Taylor's realization of the unsatisfactory conditions at the prisons influenced him to use the pardoning power more freely than his predecessors had done. The fact that Governors Buchanan and Turney carried this policy still further would seem to strengthen the probability of this interpretation.

The last quarter of the nineteenth century saw a decided change in the public attitude toward the treatment of children confined in penal institutions. As a result of this, Illinois established juvenile courts in 1899. Judge Ben D. Lindsey had instituted this reform in Denver and, before 1902, Milwaukee, Buffalo, New York, Baltimore and Cleveland had provided for similar institutions.[24]

When Robert L. Taylor became governor in 1886, a fourth of the inmates of the main prison at Nashville were twenty-one years old or under,[25] and records show that some were as young as twelve years.

It is not surprising that "Bob" Taylor should be indignant at the practice of confining children in the same quarters with

[23]

Years December 1	Total deaths in prisons	Average per year
1880-1882	89	42½
1882-1884	205	102½
1884-1886	156	78
*1886-1888	*93	*46½
*1888-1890	*78	*39
1890-1892	133	66½
1892-1894	120	60
1894-1896	278	139
*1896-1898	*106	*54

* Taylor's administrations. See Reports of prison officials for years indicated in *Appendix* to House or Senate Journals of the General Assembly of the State of Tennessee.

[24] Arthur M. Schlesinger and Dixon Ryan Fox, *A History of American Life*, XI, 182-183.

[25] See Report of Chaplain, *op. cit.*

8

hardened criminals. In his message to the legislature in 1889, he described the procedure as "barbarous and cruel." He held that "to place a child in the society of felons for years is a cruel murder of the moral instincts, that might be awakened under proper influences." He declared that the state had no higher duty than to provide a "reformatory institution where these young criminals may be educated away from crime"; and advised the legislature that he had "made it a practice to turn them out."[26] The legislature sought to remedy the situation by passing an act which required all convicts under 18 years to be kept in the main prison "separate and apart from older and hardened criminals." The chaplain was permitted, after working hours, to "furnish instruction in educational and moral training" for any under 18 years who might desire to take advantage of it, providing that no more than two hours per day be devoted to this training. The act required lessees to provide a suitable place for such a school, within the prison walls.[27] Needless to say, the provisions of this act did not satisfy the governor, and as he left office in 1891, he renewed his recommendations for a reformatory with the declaration that Tennessee was not "in pace with more advanced efforts along this line." He further stated that "In the absence of any such provision, I have felt it a duty I owed to humanity and society to pardon children as fast as they arrived at the Penitentiary."[28] In this message he further recommended a school for youthful imbeciles where they might be treated scientifically. Many cures had been effected by these methods in other states, he declared.

When Taylor was inaugurated governor in 1897, after an interval of six years, he returned to the subject of a reformatory in his first message to the legislature with these words: "I have declared on the hustings in the presence of the people that it is a crime against humanity to send children to the penitentiary" to mingle with hardened criminals. He warned the legislature that until it provided a reform school, "separate and

---

[26] Governor's Message, *Appendix to the House Journal,* 46th General Assembly, 1889, pp. 5-7.

[27] *Acts,* 46th General Assembly, Tennessee, 1889, Chapter 24, Section 11.

[28] Governor's Message, *Appendix to the House Journal,* 47th General Assembly, 1891, pp. 5-7.

apart from the penitentiary," he saw no other course than that which he had followed in his former terms as governor. He suggested such rules for the management of the proposed school as were found to be in successful operation in other states.[29] The plea fell on deaf ears and when, in 1899, he delivered his final message as governor of Tennessee he again urged the establishment of a reformatory. In doing so, he declared again that the practice of sending children of tender age to the penitentiary was "not in keeping with civilization."[30]

The legislature appointed a joint penitentiary investigative committee at the beginning of his final term. Among a number of other things this committee reported that it found among the convicts at the old prison a large number ranging from 12 to 21 years of age, besides several old and decrepit men. The committee recommended that some twenty or thirty of this class be granted clemency and its members themselves "called personally upon the Governor asking their pardon."[31] The committee did not state what the action of the governor was with regard to its request, but it does no violence to the imagination to picture some twenty or thirty new pardons bearing the name of Robert L. Taylor. In all probability, statisticians were able to tabulate some twenty or thirty pardons to the discredit or credit of "Bob" Taylor and critics could more truthfully refer to him as "the pardoning governor."

One writer on Tennessee history has described the progress of education during the administrations of Robert L. Taylor in these words: "The strong tendency, already noted in the administration of Governor Bate, with regard to improvement in the public school system, was still more marked in Taylor's administration."[32] An outstanding authority on the history of public schools in the state, speaking of the Taylor period, says: "There is evidence that during this period attention was being

---

[29] Governor's Message, *Appendix to the House Journal*, 50th General Assembly, 1897, pp. 96-99.

[30] Governor's Message, *Appendix to the House and Senate Journal*, 51st General Assembly, Tennessee, 1899, pp. 411-427.

[31] "Report of the Joint Penitentiary Investigative Committee, *Appendix to the House Journal*, 50th General Assembly, Tennessee, 1897, p. 886.

[32] Moore and Foster, *op. cit.*, I, 571.

given to the subject of better preparation of teachers."[33] The revenue law of 1887, the first act signed by Governor Taylor, increased the state levy for school purposes by 50 per cent.[34] This year, too, saw the formation of the Public School Officers Association.[35] The records show that during the four-year period of Taylor's first two administrations, there was a decided increase in the number of pupils enrolled in public schools, as well as in the average daily attendance and the average number of days taught. There was also an increase in the number of school houses, in the estimated value of school property, and in the total amounts of money received for school purposes. The number of teachers increased as did the amount paid in salaries to teachers and their average monthly pay.[36]

It must be recognized that this development in public education in Tennessee began before Taylor's administration and has continued since that time. It would, in fact, be misleading to attribute to Governor Taylor any extraordinary influence upon the course of education in Tennessee. Yet the fact is indisputable that this spokesman of Tennessee's rural Democracy was in thorough accord with those who sought to advance the state's educational system. Because of his long leadership, it is interesting to note some of his ideas on education and some of his official acts touching on the subject.

In his first message to the legislature, in 1887, Taylor emphasized the importance of the public school system but contented himself with urging the legislature to give careful consideration to suggestions made by the state superintendent looking toward the improvement of schools.[37] Two years later, however, he asked the enactment of a law requiring that "the elements of scientific agriculture be taught in the public schools." He be-

---

[33] Robert Hiram White, *Development of the Tennessee State Educational Organization, 1796-1929*, p. 139.

[34] *Ibid.*, p. 210.

[35] *Ibid.*, p. 138.

[36] Reports of the Superintendent of Public Instruction, *Appendix to the Senate Journal*, 45th General Assembly, Tennessee, 1887, pp. 7-11, and *Appendix to the House Journal*, 47th General Assembly, Tennessee, 1891, pp. 8-10.

[37] Governor's Message, *House Journal*, 45th General Assembly, 1887, pp. 368-369.

lieved that too few appreciated the fact that farming was a science, and held that this should be impressed upon the minds of the young if the state's agricultural resources were to be developed to the fullest. He also asked action by the legislature "to insure closer collection of poll taxes and to require Trustees to be more careful to keep inviolate and to rightfully appropriate to its proper use, all money collected for school purposes."[38] This solicitude for the schools of the state appears in all his messages and one of the chief benefits from improved assessment and revenue laws, he constantly held, would be adequate revenue for a splendid system of free schools. Upon his retirement from office in 1891, he called attention to "the wonderful progress of the public school system" during his two terms as governor and urged "all possible support and encouragement to public education."[39]

Governor Taylor took a real interest in what is now the George Peabody College for Teachers. At that time it was called State Normal College, though it received support from the Peabody foundation. It was at his suggestion, made during his first administration, that the name was changed to Peabody Normal College. The assigned objects of this change were to perpetuate the name of the founder and also to draw students from other Southern states.[40] The trustees of Peabody Institute at Baltimore owned three hundred bonds of the state of Tennessee which, under the state debt settlement, were reduced by one-half both as to face value and interest rate. Similar bonds, held by educational institutions of the state, had been held at par. The trustees asked for the same treatment of bonds owned by Peabody Institute. Governor Taylor, in his message of 1887, advised the legislature that he considered the request reasonable and that it should be met. This was especially true, he believed, in view of the benefits the state

---

[38] Governor's Message, *Senate Journal,* 46th General Assembly, 1889, pp. 28-29.

[39] Governor's Message, *Appendix to the House Journal,* 47th General Assembly, 1891, pp. 8-9.

[40] Report of the Superintendent of Public Instruction, *Appendix to the House Journal,* 46th General Assembly, 1889, pp. 430-431.

had already received from the Peabody fund.[41] On another occasion Taylor showed his interest in Peabody College. Upon the death of Rev. Eben S. Stearnes, Chancellor of the University of Nashville and President of Peabody Normal College, early in 1887, the Peabody Board requested to be heard before a new president was appointed. Governor Taylor, with his superintendent of public instruction, went to New York, conferred personally with the Peabody Board and, upon its suggestion, named Professor W. H. Payne of the University of Michigan to the vacant post.[42] How far Taylor was influenced in his dealings with the Peabody Board by the thought of future benefits that might come to the state from this source is problematical. Certainly, his conduct was in line with his well known philosophy that more is to be gained by coöperation and conciliation than by antagonism.

Governor Taylor's attitude toward the University of Tennessee is most interesting. He stated in his first message to the legislature that he thought the state university should give "that practical education to which it was at first intended to be chiefly devoted." He held that it should be a "practical school for practical training, and not an ideal institution for a constituency that does not exist."[43] So strong was his position on this point that one newspaper declared that he favored abolishing the classical department and devoting the school entirely to the sciences, agriculture, and technology.[44] Whether or not the governor favored going to this extreme, he did recommend a thorough reorganization of the state university and when the legislature failed to take action he appointed Dr. Charles W. Dabney, Jr., to the presidency of the institution. He, in the words of the governor, "effected a complete revolution of method and arrested the decay that up to two years ago

---

[41] Governor's Message, *Senate Journal*, 45th General Assembly, 1887, pp. 303-304.

[42] Report of Superintendent of Public Instruction, *Appendix to the House Journal*, 46th General Assembly, 1889, p. 307.

[43] Governor's Message, *House Journal*, 45th General Assembly, 1887, p. 370.

[44] *Nashville Banner*, February 26, 1887.

marked its gradual downfall."[45] Whether the credit should go
to the governor, trustees, president of the university or to a
hearty coöperation of all together with funds advanced by the
United States government and by friends of the university,
the four years of Taylor's administrations saw a marked activity at the institution. Besides repairs to old buildings, the
following new ones were constructed: the mechanical department
with $7,000 worth of machinery, building and fixtures for the
experimental station of the agricultural department, Y. M.
C. A. building with gymnasium, and a residence for the president. Reports of the university declare that the "reorganization was thorough and complete"; courses in agriculture and
related sciences were made more perfect and the course in
mechanics was made practical and effective. They show the institution of several new courses "bearing directly upon the
other great resources of the state, like mining and manufacturing." In addition, the departments of law and teacher training
were added. In spite of the governor's supposed desire to abolish
the academic school, the report shows that, between 1888 and
1890, three professors and six instructors were added to that
department.[46]

Undoubtedly, the development at the University of Tennessee
during this period was due, in a great degree, to the forces
then at work for educational advancement and technical training in Tennessee as well as in other states. It is certain, too,
that President Dabney and the trustees of the university had
a tremendous influence in shaping this period of the university's
history. After allowing due credit for all this, one cannot but
be curious as to the part played by this "cat-gut tickler of the
mountain" whom the "wool-hat boys" had elected governor of
Tennessee. There can be no question but that the trend of that
development was along the lines laid down by Taylor in his first

---

[45] Governor's Message, *Senate Journal,* 46th General Assembly, 1889,
p. 29.

[46] Reports of the Trustees, President, etc., of the University of Tennessee,
for 1886-1888, *Appendix to the House Journal,* 46th General Assembly,
1889, pp. 444-447; for 1888-1890, *Appendix to the House Journal,* 47th
General Assembly, 1891, pp. 7-32.

message. When he came to the end of his four years in office, he was able to report to the legislature that he had found the university "literally in ruins, buildings decaying, work languishing, almost ready to succumb. . . ." Doctor Charles W. Dabney, Jr., had been called to head the institution and had "wrought a wonderful transformation."[47]

On December 20, 1886, a month before Governor Taylor assumed office, the state treasury showed an overdraft of $64,-532.62. Four years later, a month before he retired from office, there was a balance of $79,765.86.[48] This does not prove that Taylor was a financial wizard, but it does indicate that he faced an important problem in state finance. In his first message to the legislature, he urged a revision of the state's revenue laws. He complained that small real estate holdings were taxed at nearly full value while large estates were frequently taxed at less than half value and that the greater part of personal property was not taxed at all. His remedy was to tax all property, real and personal, at full value. By this means, he thought, the rate could be reduced by half and still yield an increased revenue to the state. He admitted that the problem was an old one which had never been solved satisfactorily but held that to be no reason for not solving it or, at least, making an attempt to improve the system of taxation.[49] In line with the governor's suggestion, the legislature passed "An act to provide more just and equitable laws for the assessment and collection of revenue," one of the chief provisions of which was that land and personal property be assessed at cash value and stocks and bonds at market value. Another section provided for county tax assessors who were to assess all species of property at cash value.[50] At the beginning of Governor Taylor's second administration in 1889 he was able to report

[47] Governor's Message, *Appendix to the House Journal,* 47th General Assembly, 1891, p. 9.

[48] Biennial Report of the Treasurer, *Appendix to the House Journal,* 46th General Assembly, 1889, p. 135 and *Ibid.,* 47th General Assembly, 1891, p. 25.

[49] Governor's Message, *House Journal,* 45th General Assembly, Tennessee, 1887, pp. 367-368.

[50] *Acts,* 45th General Assembly, Tennessee, 1887 Chapter 2, pp. 24-56.

to the legislature an increase of nearly a quarter of a million dollars in the current treasury receipts for the biennium. This was due, he declared, to the natural increase in property, closer collections, and prompt settlements by trustees. It also demonstrated, he thought, a better ability of the people to pay. The assessment law of 1887 which increased property valuation and ferreted out new property, would show its effect in current collections, he believed.[51] Yet, in spite of increased revenue, the governor was dissatisfied with the assessment law of his first administration and feared that there had not been exact equality. He conceived it the duty of the legislature "to see that all citizens stand equal, that no interest is over taxed." He believed that lands should have first concessions but that industrial enterprise "should have the least possible embargo laid upon it."[52] The legislature of 1889 revised both assessment and revenue laws to a limited extent. The chief changes in the latter seem to have been increases in corporation taxes.[53] In its zeal to levy upon corporations, the legislature had gone too far and had taxed both the property and stock. A year later, February 11, 1890, Governor Taylor was forced to call an extra session to remove this double taxation. In his message upon the subject he set forth this very interesting principle: ". . . double taxation is unconstitutional. Yet . . . when property is justly taxed *ad valorem* and still there are privileges predicated upon this property from which extraordinary profits are made, the state may with propriety and fairness tax such extraordinary privilege." He appeared somewhat despondent when he declared that "nothing will be satisfactory short of a complete revolution in the taxing system," evaluating everything at its true worth and reducing rates accordingly.[54]

After an interval of six years, Taylor was again elected governor in 1896. In his first message to the legislature he emphasized again his belief that "every form and item of property" must be taxed at actual value before the system

[51] Governor's Message, *Senate Journal*, 46th General Assembly, Tennessee, 1889, pp. 25-26.
[52] *Idem.*
[53] *Acts,* 46th General Assembly, Tennessee, 1889, chapters 96 and 130.
[54] Governor's Message, *Acts,* 46th General Assembly, 2nd Session, 1890.

could be secured against inequalities. This, he believed, would allow a reduction in rate "so as to invite investment and enterprise from other sections." He returned to the subject in his final message in 1899 with the assertion that assessment of all property at full value "would relieve the hardship on the small property holder, who is usually taxed near full value."[55] Another reform, favored by Governor Taylor during his third administration, was the discontinuance of the back tax attorney. He believed that county trustees should be given sufficient power to clean up the delinquent tax list and then should be compelled "to keep it clean."[56]

When Taylor retired from office in 1891 he was able to report to the legislature an increase of $123,000,000 in taxable property during his two administrations with a corresponding increase in revenue of nearly a half million dollars. He believed the state could meet its current expenses and pay interest on the debt without making further losses and, as has been pointed out, there was a modest balance in the treasury. During the six years between his second and third administrations, the legislature had reduced the state tax rate by one-third, and when he became governor in 1897, he found a floating debt of $850,000 which he believed was "due solely to this unwise reduction" of rate. The legislature ignored his request that the former rate be restored and when he retired from his final term in 1897 this debt remained.[57]

If the tax and finance policies of Governor Taylor were to be expressed in a sentence, this might be said: he favored meeting all the honorable obligations of the state, administered economically but along the then modern lines, by a system of taxation that would bear equally upon all forms of property. He opposed repudiation of obligations, favored new expenditures that were necessary to bring Tennessee in line with more advanced states, opposed resorting to loans, and opposed reduction of taxes until the state was in sound financial con-

[55] Governor's Message, *Appendix to the House Journal,* 50th General Assembly, 1897, pp. 96-99 and *Appendix to the House and Senate Journal,* 51st General Assembly, 1899, pp. 411-427.

[56] *Ibid.,* 1897, pp. 96-99.

[57] *Ibid.,* 1897, pp. 411-427.

dition. He believed that all this could be accomplished when and only when all property of every kind was taxed at full value. He resented the inequalities of assessment, believed the poorer classes bore an unjust burden of government, did not hesitate to point out weaknesses in assessment and revenue laws passed during his administrations together with faults of administration and, finally, seemed to despair of ever securing absolute justice in taxation. In spite of this despair, he unhesitatingly attacked the problem with each session of the legislature.

During Governor Taylor's last term in office, 1897-1899, the question of railroad taxation became acute. A special session of the legislature was convened in 1898 to deal with the problem and in his message to that body, Taylor reviewed the history of attempts to tax these corporations along with telephone and telegraph companies. This document throws considerable light not only on the immediate problem but also on Taylor's views on the use of the injunction by federal courts to regulate taxing powers of the states.

Prior to 1875, the governor declared, the railroads of Tennessee had never paid a cent of taxes to the state. An act of that year, strengthened by subsequent amendments and alterations, had been designed to bring this property under taxation. In spite of all efforts, the assessments on railroads continued to be far below their true value. The ineffectiveness of all attempts to remedy the situation, Taylor held, was due to defects in the law, systematic disregard of law by the railroad companies together with their efforts to evade requirements and defeat execution, and finally, some officials, charged with enforcement of the law, did not perform their duty. In 1895 Governor Turney had undertaken to assess these corporations at their true value but, having no data, had instituted investigations on the subject. Taylor then presented a summary of the findings of Governor Turney. To illustrate, the Louisville and Nashville Railroad was assessed at the rate of $13,420 per mile while the average per mile value, based upon cost of construction, net earnings, bond and stock values, and company's own valuation, was $40,994. The company's own valuation, it was found, was $48,730 per mile or 3.6 times the assessed value. The investigation revealed that between 1887 and 1895, the per cent of annual average increase of assessed property other than railroads, including lands, town lots, and other property, had been 39.6 while that of railroads was 4.3.

The task of assessing railroads at their true value had been assigned to the state board of assessors but that body had withheld its report until 1897. Upon receiving this report, the legislature of that year had created a railroad commission to assess the property of the carriers as well as that of telephone and telegraph companies.[58] The foreign corporations applied to federal courts for injunctions against state officials seeking to collect under this act and domestic corporations sought the same in state courts. The injunction of the federal court annulling the assessment, to use Taylor's words, "has excited alarm and apprehension among our citizens" and the decision "has given me great concern." He described the ruling of the court as "far in advance" of other decisions of federal courts involving state taxation, and it went a long way, in his opinion, "to paralyze the authority of the State to collect taxes from foreign corporations." At this point the governor gave his view on the constitutional question involved. He said: "It was never contemplated by the authors of the Federal Constitution that the authority of the States to tax property within their limits should thus be interfered with. And the substitution of the will or judgment of the Federal Courts in the matter of valuing property for taxation, for the will of the State, is a clear violation of its terms." The very existence of government, he held, depended upon the power of the state to assess and collect taxes.

It was in the face of this injunction that Governor Taylor called the special session to pass legislation meeting the various

---

[58] *Acts,* 50th General Assembly, Tennessee, 1897, Chapter 10: An Act to create a Railroad Commission, define its duties and powers, to prohibit extortion, unjust discriminations and undue or unreasonable preferences by railroads on charges, to secure just and reasonable rates and charges, with provisions for enforcement. Chapter 5: An act to provide just and equitable laws for the assessment and collection of revenues . . . from railroad, telegraph, and telephone companies.

phases of the situation.[59] Between the time that the governor
had written his message and that of its delivery to the legislature, the federal court had granted an injunction in the case
of domestic corporations. This action took the proceedings out
of the state courts and, Taylor declared, turned over to the
federal court "the administration of the taxing power of the
State." This was the last straw, in the eyes of Governor Taylor,
and called forth this rather vigorous expression of opinion to
the general assembly: "What has been done by the railroads
and other companies resisting taxation is calculated to arouse
your just indignation. The dignity of the State has been insulted and her just authority defied. A determined effort has
been made to escape an obligation which every citizen in one
form or another, must bear—fair and just taxation." In spite
of such provocation, however, the real Taylor asserted himself.
The man of moderate views, who was able to harmonize discordant elements, was incapable of going to extremes. Just
indignation did not justify unjust use of authority and his
message closed with these words: "But while this is true, your
legislation, whatever it is, should not be conceived or matured
in the spirit of anger or resentment. Under the limitations of
the Constitution, all legislation must be just and impartial."
Thus he admonished the legislators to be "guided with wisdom
and tempered with moderation."[60]

Taylor could advise a course of moderation, but he could not
forget what he conceived to be a violation of the dignity and
authority of Tennessee by railroads and federal courts. At the
close of his third and last administration as governor and in his
final message to the legislature, he returned to the subject "calculated to arouse . . . just indignation." He pointed out that
the constitution contemplated assessment of all property at
true value. He recalled the fight of the railroads to escape this
and reminded the legislators that the subject was still in liti-
gation. He closed his discussion of the matter in these words:

[59] See, *Acts,* 50th General Assembly, Tennessee, 2nd Session, 1898, Chapters
4 and 5.

[60] Taylor's message, from which above excerpts and quotations are taken,
is found in *Acts,* 50th General Assembly, Tennessee, 2nd Session, 1898,
pp. 10-30.

"The Federal courts have encroached upon the powers of the state until it seems that local self-government must soon perish among its worshipers." Andrew Jackson might have used the same words when he refused to force Georgia to obey the United States Supreme Court in the Indian dispute. Andrew Johnson might have used them when he vainly defended the rights of the states during Reconstruction days. Since Taylor spoke, many men, whose pretensions to statesmanship far overshadow those of "Our Bob," have expressed views that are not greatly dissimilar.

At the beginning of his second administration in 1889, Governor Taylor recommended the enactment of a "well-devised registration law to prevent duplicate voting in cities."[61] The legislature of that year passed three acts dealing with the subject of election reform. One required the registration of voters in towns and cities as well as in civil districts of over 500.[62] Another provided for separate ballot boxes and officials in elections for president and congress from those for governor and the legislature.[63] The third act was designed to provide "more stringent regulation for securing the purity of elections" and applied to counties of over 70,000 population and cities of over 9,000. This act instituted a modified form of the Australian ballot and provided for semi-secrecy in marking it.[64] In his message to the special session of the same assembly a year later, Taylor reminded it that the new system was an experiment, "studied by thoughtful men of the nation," and suggested certain minor changes. His reference to the educational test is interesting, though not altogether clear. After declaring that the constitutionality of the question could only be decided by the courts, he stated that regardless of its constitutionality, "the limitation is decried by many of our fellow citizens whose opinions are entitled to great consideration."[65] This might be interpreted as indicating the governor's doubt on the educa-

---

[61] Governor's Message, *Appendix to House Journal*, 46th General Assembly, 1889.

[62] *Acts*, 46th General Assembly, 1889, Chapter 207.

[63] *Ibid.*, Chapter 218.

[64] *Ibid.*, Chapter 188.

[65] Governor's Message, *Acts*, 46th General Assembly, 2nd Session, 1890.

tional test, but such an assumption would be open to serious question. In his message of 1891, Taylor again took up the matter of election laws. After calling attention to laxness of officials on poll tax requirements and suggesting more stringent laws to prevent it, he discussed the "conflict between Federal and State authorities" over the management of elections. This, he held, threatened the stability of the republic. In order to forestall any reason for federal interference, he believed the laws should be improved "to insure full, fair, and complete" expression of the people's will.[66]

Following the campaign of 1896, in which Taylor was Democratic nominee for governor for the third time, his Republican opponent filed a petition with the general assembly, for a recount, charging fraud.[67] Within a few days after the filing, and before the time for Taylor's inauguration, the legislature passed an act requiring a bond of $25,000 to be posted by contestants before filing or making objections "conditioned upon the faithful, bona fide and successful prosecution of such contest." The legislature, in joint session, could declare the bond forfeited if it were decided that the contest was not brought in good faith or if it should appear "malicious or unwarranted, or made for political effect, or without reasonable cause."[68] As a result of this act, the Republican candidate dropped the contest. Taylor, in his message a few days later, took up the matter of election laws. He called attention to the enormous sums of money which had flooded the state during the recent campaign.[69] He feared that the ballot box would be debauched should such practices continue and urged the legislature to devise laws "so searching and comprehensive in their scope, and so severe in their penalties" against the use of money in elections "as to at once crush out this insidious evil."[70]

---

[66] Governor's Message, *Appendix to the House Journal,* 47th General Assembly, 1891, pp. 11-12.

[67] *Senate Journal,* 50th General Assembly, 1897, pp. 13-14.

[68] *Acts,* 50th General Assembly, 1897, Chapter 79.

[69] It should be remembered that this was the famous Bryan-McKinley campaign in which Mark Hanna played so important a part.

[70] Governor's Message, *Appendix to the House Journal,* 50th General Assembly, 1897, pp. 89-91.

The general assembly, in line with the governor's suggestions, passed five acts dealing with the subject. Four of these had to do with the machinery of elections but the fifth struck at attempts to corrupt the ballot box. It was made unlawful to give or receive bribes or promises of place or office, directly or indirectly, as was betting with voters with intent of influencing their attitude toward elections. The act further made it unlawful for employers to attempt to influence employees through intimidation, threats, or through printed matter of any kind enclosed in pay envelopes.[71] However questionable may have been its own methods, agrarian Tennessee it was felt, must protect itself against industry in politics.

An attempt to present Robert L. Taylor in the light of a professional reformer would do violence to the facts. Yet no study of his administrations can ignore various suggestions he made in his messages to the legislature. Some of the more important have been discussed. Others should be noted.

At the beginning of his first administration he attacked the iniquitous fee system as it applied to courts and urged that district attorneys and clerks of courts be placed on salaries only, as a first step in reform. This would end, he believed, the swarm of witnesses about magistrate's courts and court houses, especially in cities. It would stop the "innumerable warrants, indictments, and multiplied processes issued in frivolous cases" and the "endless stream of unnecessary court costs of every description." He also believed that the practice in circuit courts of summoning all witnesses for the term to be present the first day, to be held until needed, was extravagant. Cases should be set for certain days and necessary witnesses summoned for that day only. He further held that it was "high time" for the legislature to curb the power of grand juries when the grand jury room became "a tub mill to grind out and pile up multiplied frivolous cases at an enormous public expense."[72] When laws were passed in his final administration, ten years later, proposing to reduce costs of criminal prosecution and to reform the

---

[71] *Acts,* 50th General Assembly, 1897, Chapter 14.

[72] Governor's Message, *Appendix to the House Journal,* 45th General Assembly, 1887, pp. 91-94.

fee system, he found them not altogether satisfactory. In his final message in 1899, he suggested that they be improved.[73]

Taylor showed a constant interest in the work of the bureau of agriculture, statistics, mines and immigration. While he held that agriculture was rightly the predominant interest of the bureau, he urged liberal appropriations to attract capital and labor by spreading statistics on the resources of the state. He wanted a new work on the geology of Tennessee to replace that published in 1869. He believed that the state should have a creditable exhibition of its resources at the Columbian Exposition in Chicago, and hailed the Tennessee Centennial Exposition as a rare opportunity to attract capital by a full and adequate display of the state's possibilities. He asked increased powers and revenues for the state board of health, he wanted a law providing for the registration of births, marriages, and deaths, declaring that "all the more enlightened states and nations possess such statistics" and that Tennessee had imperative need of them. He recommended stricter laws for the conservation of fish and game, and he thought that coroners should have power to investigate fires of suspected incendiary origin. He urged the legislature to provide a home for needy ex-Confederate soldiers. "We have been contented too long to feed them upon talk and clothe them with praise, it is time now to stifle their cries with bread instead of blarney." As he retired from office he felt that he could recommend with propriety that the state provide a governor's mansion "befitting the dignity and honor of the State." By 1891 he was convinced that the constitution should be revised to meet modern conditions. Though he believed the time not ripe for calling a convention, he asked the legislature to pass resolutions looking toward one in four years time. In this way the matter would be placed before the people.[74]

A study of Robert L. Taylor as governor reveals, it seems, a man with solid ideas of state government. His most enthusiastic admirers would hardly claim for him the rank of statesman of

[73] Governor's Message, *Appendix to House and Senate Journal*, 51st General Assembly, 1899, p. 412.

[74] These suggestions and recommendations are found in the various messages of Governor Taylor to the legislature, *op. cit.* Some of them appear in more than one message.

the first order. On the other hand, he towers above the mere "fiddler" and jester so often associated with his name. He came into office at a time when modern ideas of social obligations of the state were making rapid growth throughout the country and found himself in complete sympathy with them. He found a state that had been retarded in its natural development for a quarter century by war and its aftermath. Large expenditures were necessary to bring it abreast of the times. Yet the state's finances were far from satisfactory. Interest on its debt was a formidable item, to say nothing of making provisions to pay bonds when due. The economic life of the state was based largely on agriculture, yet conditions already existed that were to bring about the great agrarian movement of the eighties and nineties. Taylor understood the financial condition of the state and its people. He never allowed the zeal of the reformer to obscure solid facts of reality. The fact that he could temper his demands for improvement to meet actualities shows him no less sincere in his demands. In state affairs he was not an impractical idealist.

In his insistence upon equitable taxation, Taylor showed his concern for the groups which had elected him. He constantly pointed out that the small property-holder, particularly of real estate, bore an unjust burden at the hands of the state. He hoped to lighten the burden of this group by forcing other forms of property to pay their just dues. He did not demand discrimination in favor of his followers but only that discrimination against them be discontinued. Taylor's attitude on education likewise showed his interest in the agricultural elements in the state's population. Agriculture was a science, he believed, and should be taught as such, not only to those who were able to attend the state university but to children in the common schools. In this way the economic condition of the farming classes would be improved and the greatest resource of the state would be better developed. At the same time, he did not lose sight of the need for training in the other sciences. Courses should be offered that would lead to mining and manufacturing. Taylor's assault upon the fee system and particularly his insistence that witnesses be summoned only on days they were needed is perfectly understandable to those who have heard farmers complain of the waste and inconvenience of the latter practice. In a word, Governor Taylor spoke the language of the small farmers of Tennessee yet could always appreciate the importance of other interests.

It cannot be overemphasized that Robert L. Taylor came to the governorship at a time when new conceptions of a state's obligations to its citizens were becoming widespread. Old methods were no longer adequate and new ones had to be adopted. Throughout his administrations, Taylor showed that he was cognizant of the progress made in other states and had no illusions as to Tennessee's backwardness in effecting reforms along this line. He constantly urged that reforms which had been successful in other states be studied with a view of adapting them to conditions in Tennessee. Governor Robert L. Taylor was practical, informed, progressive.

CHAPTER VI

THE AGRARIAN MOVEMENT

THE SERIES of agrarian movements which swept over the agricultural areas of the United States at short intervals from 1870 to 1896 naturally made their influence felt in the Southern states. On the other hand, the effects of these movements were greatly modified by the local conditions existing in that section.[1] The drastic changes in the economic and social order which followed 1865 could scarcely fail to exert a tremendous influence throughout the remaining decades of the nineteenth century.[2]

The political results of the various agrarian crusades were greatly modified in the South by the ever-present race question. Threats to white supremacy had solidified the Southern people politically and no movement, whether industrial or agrarian, could ignore that fact. The execution of any political program depended upon the ability of its adherents to capture the machinery of the Democratic party, which, as has been pointed out, had fallen into the hands of conservatives in the period following Reconstruction. Their hold upon the states was more

---

[1] Among the works which may be regarded as indispensable to an understanding of the agrarian movements in the United States are Frank L. McVey, *The Populist Movement;* Solon J. Buck, *The Agrarian Crusade;* Solon J. Buck, *The Granger Movement.* A recent study is that of Hicks, *The Populist Revolt,* Minneapolis, 1931. This is valuable not only for the author's treatment of his subject but also for the very complete bibliography contained in it. Other works with a more local setting are Herman Clarence Nixon, "The Populist Movement in Iowa," *Iowa Journal of History and Politics,* XXIV, 3-107; Brooks, *op. cit.;* Arnett, *op. cit.;* Francis B. Simkins, *The Tillman Movement in South Carolina.*

[2] In addition to Arnett, Brooks, and Simkins, *op. cit.,* see Walter Lynwood Fleming, *The Sequel of Appomattox, A Chronicle of the Reunion of the States;* Nathan Fine, *Labor and Farmer Parties in the United States,* p. 73.

secure in the lower South, where the race problem was more acute and the one-party system was more completely established.

By the early eighties, however, the agrarian groups had shown signs of revolt. Goaded by years of agricultural depression, they had begun to take stock of their condition and to question the leadership of their generals, colonels, and majors. Rumblings of discontent were heard which were soon to develop into uprisings, "political rather than social," against those who dominated the political life of the states and who seemed to be directing the economic trend. These uprisings took the form of fights to secure control of the Democratic party. "It was a fight of the outs against the ins. The outs were made up chiefly of small farmers in the richer agricultural sections . . . and the bulk of citizens of the upland regions. The ins consisted of the office-holding class, of conservatives who dreaded any division among the whites . . . and in general, of such as found in the existing order the means of welfare or a stay to their pride."[3] By 1886 "Private" John Allen of Mississippi was in congress, sent there two years before by the former privates of his district. In Georgia, Dr. William H. Felton, "the archinsurgent of this era," had been making his fiery attacks upon the "supreme caucus," the "court-house rings" and the "developers of resources."[4] Tom Watson was laying the foundations of his long career of dissent and was preparing to lead the embattled farmers in their uprisings of the coming decade.[5] By 1886 the farmers of South Carolina had started their drive against the firmly entrenched conservatives. Their immediate objective was the "capture of the machinery of the Democratic party" for the coming election. They failed in this objective, but they were gradually developing the awkward, one-eyed "Farmer of Edgefield" into the forceful Ben Tillman who was to crush the old oligarchy and dominate the Democratic organization in that state for many years.[6] It has already been seen how the "wool hat boys" of Tennessee nominated "Bob" Taylor over the op-

---

[3] W. G. Brown, *The Lower South in American History*, p. 256.
[4] Arnett, *op. cit.*, pp. 34-35.
[5] *Memorial Addresses: Senator Watson*, Washington, 1924, pp. 12-13.
[6] Simkins, *op. cit.*, pp. 59-61.

position of party press and leaders. It must not be assumed that "Private" John Allen, Tom Watson, Ben Tillman and "Bob" Taylor were similar in their views or methods, but they did represent, it seems, dissatisfaction with the old, conservative dictators of the Democratic party in their respective states.

Tennessee differed from the states of the lower South, as well as from those of the West. It is a noticeable fact that, as a rule, the agrarian revolts developed their greatest bitterness and strength in areas which relied on a single source of farm income.[7] Except for comparatively small sections devoted to cotton and tobacco, agriculture in Tennessee was reasonably well diversified, as was the growing of livestock. Exploitation of timber resources, together with the development of mineral resources, particularly in East Tennessee, supplemented farm production. At the same time, more and more capital was being invested in the state's manufactures. The presence of the Negro gave rise to social conditions in Tennessee that did not exist in the West, yet in no sense was the race problem as formidable as in the lower South. Politically, the state differed from the other sections mentioned. Though the Democrats controlled under normal conditions, the Republican party was of sufficient strength to threaten Democratic control whenever a considerable faction of that party became alienated. All these factors contributed to the reactions of Tennessee to agitations by agricultural leaders.

A few comparative figures show the fact that Tennessee farmers were gradually recovering from the effects of war and reconstruction in spite of conditions unfavorable to agriculture. In 1890 the average value per acre of land in the state was only 93 cents below that of 1860 and was $4.00 more than that of 1870.[8] The value of livestock in 1890 slightly exceeded that of 1860 and represented an increase of 36 per cent over the same item in 1870. Farm implements and machinery in 1890 were valued at some $1,500,000 more than in 1860 and at more than

---

[7] This fact is pointed out with respect to Iowa in Nixon, *op. cit.*, pp. 4-6. The votes in elections of 1892 and 1894 are illustrative. See Hicks, *op. cit.*, pp. 263, 337.

[8] *Census Reports,* V, Twelfth Census of the United States, taken in the year 1900, agriculture, Part 1, pp. 694-695.

twice as much as in 1870.[9] At the same time, Tennessee suffered from the general agricultural depression and the decrease in prices on agricultural commodities. The total value of the state's farm products in 1890 was 36 per cent below that of 1870.[10]

A brief review of earlier agrarian movements in Tennessee reveals that the Grangers gained considerable strength in the state. At one time there were 1,042 granges in the state and this number, in relation to population, compared with such states as Illinois, Ohio, Michigan, Wisconsin, Minnesota, the Dakotas, Florida, Arkansas, and Texas.[11] The Grange, however, was primarily social rather than political in purpose. This may explain both its strength in the state and its lack of political significance. In contrast with the Grange, the Greenback movement was political in nature. On three different occasions the party nominated a candidate for governor in Tennessee. In 1878 it polled approximately 10 per cent of the vote cast, in the presidential year of 1880 only 1½ per cent of the total vote was Greenback, and in its final appearance in 1882 the party polled some 4 per cent of the total. At no time was the Greenback

---

[9] *Ibid.*, pp. 698-701.

[10] *Ibid.*, p. 703.

[11] Buck, *The Granger Movement*. The following table, given by Mr. Buck, shows the grange strength in the several states in relation to the agricultural population.

Number of granges per 100,000 of population engaged in agriculture:

Over 500	250 to 500	150 to 250	75 to 150	Under 75
Kentucky	Tennessee	Mississippi	S. Carolina	New York
Indiana	Florida	Alabama	Louisiana	Rhode Island
Missouri	Vermont	Georgia	Maryland	
Iowa	Ohio	N. Carolina	Delaware	
Kansas	Michigan	Virginia	New Jersey	
Nebraska	Illinois	W. Virginia	Massachusetts	
Colorado	Wisconsin	Pennsylvania	New Hampshire	
Montana	Minnesota	Nevada	Maine	
Idaho	N. Dakota			
Washington	S. Dakota			
Oregon	Arkansas			
	Texas			
	California			

strength sufficient to influence the results.[12] The fact that this party made its appearance at a time when the state debt fight overshadowed all other issues may have contributed to its weakness in Tennessee.

The interval between the passing of the Greenbacks and the appearance of the Farmers' Alliance as a political factor in 1890 saw the rise of Robert L. Taylor to the governorship of Tennessee. How far the Taylor movement was aided by the agricultural unrest of the times is a matter of opinion. There can be no question, however, as to the general dissatisfaction with party leadership existing among rural Democrats of the state prior to Taylor's nomination in 1886. The study of his campaigns and administrations has revealed that he made his appeal to this group as candidate and represented its views as governor to such an extent as to hold its allegiance to himself and to the Democratic party.

By the time Taylor had completed his second term as governor, the Farmers' Alliance had reached its full strength in Tennessee and was able to capture the Democratic gubernatorial nomination. The organization which accomplished this was officially known as The Farmers' Alliance and Industrial Union and represented a union of the Agricultural Wheel and the Farmers' Alliance, two farm organizations of similar character. The national Agricultural Wheel, which had originated in Arkansas in 1882,[13] made its appearance in Tennessee during 1884. As was natural, it was introduced into West Tennessee, where it grew rapidly in numbers and influence until its union with the Alliance five years later. The organization included some 1,333 subordinate wheels in Tennessee, but its strength lay

---

[12] Election Returns, MS vol., in the office of the secretary of state, Nashville, Tennessee. The votes were as follows:

1878		*1880*		*1882*	
Democrat	89,018	State Credit Dem.	79,191	Democrat	118,821
Republican	42,328	Low Tax Dem.	57,424	"Sky Blue"	
Greenback	15,196	Republican	102,969	Dem.	4,599
		Greenback	3,641	Republican	90,850
				Greenback	9,072

[13] Buck, *The Agrarian Crusade*, p. 116.

very largely in the western section of the state.[14] Though the
National Farmers' Alliance and Coöperative Union of America
began its existence in Texas before the Wheel originated in Arkansas,[15] it did not appear in Tennessee until three years after
the first Wheel was organized. The first Alliance in the state
was established in Middle Tennessee in 1887. Due to the fact
that West Tennessee was pre-occupied by the Wheel, the Alliance gained its greatest strength in the middle section of the
state from whence it spread eastward. Its growth was rapid and
within a year after its appearance, there existed several hundred subordinate Alliances. In 1889, these were united into a
State Alliance, largely through the leadership of J. H. Mc-
Dowell, a vice president of the "Southern" Alliance for Tennessee.[16] McDowell was evidently a man of superior ability and was
to play an important part in Tennessee politics within the next
few years. In December, 1888, the national organizations of the
"Southern" Alliance and the Wheel voted to unite under the
name of the Farmers' and Laborers' Union of America.[17] By the
following July, 1889, the union had been consummated in Tennessee and John P. Buchanan, of Rutherford County, was
named president of the combined organization.

The "Southern" Alliance had been based largely upon the
idea of coöperative buying and selling, but that of the Northwest had very early turned its attention to political questions.
At Chicago in 1881 the program of the latter was declared to
be "a just income tax, salary reductions for officials, election of
officials rather than appointment, regulation of interstate com-

---

[14] Corinne Westphal, *The Farmers' Alliance in Tennessee,* Unpublished
M. A. Thesis, Vanderbilt University, 1929, pp. 25-26. Joseph A. Sharp,
Farmers' Alliance and Tennessee Politics, 1890-1892, Unpublished M. A.
Thesis, University of Tennessee, 1931, pp. 29-42.

[15] Buck, *The Agrarian Crusade,* p. 115. This organization was "somewhat
different in character and quite different in origin" from the National
Farmers' Alliance, organized by the farmers of the Northwest, usually
called the Northwestern Alliance. See *ibid.,* pp. 117-118. To avoid confusion,
these organizations will be referred to as the Southern Alliance and the
Northwestern Alliance.

[16] Westphal, *op. cit.,* pp. 30-31.

[17] Buck, *The Agrarian Crusade,* p. 117. In spite of the new name, the
name Alliance was generally applied to the order. In Tennessee the term
Alliance or Farmers' Alliance was common and is so used in this study.

merce, improvement of patent laws, pure food laws, and regulation of transportation systems."[18] Again in 1887 resolutions adopted by the body favored "free coinage of silver, issue of paper money direct to the people, ultimate ownership of railroads, government ownership and operation of the telegraph, improved waterways, restriction of liquor trade, public school industrial education, improvement of agricultural colleges, and popular election of senators."[19]

With such an example set by the Northwestern Alliance and with agricultural conditions in such an unsatisfactory state, it was inevitable that the Southern branch of the organization should enter politics as a means of bringing about desired reforms. It was inevitable also that its activity should be directed toward the capture of control in the Democratic party. This took place in various Southern states in 1890. As a result, Ben Tillman and almost the entire Tillman ticket won the Democratic nominations in South Carolina.[20] The organization won a signal victory in Missouri, where all Democratic congressmen and a majority of the legislature were pledged to support the Alliance program. Eight of the nine members of congress from North Carolina were so pledged, as were half of those from Virginia, four of eleven in Kentucky, and two of seven in Mississippi.[21] In Alabama the Alliance made a desperate attempt to name the Democratic candidate for governor. Though its representative had the support of more delegates than either of the four opposing candidates, he was unable to command the necessary majority, and his defeat was effected by a consolidation of the opposition after a long struggle that threatened the disruption of the party.[22]

In Tennessee the Alliance put forward John Price Buchanan as its choice for the Democratic gubernatorial nomination in

---

[18] W. W. Jennings, *A History of Economic Progress in the United States*, p. 420.

[19] *Ibid.*, p. 421.

[20] Simkins, *op. cit.*, p. 127.

[21] Arnett, *op. cit.*, p. 123.

[22] *Nashville American*, May 29, 1890, and succeeding issues. A full description of the Alabama fight is found in Charles Grayson Summersell, *A Life of Reuben F. Kolb*, Unpublished M. A. Thesis, University of Alabama, 1930.

1890. He was opposed by Josiah Patterson of Memphis, Jere
Baxter of Nashville and by John M. Taylor.[23] Buchanan was
born in Williamson County in 1847. He was descended from a
pioneer family of Middle Tennessee, had been a private in the
Confederate army and had, since the close of the war, devoted
his time to his farm in Rutherford County. He had been a consistent Democrat and had served two terms in the legislature.[24]
He had been president of the state Farmers' Alliance before its
union with the Wheel and continued to head the combined organization. He held this position at the time of his nomination
for governor.

Patterson was a native of Mississippi, and had served with
distinction in the Confederate army as colonel of a Mississippi
regiment. He began the practice of law in his native state after
the war but had moved to Memphis where he soon established a
successful practice. He had served a term in the legislature, was
an ardent admirer of Senator Isham G. Harris and was regarded as one of the Senator's devoted followers.[25] Patterson made
his bid for the nomination with old fashioned Democratic appeals. He pointed out to Alliance men and farmers that "every
tenet of the Alliance . . . was a principle of Democracy" and,
in line with this, urged some needed reforms in the revenue system and against trusts or combinations.[26] His supporters declared that his nomination would be a victory for "Southern
ideas of home rule" as against the Republican policy of federal
interference in state affairs.[27] Patterson was looked upon as the
candidate of the Harris wing and, as such, was opposed by the
industrialists who termed him the machine candidate.[28]

Baxter was the avowed candidate of the industrialists. In his
opening speech, he frankly espoused the industrial idea. He announced himself as a "business candidate for Governor" who

[23] It does not appear that John M. Taylor was in any way related to
Robert L. Taylor.
[24] Gentry R. McGee and C. B. Ijam, *A History of Tennessee from 1663
to 1930*, p. 251.
[25] Speer, *op. cit.*, pp. 266-268.
[26] *Nashville American,* April 27, 1890.
[27] *Memphis Appeal,* July 17, 1890.
[28] Illustrations of this opposition may be found in the *Chattanooga Times,*
July 16-20, 1890.

believed in carrying business principles into politics and in developing the country with railroads, mines and manufactures. A leading Harris editor summed up his speech in these words: "The tenor of his speech was that business was more important than political principles in a state government. . . ."[29] Baxter was the natural champion of industrialism. The son of a wealthy Nashville family, by 1880 he was vice president of the Memphis and Charleston railroad and was promoted to the presidency of that company within a year. He organized and was president of a coal company with large holdings in North Alabama. His company had built the Sheffield and Birmingham railroad for the purpose of transporting its coal to Birmingham, and Baxter became its president. He owned a large farm near Nashville and, for this reason, felt that he could talk to rural voters as one farmer to another.[30]

John M. Taylor did not play an important part in the canvass. He announced his candidacy as an "Upper-case Democrat" whose only claim for preferment was that he had "always voted the ticket straight and had always done his duty in maintaining the principles of the party and promoting its interests."[31]

The setting of the pre-convention campaign of 1890 is strikingly similar to that of 1886. The Colyar and Harris wings of the party contended for supremacy under the leadership of Baxter and Patterson respectively while the rural elements in the state, organized to a large degree under the Farmers' Alliance, supported Buchanan. These were the same people who had supported Robert L. Taylor against the factionalists. It does not appear that Taylor, then governor, took any part in the campaign although Baxter supporters claimed that the governor favored their candidate,[32] supposedly in retaliation against the Harris followers who had fought him so bitterly in 1888. If Governor Taylor did support Baxter, it escaped the notice of the Alliance forces, for no mention was made of it in that organ-

[29] *Nashville American*, April 27, 1890.

[30] Speer, *op. cit.*, pp. 757-759.

[31] *Nashville American*, April 16, 1890. See also *Knoxville Tribune*, June 19, 1890.

[32] *Chattanooga Times*, July 16, 1890.

ization's paper, the *Weekly Toiler*, which did not hesitate to expose any who opposed its candidate.[33] It is not likely that "Bob" Taylor actively opposed the evident will of the "wool-hat boys" who had stood by him so faithfully in the two previous campaigns.

During the pre-convention canvass, very little mention was made of Buchanan's candidacy in the party press, except for an occasional news item from a rural county to the effect that delegates had been instructed for him. However, he had been making an intensive campaign in which he had appealed to the farmers on the principles of the Alliance. At the same time he had vigorously asserted his Democratic orthodoxy. It is noticeable that, during the campaign for the nomination, Democratic papers stressed the importance of party solidarity. Nothing was said about Buchanan or his Alliance ideas that would make it embarrassing to support him as a nominee or that would tend to drive the Alliance people from the party in case of their defeat. The following editorial illustrates this policy.

. . . The farmers of the South have many righteous demands to ask of the legislators of the country. In order to effect their purpose they have organized in almost every state. But the farmers of the South are above all, Democrats. They are white men and believe in the white man's party. They are not an organization for wrecking the Democratic party. They have organized to get a common view of the situation, and in order to give emphasis to their demands. They will succeed but it will be only by the success of the Democratic party. The Democratic party is their hope for everything desirable, their protection and guarantee against legislation wicked and in the interest of the classes.[34]

This did not differ greatly from Buchanan's own view of the situation as expressed to the convention which nominated him. "Though the contest may be severe," he said, "as long as the power of speech may redeem it, I will be heard proclaiming to the people the principles of Democracy as enunciated by Jackson, Polk, and Johnson. . . . The principles of Democracy are

---

[33] *Weekly Toiler*, June and July, 1890.
[34] *Nashville American*, June 2, 1890.

eternal. . . . The Democratic party is opposed to allowing the National and State governments being converted into huge machines of legalized robbery for the aggrandizement of the few and the oppression of the many."[35]

This conservative position of the Alliance candidate was not at variance with his previously expressed views. In his annual address as president of the state Farmers' Alliance the year before, he had declared that the three great purposes of the organization were to benefit each farmer individually, the whole body of farmers, and all persons in pursuit of any legitimate and honorable business, in a word, "equal and exact justice to all." In this address, made before he had been mentioned as a candidate for governor, he declared it the policy of the Alliance to coöperate with the manufacturers of Tennessee by buying from them, through Alliance agencies, such products as could be supplied by them at reasonable prices. The farmers' organization, he said, wanted the "manufactures" of the state developed to where they could supply the greater part of the state's needs. The political purpose of the Alliance, as stated in this address, was to break the control of monopolists who, through corruption and bribery, had subverted government to the great injury of farmers and laborers.[36] This same conservative attitude was expressed a year later by the *Toiler*, official publication of the Alliance and edited by McDowell. In a leading editorial entitled "Let the Spirit of Conservatism Prevail," McDowell urged farmers to remember the Alliance pledge of justice to all honorable and legitimate vocations. He explained his position further: "The development of the resources of our great state and the prosperity of every legitimate industry should be made a common cause in which every class is equally interested. We need more railroads, more factories and more capital to develop the hidden resources of mother earth."[37] It is important to contrast this attitude of Tennessee farmers with that of the Northwestern Alliance, which had demanded government ownership of railroads and telegraphs three years

[35] *Nashville Banner*, July 19, 1890.
[36] *Weekly Toiler*, July 31, 1889.
[37] *Ibid.*, July 23, 1890.

before at Chicago. The views of the Tennessee Alliance were not greatly different from those which Robert L. Taylor had frequently expressed. They have a striking similarity to the view of President Andrew Jackson, as expressed in his inaugural address, that the national welfare demanded equal consideration for the interests of agriculture, commerce and manufacturing.[38] It is not surprising that the Democrats of Tennessee, who had supported Jackson, Johnson, and Taylor, found it possible to support Buchanan on a program such as he and the Alliance had advanced.

As convention time drew near it became evident that Buchanan would take the lead in the early balloting. It was freely predicted, however, that his delegates would not stand the pressure of machine politics and would desert him before his nomination could be effected. It was thought by some that the farmer delegates would be "weak and gullible" and could easily be led away from their candidate "by the arts and wiles of political lobbyists."[39] Such did not prove to be the case. The strength of the four candidates, as revealed on the first ballot, remained relatively unchanged through twenty-five ballots extending over three days. At last the withdrawal of John M. Taylor broke the deadlock and Buchanan was nominated on the 26th ballot.[40] Though the nomination of its candidate was hailed as a great victory by Alliance men, it seems likely that one editor viewed the situation correctly when he declared that Buchanan could not have been nominated had it not been for the bitter fight between the Baxter and Patterson factions.[41] Another paper, which had supported Baxter, took satisfaction in the view that Buchanan's nomination was a rebuke to the machine which had supported Patterson and which had demanded an "upper-case Democrat."[42] Baxter and Patterson, it will be remembered, were

---

[38] Richardson, *op. cit.*, II, 437.

[39] *Nashville Banner*, July 12, 1890 and *Nashville Review* (Republican), quoted in *Nashville Banner*, July 11, 1890. See also *Memphis Avalanche, Memphis Appeal* and *Chattanooga Times*, July 12 to July 18, 1890.

[40] *Nashville Banner*, July 16-19, 1890 and *Chattanooga Times* for same dates. The vote, omitting fractions, on the first ballot stood, Buchanan 757, Patterson 370, Baxter 297, Taylor 177.

[41] *Nashville Banner*, July 19, 1890.

[42] *Chattanooga Times*, July 20, 1890.

the candidates of Colyar and Harris wings of the party. The old state's rights Democrats and the industrialists of the New South were still fighting for party control and again the small farmer element had capitalized on the enmity between the two factions. This difference should be noted, however, between the victory of Buchanan and that of Robert L. Taylor. The former had won through the well directed efforts of a powerful organization. Taylor had consolidated and led the same groups by means of his personal popularity and at a time when no organization existed among them.

The platform adopted by the Democratic convention, to which the Alliance and its candidate subscribed, reflected the conservatism of the Tennessee farm movement. On national issues, it declared against the importation of pauper labor and for the reservation of public lands for homestead purposes. Similar views on these subjects appeared in the national platforms of both Democratic and Republican parties in 1888 and 1892.[43] With reference to the currency, soon to become such an important issue, the state platform called for a currency of gold, silver, and paper, convertible into coin at the option of the holder. It also demanded free coinage of silver on the basis originally fixed by law, and that the silver and gold dollar be equally a unit of value.[44] The bitter McKinley-Bryan campaign of 1896, together with the subsequent discrediting of bi-metalism and glorification of the gold standard, has served to obscure the fact that, prior to that year, both parties had been committed to bi-metalism. In fact, the Tennessee Democratic-Alliance currency plank of 1890, far from being radical, was strikingly similar to the pronouncements of both major parties in their national platforms.[45] Without entering into a discussion

<hr>

[43] Porter, *op. cit.*, Democratic platform of 1888, p. 141; of 1892, pp. 162-164. Republican platform of 1888, pp. 148-149; and of 1892, pp. 175-176.

[44] *Nashville Banner*, July 16, 1890.

[45] For the sake of clarity the following quotations from the national platforms are given: *Republican*, 1888, "The Republican party is in favor of the use of both gold and silver as money, and condemns the policy of the Democratic Administration in its efforts to demonitize silver." Porter, *op. cit.*, p. 150. *Republican*, 1892, "The American people, from tradition and interest, favor bi-metalism, and the Republican party demands the use of both gold and silver, as standard money, with such restrictions and under such pro-

of the merits of the currency controversy, it is evident that the Tennessee platform of 1890 was far from radical, judged by views of the major parties of the country.

The demands of the Democratic-Alliance platform relating to state affairs are worth noting. They were: extension of the free school system; strict economy with expenses reduced to the minimum; just and equal taxation of all persons, corporations, and property subject to taxation; amendment of lien laws so as to secure full protection to laborer and mechanic; establishment and development of good roads; a welcome of capital and labor to the state; and, finally, modification of the penal system to eliminate competition with free labor.[46]

The platform was accepted by all factions of the party. One editor was relieved because it was not a transcript of the Alliance code, but "predicated solely upon the immortal doctrines of Thomas Jefferson."[47] Another paper, which had opposed Buchanan, called the document "broad, comprehensive and clear." It held that the platform was conservative without fear or evasion yet, at the same time, positive and bold but not defiant or aggressive. With such a platform, it declared, all can support the ticket regardless of who is nominated.[48]

Buchanan was accepted as the Democratic nominee by the party press, though there was a noticeable lack of enthusiasm in some quarters. The *Banner* at Nashville was of the opinion that "The farmers compose the mass of voters in the state, and

---

visions, to be determined by legislation, as will secure the maintenance of the parity of values of the two metals so that the purchasing and debt-paying power of the dollar, whether of silver, gold, or paper, shall be at all times equal. The interests of the producers of the country, its farmers and its workingmen, demand that every dollar, paper or coin, issued by the government, shall be as good as any other." *Ibid.*, p. 174. *Democratic,* 1888, Silent on the subject. *Democratic,* 1892, ". . . We hold to the use of both gold and silver as the standard of money of the country, and to the coinage of both gold and silver without discriminating against either metal or charge for mintage, but the dollar unit of coinage of both metals must be of equal intrinsic and exchangeable value . . . and we demand that all paper currency shall be kept at par with and redeemable in such coin. . . ." *Ibid.*, p. 162.

[46] *Nashville Banner,* July 16, 1890.
[47] *Memphis Appeal,* July 19, 1890.
[48] *Memphis Avalanche,* July 17, 1890.

10

there can be advanced no good reason why a farmer should not be made Governor if the people want him in that place."[49] One rural editor expressed the attitude of many when he urged his fellow Democrats to stand by the nominees for, said he, "the meanest Democrat living is an angel compared to the best Republican God ever made."[50] The campaign resolved itself into an effort to stir up Democratic enthusiasm. The Republican nominee, Lewis T. Baxter, was comparatively unknown, and the joint debates between the two candidates failed to capture the popular imagination. One authority in Tennessee history described the campaign as rather listless "until Governor Robert L. Taylor enlivened it by taking the stump for the democratic ticket."[51]

It appeared for a time that the Democratic nominee would be defeated because of his assumed endorsement of the St. Louis "demands" and the "sub-treasury scheme." Both the "demands" and the "sub-treasury scheme" had been put forward at the St. Louis convention of the Alliance in December 1889, to which Buchanan was a delegate. One of the "demands" not included in the state Democratic platform called for "government ownership and operation of the means of communication and transportation."[52] The rather novel sub-treasury plan proposed "that the system of using certain banks as United States depositories be abolished." It proposed the establishment of a sub-treasury in every county in the United States which offered for sale, during one year, farm products to the value of half a million dollars. Elevators or warehouses were to be located in such counties, where farmers might store their crops and receive certificates of deposit which would entitle them to a loan at the sub-treasury equal to "eighty per cent of the local cur-

[49] *Nashville Banner*, July 12, 1890. An idea of the attitude of the party press may be had from expressions in *Memphis Avalanche, Chattanooga Times* and *Nashville American*, July 19, 1890. See also quotations in the *Nashville Banner* of July 24 and 25 from *Knoxville Sentinel, Wartrace Advance, Giles County Democrat, Franklin Review and Journal, Fayetteville Sun, Jackson Times, Tullahoma Guardian, Pulaski Citizen, Obion Democrat, Gibson County Herald, Kenton Argus.*

[50] *Shelbyville Gazette*, quoted in *ibid.*, July 25, 1890.

[51] Moore, *op. cit.*, I, 575.

[52] Buck, *Agrarian Crusade*, pp. 129-130.

rent value of the products deposited." Other provisions fixed
the annual interest rate on all such loans at one per cent and
allowed one year for redemption of the deposited products.[53]

By this plan, it was hoped to enable farmers to hold their
crops for better prices and, further, to provide flexibility to the
currency through the certificates of deposit. The first principle
has been applied boldly in the "New Deal" by Franklin D.
Roosevelt and the latter principle, with respect to commercial
paper, was adopted in the Federal Reserve system by Woodrow
Wilson, but both ideas appeared extremely radical in 1890.
Buchanan's endorsement of the sub-treasury plan, prior to his
nomination for governor, was ignored in the early stages of the
campaign. As early as August, however, certain county Alliances, notably that of Williamson County, began to question
local candidates as well as those for the legislature and congress
as to whether they subscribed to Alliance principles, including
the sub-treasury plan. Almost immediately the *Nashville Ban-*

GOVERNOR'S ELECTION 1890
White—Democratic   Vertical—Republican

ner wanted to know whether the candidate for governor was
willing to declare himself on the subject, holding it unfair to
exempt the head of the ticket from answering questions which
other candidates were required to face. Buchanan's refusal to
state whether or not he endorsed the plan infuriated that paper,
which had not been unfriendly to him up to that time. It became bitter against him and almost frantic in its demands that
he declare his position. A few smaller papers joined the *Banner*
in its demand and many others began to question why their
candidate did not speak out on a question that seemed so im-

---

[53] *Idem.*

portant.[54] Buchanan, however, remained as silent on the subject as was the Democratic platform. Though he had favored the idea as a citizen and an Alliance official, he refused to commit himself as nominee. It seemed for a time that the sub-treasury plan would be his undoing, but the more stalwart party papers and orators came to his rescue. The campaign developed into a party crusade and Buchanan was elected by a majority nearly ten thousand greater than that of Taylor's in 1886, although the latter had polled some 13,000 more votes in that off-year election than Buchanan did in 1890.[55]

Not only did the Farmers' Alliance succeed in naming the governor but it had shown impressive strength in the various legislative contests. Of the thirty-three members of the state senate, fourteen were listed as Alliance men while forty of the ninety members of the lower house belonged to the order. The combined total of fifty-four Alliance men in the two houses included four Republicans and fifty Democrats. Although the Alliance fell a few votes short of a majority in either house, there were a number of farmers in the legislature who were not members of the order.[56] Thus it was that the assembly was distinctly agrarian in character.[57]

Governor Buchanan delivered his first message to the legislature on February 10, 1891,[58] and in it outlined his program of proposed legislation and reform. The new Democrat-Alliance governor made no startling suggestions. He declared that the wide-spread nature of agricultural distress proved that its

[54] *Nashville Banner*, August, September and October, 1890.

[55] *Elections Returns, op. cit.* The vote in the two elections was:

	1890		1886
Democratic—Buchanan	113,549	126,628—R. L. Taylor	
Republican—Baxter	76,081	109,837—A. A. Taylor	
Prohibitionist—Kelly	11,082	. . . . . .	
Total vote	200,712	236,465	

[56] Charles A. Miller (Comp.), *Official Manual of Tennessee*, pp. 246-248. See also Sharp, *op. cit.*, pp. 98-99.

[57] In the congressional elections, the Alliance endorsed the regular Democratic nominees. See Sharp, *op. cit.*, p. 74.

[58] Governor's Message, *House Journal*, 47th General Assembly, Tennessee, 1891, pp. 149-165.

causes were national rather than local and, for that reason, state legislatures were powerless to deal with them. He held that a shortage of the money supply had produced financial stringency and that the national government alone could remedy this evil.

On many state problems Buchanan's recommendations did not differ greatly from those previously made by Governor Taylor. He held that the big task in matters of taxation was to make existing laws more effective, and proposed a state board of equalization. He urged the establishment of a reformatory for youthful criminals and held that a new penitentiary was the state's greatest need. On the important question of leasing convicts to private concerns, he, like Taylor, recognized the objectionable features of a system which brought unfair competition to free labor, particularly to miners. Though he saw the necessity of a change in the penal system he, like Taylor, believed that the financial condition of the state made it "unfeasible" at the time. He recommended a liberal policy toward the state's charitable institutions. He suggested the publication of a new geological survey for the purpose of advertising the state's natural resources. The subject of public education received a large share of the governor's attention. He urged the greater development of the state school system and larger appropriations to its various activities. He advocated increased taxation if this were necessary to provide adequate funds for the schools. He further believed that courses in civil government should be taught. At this time the so-called Force bill was before congress and was arousing wide discussion, particularly in the South. A sentence in the governor's message throws interesting light on some of the reactions in the Southern states to this hated bill. In discussing an appropriation for a Tennessee exhibit at the World's Fair to be held in Chicago he said: "While I fully endorse the action of the Legislature of Tennessee and of other states in refusing to make appropriations until the Force Bill is disposed of," he thought the fate of the bill was sealed and that the appropriation could be made at that time. It would appear that the legislature was not so optimistic on the subject for it confined its action to granting authority to the county courts to make such appropriations as they might see fit. Three of Buchanan's suggestions reflected his particular interest in agriculture. He urged the retention of the state's agricultural department in spite of agitation for its discontinuance and, also, that its appropriation be increased by $2,000 to provide for the inspection of fertilizers. He believed that the dairy interests of the state would be encouraged through laws preventing the adulteration of its products. Finally, after commending the state board of health, he urged its further development with the view of preventing and curbing live-stock diseases. One of the most noteworthy of Buchanan's suggestions was the proposal to subject state banks to state inspection. This, it seems, reflects the common suspicion of banks, existing among agrarians of the time.

Though the farmers of Tennessee apparently had little sympathy with the more radical measures of the agrarian program, as it developed in the Northwest, they were aroused on the subject of "trusts" or combinations for price fixing purposes. This attitude naturally led to a suspicion of corporations generally. Buchanan evidently reflected the views of his constituents in his message. He held that the state had the public welfare, and not private aggrandizement, in view when it provided for the creation of corporations. Large enterprises, beyond the scope of individual endeavor, afforded the only excuse for incorporation. It was never intended, he thought, for corporate bodies to "usurp the offices of a citizen or to relieve him of responsibility." As matters stood, he believed, the chief reasons which led men to incorporate were "to limit their liabilities and to increase their powers." To remedy this evil, he suggested that charters be granted to none but public or quasi-public corporations and to those whose field was beyond individual endeavor.

The Democratic-Alliance governor seems to have voiced a fundamental difference between agrarians of South and West when he declared that the "trust" evil was largely the result of the "national policy of protection." He believed that genuine relief would come only when that policy was abandoned.[59]

---

[59] For an interesting discussion of this difference between Southern and Western Agrarians in their view of the tariff question, see Hicks, *op. cit.,*

It is significant that the western controlled Populist party, in its national platforms of 1892 and 1896, failed to include the tariff among the many evils denounced.[60] Though the governor believed that "trusts" resulted largely from the protective system, he believed the state could do something toward curbing them and advanced a rather novel plan. He proposed a law requiring each existing corporation to "submit by oath to a statement" that it was not and would not become a party to a trust or combination seeking to establish prices at variance with the law of supply and demand. He proposed that any corporation which refused to submit to such an oath would forfeit its charter. He believed that such a law would not harm honest corporations and would "be of service to the public welfare." In line with this policy of curbing the "trusts," he proposed uniform textbooks for the state.

The governor's message was well received. One Democratic paper in East Tennessee pronounced it a sound, sensible, conservative document which proved that the people had made no unpardonable mistake in choosing a "common farmer" to be their governor. Continuing, the paper declared that he exhibited no narrow spirit, advocated no radical changes, urged no extreme measures, but offered many suggestions worthy of endorsement by the legislature.[61] The *Nashville Banner* which had waged such a bitter fight against the governor, declared that the message should be commended, in the main, as "a well considered, broad minded" treatment of public questions though it doubted the wisdom of some recommendations. It described the governor's proposal that corporations be required to take oath not to become a party to a "trust" as a "unique suggestion" of doubtful value.[62] A staunch Republican paper pronounced the message "a strong, common sense state document" which did credit to the heart and mind of the governor.[63]

pp. 80-81. Nixon, *op. cit.*, gives little indication that the tariff played an important part in the Populist movement in Iowa. See also Buck, *The Agrarian Crusade*, pp. 35, 132.

[60] Porter, *op. cit.*, Populist platform of 1892, pp. 166-169; of 1896, pp. 196-200.

[61] *Knoxville Tribune*, February 14, 1891.

[62] *Nashville Banner*, February 10, 1891.

[63] *Knoxville Daily Journal*, February 11, 1891.

A brief review of legislative acts relating to railroads, corporations and "trusts" will give some idea of the reactions of the farmer-controlled Assembly of Tennessee. Only two acts were passed affecting railroads, and these show no trace of the radical animosity toward the carriers evinced in the West. One act authorized railroads to acquire branches or lines which would connect with or form an extension to their systems. The act was not to be construed as authorizing the acquisition of parallel or competing lines.[64] The other amended an act of 1881 empowering roads to acquire lines and property of other railroads by a three-fourths vote of the capital stock. The amendment required that three-fourths of the capital stock must be present and voting, either in person or by written proxy, before such acquisitions could be made.[65] In addition to these acts dealing with transportation matters, the legislature created a commission to make surveys and gather data to be presented to the federal government along with requests for the construction of a canal connecting the Cumberland and Tennessee rivers and another joining the Tennessee and Mississippi.[66] The assembly also favored more stringent control and supervision over means of transportation than had been exercised by the interstate commerce commission.[67] These mild measures represent the extent of the Alliance crusade against railroads in Tennessee.

The legislature, like the governor, reflected popular condemnation of "trusts" and suspicion of corporations. It passed an act requiring each foreign corporation which desired to do business or own property in Tennessee to file a copy of its charter with the secretary of state and to cause an abstract of this to be filed with the register in each county in which it proposed to do business or own property. The act further provided that when a corporation complied with those requirements it became, to all intents and purposes, a domestic corporation, subject to the jurisdiction of the laws of Tennessee, exactly as if it were created under the laws of the State.[68] The assembly also passed

[64] *Acts*, 47th General Assembly, Tennessee, 1891, Chapter 125.
[65] *Ibid.*, Chapter 61.
[66] *Ibid.*, Chapter 204.
[67] *Ibid.*, H. J. R. No. 28. See also Sharp, *op. cit.*, pp. 124–125.
[68] *Ibid.*, Chapter 122.

an act "to declare unlawful all trusts, pools, contracts, arrangements, and combinations in the restraint of trade, production, manufacture, or sale" and to fix liability and punishment of such persons and corporations as might violate it. Under the act, officers and stockholders were personally liable, and the corporation charter was subject to forfeiture. Not only that, but all officers and stockholders were jointly and severally liable for all debts or obligations of each and every person connected with the corporation "as if all were partners."[69]

The revenue bill of 1891 aroused indignation in some quarters and is important in that it shows a disposition on the part of the farmer-controlled legislature to tax corporations more heavily than had been done. A Republican paper in Knoxville was particularly violent in its denunciation of the "Proposed Legislative Outrage" and "Robber Revenue Bill" which, it declared, would kill off corporate industry. In illustration of this "unblushing steal," it cited the Telephone Company of Knoxville on which the tax was raised from $400 to $5,000. It also complained that street car companies of Knoxville, Chattanooga, Nashville, and Memphis were taxed at around $5,000.[70]

Two other resolutions of the legislature throw light on the agrarian attitude in Tennessee. One requested the state's senators at Washington to oppose the Conger lard bill which, it declared, was class legislation against the manufacturers of cotton seed oil.[71] Another resolution called upon the state's representatives in congress to support an amendment to the national constitution calling for the direct election of United States senators.[72]

Governor Buchanan, in his final message to the legislature in 1893, made some further suggestions on state problems which are worth noting. These were made at the end of his term, after he had been defeated for reëlection with the endorsement of the Populist party of Tennessee. He suggested that executive officers be elected for four years. Another suggestion, surprising in

---

[69] *Ibid.*, Chapter 218.

[70] *Knoxville Daily Journal*, March 21, 22, 1891.

[71] *Acts*, 47th General Assembly, op. cit., S. J. R. No. 7.

[72] *Ibid.*, H. R. No. 38. See also Sharp, *op. cit.*, pp. 103-104.

view of the usual agrarian attitude, was that the legislature be
elected for a term of four years, that its members be paid stipu-
lated salaries instead of *per diem*, and that the length of the
legislative session be unlimited. On the subject of election laws,
he believed that there should be more safeguards about the
counting of ballots, that restrictions which practically amount-
ed to an educational qualification should be removed, and that
rigid restrictions on the technical marking of ballots should be
done away with. These, he held, practically disfranchised many
unskilled and careless voters and placed too much power in the
hands of election officials. He further believed that the convict
lease system should be abolished and that the time had come to
call a constitutional convention. He renewed his suggestion for
the inspection of state banks.[73]

The end of the legislative session of 1891 found Buchanan,
the Democratic-Alliance governor, in general public favor.
Though there had been some severe criticism of the revenue bill
and though one paper had declared the General Assembly of
that year to be below the usually low level of legislatures,[74] the
governor had escaped pointed criticism. A Memphis editor, who
had opposed the governor's nomination, declared at the end of
the legislative session that the Buchanan administration, so far
as it had gone in its public acts, was bound to be one of which
the whole people would be proud. Speaking of the governor, the
editorial stated: "He has laboriously and intelligently addressed
himself to his executive duties, won respect and made friends
every day since his inauguration."[75]

In spite of this auspicious beginning, Buchanan's troubles
were soon to begin. Repeated uprisings on the part of miners in
the coal fields of East Tennessee against leased convict labor
proved to be an annoying problem to the state administration.
Although the governor was not responsible for the disturbances,
they doubtless detracted from his prestige and contributed to
his defeat for a second nomination. During the month of July,

---

[73] Governor's Message, *House Journal*, 48th General Assembly, Tennessee,
1893, pp. 35-60.

[74] *Nashville Banner*, March 31, 1891.

[75] *Memphis Commercial*, quoted in *ibid.*, March 31, 1891.

1891 strikes occurred in the mines of the Tennessee Coal Mining Company at Briceville. The grievances which led to the strikes were the refusal of the company to comply with the law allowing miners to have check-weighmen of their own choosing and the practice of the company in paying in scrip instead of money. The company immediately leased a number of convicts from the state and proceeded with the operation of the mine. On July 14 a mob of miners or their sympathizers took possession of the stockades in which the convicts were held and forced the warden to remove them to Knoxville. Governor Buchanan called two companies of the militia and went himself to the seat of trouble. He returned the convicts to the stockade and warned representatives of the miners that he would maintain order and protect the dignity and honor of the state. He urged them to seek redress through lawful means. Upon the Governor's return to Nashville a second outbreak occurred at Briceville and at Coal Creek and again the wardens were forced to remove the convicts. Buchanan, this time, called out the entire state guard and restored the convicts to their stockades. His authority for doing this was in doubt, and he called a special session of the legislature to grant him the necessary powers. He also urged that body to pass laws looking toward a redress of the grievances which had occasioned the troubles. Miners were not satisfied with the actions of the legislature, and after its adjournment two more outbreaks occurred, the trouble extending to other mines. The governor promptly called out the entire state guard and suppressed the disorders. Several leaders of the insurrection were tried and convicted and others fled the state. Aside from the effect of these troubles upon the political prestige of Buchanan, their importance in this study lies in their revelation of the agrarian's attitude toward labor troubles. The moderation which had marked Buchanan's course up to that time was evident from the first. He did not hesitate a moment to enforce the law although he realized the justice of many of the miners' complaints. At the same time, he sought to secure redress of those wrongs.

The Farmers' Alliance as an active factor in Tennessee

politics came to an end with the close of Buchanan's administration, after which it merged into the Populist movement.
The processes by which this came about are studied in the
succeeding chapter. However, it was under the Alliance that
the agrarian movement reached the high tide of its political
influence in Tennessee. Its program, both as stated in the campaign of 1890 and as translated into legislative acts, was
essentially conservative. Its only chance for success, in a political way, lay in the control of the Democratic party. This
had been made easier by the fact that the small farmer group,
of which the Alliance was largely composed, had gained a
commanding position in the party under the leadership of
Robert L. Taylor.

As has been pointed out, the Buchanan program was no
radical departure from that of Taylor. If allowance be made
for normal change in issues from year to year, it seems reasonable to say that the Alliance movement was a continuation of
that which had resulted in Taylor's success. The movement
was essentially conservative as compared to similar movements
in the West and in many other Southern states. It was an application of old Jacksonian and Johnsonian views to the then
modern issues. Its remedy was negative rather than positive.
Government was to discontinue those policies which produced
an inequitable division of wealth rather than resort to radical
measures tending to penalize the favored class for the benefit
of the less favored. As was frequently asserted in the campaign
of 1890, the ideal was exact and equal justice to all. Two
sentences in Buchanan's inaugural address illustrate in a striking way this attitude of the Tennessee agrarian. One read:
"The Jeffersonian non-interference theory of government is the
wisest, leaving people to be happy in their own way without
undertaking to do for them what they can do better for themselves." Relief did not lie, he believed, in the passing of laws
but in the proper enforcement of existing ones. According to
his view, "The weakness of state government does not arise
so much from the inefficiency of law as from the inefficiency

of the execution of the law."[76] Capital was welcomed to the state, industries invited and railroads encouraged so long as they bore their just share of taxation and did not seek unfair returns through monopolies or "trusts." The inaugural words of Buchanan upon this point are significant. Pointing toward the statue of Andrew Jackson, he declared: " . . . the spirit which led him as Chief Executive of the nation to crush with an iron heel monopoly as it reared its ominous crest, that spirit which struck at whatever was opposed to the good of the people as at a personal enemy, will never die. Today it 'stalks abroad' and lives in the hearts of the people."[77] This Democratic-Alliance governor spoke for the small farmers of Tennessee. He declared a political doctrine that was familiar to them, for they had heard it from Andrew Jackson, Andrew Johnson and Robert L. Taylor.

---

[76] Inaugural Address, *House Journal,* 47th General Assembly, Tennessee, 1891, p. 56.

[77] *Ibid.,* p 58.

CHAPTER VII

THE DEFEAT OF POPULISM

As BUCHANAN entered upon the second year of his administration, the Populist party made its appearance; and it functioned as a state organization for the first time in the campaign of 1892. The fortunes of that party and its influence on politics in Tennessee were affected largely by local conditions as well as by the personalities of those who directed it and by the political traditions of the people.

An understanding of the state campaign of 1892 must be based upon the fact that Buchanan, the executive, had given general satisfaction. The attitude of the press upon this point at the close of the legislative session of 1891 has been indicated. Though his course in the labor disturbances of 1891 doubtless lost him some support, there seems to have been a disposition to regard the first year of his administration as a success. An influential paper of Chattanooga voiced this in the early months of 1892 as follows: "The *Times*, as yet, has no candidate for governor. We have, as a whole, been satisfied with Governor Buchanan's management of the state's executive business." It added that unless some unforseen circumstances arose, it saw no reason for violating the second term rule.[1]

Opposition to Buchanan, however, had appeared in January of 1892. The *Nashville American* had taken the lead in this

[1] *Chattanooga Times*, February 27, 1892. For similar expressions of confidence, see *Morristown Gazette* quoted in *Knoxville Tribune*, July 9, 1892, *Murfreesboro Free Press*, *Murfreesboro Home Journal*, *Murfreesboro News*, *Manchester Times*, *Clarksville Tobacco Leaf*, *Somerville Reporter and Falcon*, *Gibson County Democrat*, *Jackson Whig*, *Athens Post*, *Cannon Courier*, *Stewart Courier*, *Gibson County Herald*, *McMinnville New Era*, *Bedford County Times*, *Memphis Scimitar* and *Memphis Commercial*, quoted in *Nashville Banner*, February 23, 24, 1892.

movement. Although it had, at the end of the legislative session, declared that there was "no doubt anywhere that the governor has done his duty," it now brought forward the name of Judge Peter Turney of the state supreme court as the man most fitted to lead the party to victory. Soon a number of party papers in various sections of the state had followed the lead of the Nashville daily in expressing doubt of Buchanan's availability and their preference for Judge Turney.[2] This opposition, guarded and of a mild character at first, grew in boldness and intensity as the weeks passed and finally reached an extreme bitterness.

Undoubtedly, the governor had given offense by some of his appointments. Although one editor had declared, early in 1891, that he commended some appointments and did not criticize others,[3] he changed his attitude some two months later with the appointment of John H. McDowell to the lucrative position of coal oil inspector.[4] McDowell, it must be remembered, was the leading spirit in the Alliance movement and had done effective work in bringing about the nomination of Buchanan. While holding the position of coal oil inspector, he had continued as an editor of *The Toiler*, leading Alliance paper of the state. It was charged in this paper that the editor of the *American* had been an applicant for the inspectorship and that his resentment of McDowell's appointment was the real reason for his opposition to the governor.[5] Although the editor of the *American* scoffed at such a charge, there can be little doubt that dissatisfaction with Buchanan's appointments had something to do with the opposition to him. A Republican paper declared that Buchanan had not changed his political

[2] *Nashville American*, from January 5, 1892, also *Johnson City Comet, Covington Leader, Camden Chronicle, Carroll County Democrat, Marion County Democrat, Obion Democrat, Franklin County News, Crossville Sentinel, Decherd Headlight, Martin Mail, Memphis Ledger, McMinnville Standard, Fayetteville Observer, Lebanon Democrat, Shelbyville Commercial, Franklin Review-Appeal, Knoxville Tribune, Pulaski Citizen, Columbia Herald, Jackson Tribune-Sun, Jackson Times*, quoted in *Nashville Banner*, February 23, 24, 26, 1892.

[3] *Nashville Banner*, January 27, 1891.

[4] *Ibid.*, April 7, 1891.

[5] *The Toiler*, quoted in *Nashville Banner*, March 8, 1892.

views since 1890 but that his failure to consult certain party leaders on the distribution of patronage had led to the discovery that he "was not a good Democrat."[6]

Regardless of whether the question of patronage had a determining effect upon the opposition to Buchanan, there can be little doubt that hostility to McDowell had much to do with it. This spokesman of the agrarian revolt in Tennessee had incurred the wrath of party leaders. The following editorial expression illustrates the extent to which denunciation of him went: "And yet this McDowell, a man who never generated a bead of perspiration with the labor of any muscles except those of his jaw, a former Republican, an associate of negroes during the days of reconstruction, a selfish, scheming, blatant demagogue, dares to lift his bewhiskered head high above the horizon of state politics and threaten the Democratic party."[7] The same editor condemned Buchanan for the fact that he allowed McDowell, who held the most lucrative Democratic office, to "keep on wagging an un-Democratic tongue."[8] Numerous party papers called upon the governor to break with McDowell and assured him the nomination as a reward.[9]

---

[6] *Knoxville Daily Journal,* August 1, 1892. The declaration that "certain appointments" had much to do with the opposition to Buchanan appeared in the *Jackson Tribune-Sun* (Democratic), quoted in *Nashville Banner,* March 8, 1892.

[7] *Nashville American,* April 30, 1892.

[8] *Idem.*

[9] When the campaign had reached fever heat and the *Nashville American* was abusing the governor as a tool of McDowell, it had this to say: ". . . when the time came for a renomination and the Democrats began to ask themselves whether or not to give Buch. a second term, there developed a queer condition of affairs. They went to Buch. and begged him to give them a chance to declare him a Democrat. He wouldn't say a word. McDowell had the key to the padlock and had left Buch. only a little room in the corner of his mouth to spit through. They said to him 'we want to renominate you' but only the same idiotic glance of the eye and the crucified expression of the soul was their response." October 31, 1892.

Another version of the affair was given the writer by Hon. C. C. Henderson, veteran newspaper publisher, political leader, and historian of Murfreesboro. Mr. Henderson was a close friend of the governor and was present at an interview which he recounted as follows: "Attorney General Norman and I were in the governor's office one day when Walter Cain of the *Nashville American* and Major Fyffe, representing a Chattanooga newspaper, came to talk to the governor about his connection with

Some, who were friendly to Buchanan, charged that the hostility toward McDowell arose from the latter's supposed ambition to succeed William B. Bate in the United States senate. Senator Bate had long been identified with the Harris wing of the Democratic party. The fact that the party papers of that group were the most intemperate in their denunciation of McDowell and vigorous in their opposition to Buchanan would lend color to this charge. However, a closer examination of the political situation, national, sectional and state, leads to the conclusion that the cause of this attitude toward the agrarian representative was more fundamental than either the personality and ambitions of McDowell or disappointment over distribution of patronage. The additional fact that papers of the Colyar faction joined, at last, in the opposition to McDowell and Buchanan and lent their support to the candidacy of Judge Turney suggests the influence which the race question exerted in Tennessee politics. Unless Populism were crushed, the Republicans would triumph over a divided Democracy and white supremacy in the state might be threatened. The fact that

---

McDowell. They told him that his continued relations with McDowell would make him an impossible candidate for the Democratic nomination and unless he would agree to break the close association, their papers would be compelled to turn their batteries upon him. We all talked it over. General Norman and I advised the governor that the best thing to do would be to tell McDowell of the situation and let him know, in a kindly way, that their relations must be put on a different footing. The governor turned to us and said 'You know that I don't give any more weight to McDowell's advice than I do to yours.' We agreed with him but told him that the public did not know that and, after all, what the public thought would determine political affairs. We told him that it could be brought about in such a way as not to do an injustice to McDowell and, at the same time, let the public know what the real situation was. It seemed for a time that the governor was on the point of agreeing with us when Major Fyffe, who was a young man and impressed us as being over-bearing, spoke up, saying: 'Well Governor, we will give you until tomorrow night to break with McDowell and if you do not, we will turn our batteries upon you and defeat you.'" Mr. Henderson continues: "General Norman and I looked at each other and knew that all was over. Old Buck, who had been sitting at his desk, got up and paced the floor for a minute and we knew that he was mad. After a short time he faced the newspaper men and said: 'Turn your batteries and be d——d. McDowell has been my friend and I will not throw him over for you.'"

11

this did occur later in North Carolina makes the fears of Tennessee Democrats understandable.

On February 22, 1892, representatives of various organizations of farmers and other dissatisfied groups met in St. Louis and really launched the Populist party. Although the Southern Alliance, with which the Tennessee organization was connected, held more seats in the convention than any other single organization, the third party move was essentially Western. Indeed, the idea had met with determined opposition from many Alliance leaders in the South and they had been influential in postponing a more definite step in that direction at Cincinnati in May of 1891.[10] But the agrarian revolt had gained too much momentum in the West. It could not be stayed by the misgivings of Southern representatives. The time had come when they must choose between allegiance to their Western friends or to the Democratic party.

Democratic leaders in the South recognized the dilemma in which Alliance men found themselves and determined to force them to make their choice of its horns. Old line Democrats had been irked at the Alliance domination of their party and had acquiesced in it only because of the ever-present race question. They now determined to force these new-comers in the game of politics either to renounce the new movement and, with it, their claims to preferment or to enter the third party and bear the odium of endangering white supremacy by dividing the white vote. This determination took active form, in the winter and spring of 1892, in all the Southern states except South Carolina. There the Alliance, politically, had been absorbed into the Tillman movement, the forceful leader of which so dominated the Democratic party of his state that there was no possibility of an effective Populist organization.[11] In some states where the threat of Populism was more real, Democrats did not hesitate to include in their platforms certain principles advocated by the third party. This was particularly true of

---

[10] For a full account of the formation of the Populist party and events leading up to it see Hicks, *op. cit.,* pp. 205-237.

[11] Simkins, *op. cit.,* p. 172.

Florida, North Carolina, Georgia and Texas.[12] The Alabama press denounced Reuben F. Kolb, spokesman of the Alliance in that state, and undertook to read him and his followers out of the party.[13] In Mississippi, it was declared, the straight Democracy gained a signal victory over the "tomfools" who wished to commit the party to "unquestionable heresies."[14]

It was inevitable that Tennessee politics should be affected by the threat of a third party. It was inevitable also that the strength of the Republican party in the state, together with that of the industrialist, old-line Whig element of the Democratic party, should have a bearing on the course of those who undertook to handle the situation. It must be remembered also that the group in the party which has been designated as the small-farmer Democrats, which had supported Taylor and which had been the mainstay of Buchanan in 1890, was wedded to the traditional doctrines of the Democratic party. The more radical demands of the new Populist party aroused in it little enthusiasm. Under such circumstances, it is not surprising that those who sought to solidify the Democratic party repudiated the "heresies" of Populism and demanded a return to genuine Democratic principles. A newspaper in Governor Buchanan's own county expressed this determination when it said: "Two years ago we truckled to the Alliance, whose every breath is poisonous to the principles of Democracy. . . . The Alliance had its iron grip on the throat of Democracy then but now . . . the snake-like grip has been broken and Democracy has come into its own again."[15] The same idea was expressed by a West Tennessee paper when it declared that the governor would never be renominated on a broad Democratic platform so long as he favored the "isms and schisms" advocated by McDowell and other Alliance spokesmen.[16]

The fight in Tennessee centered around the Ocala demands which included, among other things, the discredited sub-treasury

[12] Hicks, *op. cit.*, p. 247.
[13] Summersell, *op. cit.*, p. 48.
[14] *Memphis Appeal-Avalanche,* April 14, 1892.
[15] *Murfreesboro News,* quoted in *Nashville Banner,* July 20, 1892.
[16] *Jackson Tribune-Sun,* quoted in *ibid.,* March 8, 1892.

scheme, free coinage of silver, and government control and supervision of communication and transportation facilities. There was an additional demand that, should this control and supervision fail to remove existing abuses, government ownership be resorted to.[17] A Memphis editor illustrated the character of this fight when he declared: "It is because Governor Buchanan has failed to declare himself opposed to the heresies promulgated at Ocala and ratified at Cincinnati, Indianapolis and St. Louis that he now has opposition." The governor could have made his nomination sure, asserted this editor, had he merely expressed his opposition to undemocratic doctrines. He pointed out that the organ of the Alliance, of which Buchanan was a member, supported the governor with the assertion that he stood upon the Ocala demands and the governor had not rebuked it. Hence, concluded this editor, "The Governor has destroyed himself by his silence and by permitting his position to be defined by the advocates of the Ocala vagaries."[18] Toward the latter part of April the governor broke a silence that he had maintained with increasing difficulty. Many of his Alliance friends conditioned their support upon his acceptance of the Ocala platform. Many regular Democrats were equally insistent that he renounce it. When he finally did speak, Buchanan declared that he did and always had favored the principles set forth at Ocala. He had been silent, he asserted, because the platform on which he was elected was silent.[19] This declaration, believed one editor, made it impossible for the Democrats of Tennessee to support the governor's candidacy for renomination since he was "running as a Democrat on a third party platform."[20]

More than a month before Buchanan declared himself on the Ocala "vagaries," a hundred prominent Democrats had met at Nashville for the purpose of promoting the candidacy of Judge Turney, the man to "save the Democratic party."[21] This meet-

[17] For a full statement of the Ocala Demands, see Hicks, *op. cit.*, Appendix, pp. 430-431.
[18] *Memphis Appeal-Avalanche*, April 14, 1892.
[19] *Ibid.*, April 20, 1892.
[20] *Idem.*
[21] *Nashville Banner*, March 11, 1892.

ing appears to have been attended by representatives of both
the old Democratic factions. Ex-Governor James D. Porter
presided, and, as a former president of the Nashville and Chattanooga railroad, undoubtedly spoke for the industrialists.
Another active figure at the meeting was Edward Ward Carmack, then a prominent Memphis editor and regarded as a
spokesman of the Harris followers. It seems probable that this
meeting marked the consolidation of the hostile Democratic
factions for the purpose of combating the third party peril.

Some three weeks after the Nashville meeting and before
Governor Buchanan had broken his silence on the Ocala demands, Judge Peter Turney opened his campaign for the gubernatorial nomination at Winchester. After declaring that he
favored the Farmers' Alliance as long as it remained faithful
to its stated purposes, he denounced the present course of that
organization as leading to the formation of a third party. As
proof of this tendency, he quoted from an interview of Colonel
L. L. Polk of North Carolina, president of the Southern Alliance, in which Polk advised Tennessee Alliance men to stay away
from the Democratic party. He also referred to a purported
statement of "sockless" Jerry Simpson of Kansas to the effect
that the Tennessee Alliance would enter the third party. As
final proof of the intentions of the Tennesee organization,
Turney called attention to a circular sent to the subordinate
lodges in the state by McDowell in which they were requested
to state their preference between the Republican, Democratic,
and the proposed third party. Replies to this circular, Turney
declared, showed that 95 per cent of the Tennessee Alliance
wanted a third party. In this speech Judge Turney came out
out squarely against the Ocala demands. He declared that,
"In the main they are unsound, impolitic, unconstitutional, and
undemocratic." The judge asserted his opposition to the protective tariff and stated that he had always opposed the de-
monetization of silver. He held that this metal should form a
part of the currency but that its adoption must be made in
agreement with other nations.[22]

---

[22] *Memphis Appeal-Avalanche,* April 5, 1892.

The views of Judge Turney proved acceptable to all factions of the party opposed to Alliance domination and many papers, which had not been hostile to Buchanan's claims to a renomination, rapidly lined up for Turney. This was particularly true following the governor's endorsement of the Ocala demands. After making due allowance for the "band wagon" proclivities of press and politician, there can be little doubt that the Democracy of Tennessee had little faith in the radical program of those who were forming the third party and its leaders had determined to purge it of all taints of heresy. It must not be assumed, however, that Buchanan was without supporters within the Democratic party. One paper, supporting the governor, deplored the fact that Judge Turney "had allowed himself to be made the tool of a certain coterie of gentlemen, who, up to the nomination of Governor Taylor, have dominated the party in Tennessee for the past fifteen years." It declared this to be the same group which had done its best to prevent the renomination of Taylor in 1888 and predicted that Buchanan would defeat it as decisively as Taylor had done.[23] Indeed, it seemed for a time that Buchanan might control the Democratic convention in spite of the formidable array against him.

Events, however, were taking place which tended to make Buchanan's position extremely difficult. A sincere, earnest man, he lacked the ability of "Bob" Taylor to state a position that could be interpreted by opposing groups in such a way as to justify their support of him. Lacking such ability, he sometimes took refuge in silence which at times became embarrassing to himself and his supporters. He also lacked the ability of Taylor to relieve the tension of such a silence. He was unable to throw his hearers into convulsions of laughter with a droll story, fascinate them with "unpruned rhetoric," or divert them with a rendition of "Rack Back Davy" on the trusty fiddle.

On June 22, newspapers carried McDowell's announcement of his formal withdrawal from the Democratic and his adherence to the new Peoples or Populist party.[24] Thus, Buchanan

[23] *Murfreesboro Free Press*, quoted in *Nashville Banner*, March 5, 1892.
[24] *Nashville Banner*, June 22, 1892.

lost one of his ablest supporters in the contest for the Democratic nomination as well as the man who had brought upon him the severest criticisms. A week after McDowell's announcement, the new party held its convention in Nashville. That body overwhelmingly defeated a resolution to endorse the administration of Governor Buchanan because the governor had refused to endorse the third party. In fact, he had expressed decided opposition to the third party movement when, in a letter written in 1891, he declared: "I am sorry to hear of any Southern Democrat going into a third party for it means, to my mind, the ruin of the South, turning it over to the Republican party."[25] At the suggestion of McDowell, the convention decided not to nominate a candidate for governor at that time, but to submit the platform, which it had adopted, to Buchanan and give him an opportunity to announce himself an independent candidate on the Populist platform. With this plan of action decided upon, the convention dispersed to meet again on August 18th.

The platform which the Populists submitted to the governor was along the lines of the Ocala demands. It called for free and unlimited coinage of silver as before 1873, and for an increase in the circulating medium to not less than $50 per head. It also favored a graduated income tax, laws to prevent dealing in futures of agricultural and mechanical products, direct election of United States senators, and the abolition of the internal revenue law. On the subject of railroads and telegraphs, it called for government control and supervision but failed to mention, as did the Ocala demands, government owner-ship in case control and supervision did not prove satisfactory. The platform also demanded that state and national revenue be limited to the absolute necessity of government, favored reduction in salaries of state and county officers, and in sweeping terms, insisted upon equal rights to all and special privileges to none. Among the planks not included in the Ocala platform were opposition to federal interference in state elections, abolition of the penitentiary lease system, and the prohibition of

---

[25] Quoted a number of times in the *Nashville American* and *Nashville Banner* during the campaign.

the employment of children under 14 years of age in factories and workshops.[26]

It is significant that the Tennessee Populists failed to mention the much discussed sub-treasury scheme. They also made no mention of the Ocala demand that national banks be abolished or that lands granted to railroads in excess of their actual needs be reclaimed by the government. Tariff reduction, which had been included in the Ocala document, received no mention by the Tennessee Populists. On the whole, it might be said that the platform adopted at Nashville was more conservative than that of Ocala. The radical demands of the West were tempered to appeal to Tennessee Democrats. The omission of any reference to the tariff is difficult to explain, especially in view of the traditional attitude of rural Tennessee on the subject.

With the formation of the third party, composed of so many of Buchanan's friends, it became evident that he could not win the Democratic nomination. On July 25th a committee from Montgomery County, representing a convention of "Buchanan Democrats" which had been held at Clarksville the previous Saturday, called upon the governor and urged him to announce as an Independent candidate.[27] He did not give his decision to the committee at the time but five days later withdrew from the contest for the Democratic nomination.

In his statement announcing his withdrawal, Governor Buchanan declared that he had always believed in the principles of the Democratic party and had likewise believed that the Alliance was a much needed organization. He asserted that he had been true to both organizations and had sought to reconcile all factions. The "Sky-blue bolters" or "radicals," as he termed his opponents within the party, had inaugurated a plan of disruption. They had resorted to unfair means to control the party machinery by exacting pledges and promises and by applying iron clad tests never before used in the party, he maintained. It was now evident, he declared, that the convention would be controlled by this group and for this reason he with-

---

[26] *Nashville Banner,* June 28, 1892.

[27] *Ibid.,* July 25, 1892.

drew his name.[28] This action was taken some nine days before
the Democratic convention met but after it had become clear
that Judge Turney would receive the nomination. At the time
there were some 314 delegates instructed for or favorable to
Buchanan while those for Turney numbered 761.[29] A rather
striking fact was the absence of Buchanan delegates in West
Tennessee where the Wheel movement had first flourished and
where the Alliance was strongest. This seems to substantiate, in
a measure, the claims of regular Democrats that Alliance men
had early decided to desert to the third party and had made no
move to help Buchanan. Democrats asserted that this desertion
by his Alliance friends and not unfair practices by Turney
forces, as the governor claimed, had been responsible for his
failure to secure delegates.

Buchanan's statement of withdrawal did not indicate whether
he would run as an Independent or a Populist, and this fact led
to wide speculation as to his plans. Some papers declared that
he was already a "Populite," others that he was a poor loser,
and others extended the friendly advice that he would make a
great mistake to run as an Independent.[30] Many hailed the governor's withdrawal as a thing to be desired since it cleared the
atmosphere and forced him, if he continued as a candidate, to
align himself openly with the third party. In so doing, they
believed, he classed himself with the enemies of the Democratic
party and white man's rule. One paper which, five months before, had expressed its satisfaction with Buchanan's "management of the state's executive business" and saw no reason for

---

[28] *Ibid.*, July 30, 1892.

[29] *Chattanooga Times*, July 31, 1892. The totals were:

	Buchanan	Turney
Instructed	241¾	681¼
Uninstructed	73	80
Total	314¾	761¼

[30] *Memphis Commercial, Memphis Appeal-Avalanche, Chattanooga Times,
Knoxville Journal, Clarksville Tobacco Leaf, Shelbyville Gazette, McMinnville New Era, Cookville Press, Marshall Gazette, Obion Courier, Obion
Democrat, Maury Democrat, Manchester Home Journal, Franklin Review-
Appeal, Fayetteville Observer, Covington Leader, Brownsville States-Democrat* and *Union City Commercial,* quoted in *Nashville Banner,* August 1-6,
1892.

violating the second term rule in his case now pronounced his withdrawal "a welcome riddance." On the whole, it declared, his administration had been "a sorry failure."[31] In spite of such brave words, there was grave concern over the governor's course among the more sober Democrats. They had little fear of his success in the general election but were apprehensive lest he draw enough from the normal Democratic strength to bring about Republican success.

The Democratic state convention which assembled in Nashville on August 9th was something of a formality. Buchanan's withdrawal from the contest had left no organized opposition to Judge Turney. The time was devoted largely to arousing enthusiasm for the party and its candidate, and accounts of the proceedings give strong evidence that the Harris wing played a leading part in this. Senator Harris, who had been absent from the three previous conventions at least, was present and made a speech as did Senator Bate, and Congressman Josiah Patterson, both closely identified with the Harris forces. The convention nominated Judge Turney on the first ballot although there were 57 dissenting votes scattered among Hon. J. Sparks, Benton McMillin, Governor Buchanan and ex-Governor Robert L. Taylor. Turney's vote was 1491.[32]

On national affairs, the platform adopted by the convention was merely an endorsement of the national Democratic platform and of the party's national candidates, Cleveland and Stephenson. On state matters, it failed to endorse the administration of Governor Buchanan and spoke on only three subjects. It favored abolition of the penitentiary lease system, uniform and equal taxation, and condemned all unjust discriminations by public or quasi-public agents or corporations.[33]

During a session of the convention, hand bills were distributed calling upon the friends of Governor Buchanan to meet in the senate chamber that evening. A number gathered and passed resolutions calling upon the governor to announce as an Independent. This action of the governor's friends was not unani-

---

[31] *Chattanooga Times,* August 1, 1892.
[32] *Knoxville Tribune,* August 10, 1892.
[33] *Nashville Banner,* August 10, 1892.

mous and some withdrew from the hall when they failed to block it.[34] Five days later Buchanan did announce his candidacy "in obedience to the demand of what I believe to be the majority of the rank and file of the Democracy, by whose suffrage I was made party standard bearer and to whom I owe allegiance." Along with his announcement, he put forward his own platform which showed unmistakably the influence of the third party program but which, in some respects, differed from the announced principles of Populism. One very important plank which the governor included and which the Populists did not mention was that on the tariff. He declared for "free commerce with all nations and a tariff restriction only when revenues from other sources are insufficient to meet the expenses of an economical government." He included two other measures of national policy which the Populists failed to mention but which appeared in the Ocala demands. They were the abolition of national banks and prohibition of alien ownership of land. Like the Populists, Buchanan made no mention of the sub-treasury scheme. In state affairs, the governor went beyond the Populist platform in declaring for a law providing for arbitration of labor disputes, for a liberal tax rate for the public school system and for a convention to revise the state's constitution. On the other hand, Buchanan did not advocate government control and supervision of telegraphs and railroads nor did he demand the abolition of the internal revenue law. He failed also to urge the limitation of revenue or reduction of officials' salaries.[35]

Attention has been called to the fact that the Tennessee Populist platform was more conservative than that of the national organization. It may be added that Buchanan's program was still more conservative. By failing to advocate government supervision and control of railroads and by his anti-tariff views, he had placed himself more nearly in accord with the traditional views of rural Tennessee. It should be said, however, that in his advocacy of free trade he went further than the Democratic party of his time had gone either in state or national platforms. Three days after the governor's announcement the Populist

---

[34] *Idem.*
[35] *Nashville Banner,* August 15, 1892.

convention reconvened at Nashville, endorsed Buchanan's platform as "in accord with the principles of the reform movement" and voted to support him for governor.

The state campaign of 1892 was overshadowed by that of Cleveland and Harrison. This was in some measure due to the character of the three chief candidates. Winstead, the Republican nominee, was apparently a very good man but played a colorless part in the campaign. Neither Buchanan nor Turney was able to catch the popular imagination or arouse enthusiasm among his followers. There was one campaigner for the Democrats, however, who never failed to stir a large following with his appeals for Democracy. Robert L. Taylor had been placed at the head of the party's list of presidential electors. A paper that had not supported Taylor in his first campaign, commended the choice of "Our Bob" as a "master stroke." Continuing it said: "Taylor will wean back to the Democratic party those who have been disgruntled and dissatisfied. He is the only man in the state who can do it, too, with any effect."[36]

In sharp contrast to Taylor's method of "weaning" Democrats back into line, the party press entered into a campaign of bitterness against the "Populites" and the Independent candidate for governor. Under the leadership of the brilliant and vitriolic Carmack of the *Memphis Commercial*, Democratic editors vied with each other in employing adjectives to describe the renegade Buchanan. The Chattanooga paper, which had found the governor's administration satisfactory earlier in the year, carried an editorial which may be taken as illustrative of the warfare conducted by the press. Within the space of a dozen lines the following terms were applied to the Independent candidate: "puppet," "figure head," "dummy," "weak," "narrow," "inefficient," "greedy," "brainless."[37] It was against McDowell, however, that the most bitter epithets were hurled. "Jehazy," as he was called, was denounced as the brains behind the governor and as the author of all the dangers which threatened white supremacy in Tennessee.

From the very first, Democratic press and orators declared

---

[36] *Chattanooga Times*, July 10, 1892.
[37] *Ibid.*, October 24, 1892.

that Buchanan had no chance of success and that his candidacy was only a scheme of McDowell's to throw the election to the Republican candidate. As final proof of this, a Knoxville paper obtained and published a letter from one Jo J. Ivins, editor of the *Knoxville Republican*, to G. W. Hill, Republican National Committeeman for Tennessee, and Hill's reply. In these two letters, ostensibly written for each other's view only, both these prominent Republicans deplored the fact that the National Republican Committee had been duped into paying McDowell $15,000 for bringing Buchanan into the contest. The letters set out all the details of the purported "deal" between McDowell and the Republicans. In addition to the $15,000 in cash that McDowell received, he was to be elected United States senator by a legislature controlled by Populists and Republicans. In return the Republicans were to have the governorship, possibly the electoral vote of the state, both delivered by reason of the split in the Democratic party, and the same legislature which made McDowell United States senator was to repeal the election laws and establish a system that would give the Republicans "permanent control of the State."[38] Needless to say, the Democratic press took the fullest advantage of the discovered deal. It mattered little that McDowell and Republican leaders denied the truth of the "facts" contained in the letters, that later Hill claimed to have made his statements only from hearsay, and that Ivins was denounced and driven from his editorial position by the Republicans. Democratic papers both within and outside Tennessee devoted much space to the "scandal."[39] The charge was not made that Buchanan was a party to the deal. The concensus of opinion was that he had been used as a "tool" by the "wily and unscrupulous" McDowell. Regardless of the truth of the facts discussed in the letters, and there seems to be strong evidence that they did not fall into Democratic

---

[38] *Knoxville Tribune, Nashville American*, October 23, 1892.

[39] *Birmingham Age-Herald, New York World, Louisville Courier Journal, Memphis Commercial, Memphis Scimitar, Memphis Appeal-Avalanche, Nashville American, Nashville Banner, Chattanooga News, Chattanooga Times, Clarksville Tobacco Leaf-Chronicle, Morristown Gazette, Franklin Review-Appeal, Johnson City Comet, Jackson Tribune-Sun,* quoted in *Knoxville Tribune,* October 26, 27, 28, 29, 1892.

hands accidentally, there was some understanding by which the Populists were to name the United States senator, according to McDowell's own statement.[40] Indeed, there were "understandings" between Populists and Republicans in a number of Southern states,[41] though they had little effect on the outcome of the elections, except in North Carolina.

An interesting episode of the campaign and one which probably did as much as any other to consolidate Democratic strength in the state was the Pulaski visit of General Weaver, Populist presidential candidate. Weaver had commanded federal troops stationed at Pulaski in 1863-1864. Reports on the baseness of his conduct at that time were circulated throughout the South. He went to Pulaski to meet his accusers face to face and deny the charge. Democratic papers urged the people of Giles County to subdue their righteous indignation and refrain from insulting their guest. This they did, but immediately after Weaver's speech a number of people met at the courthouse and adopted resolutions charging that he had, as military commander, levied assessments on non-combatant citizens, wantonly devastated the county, insulted old women and children and had made his name "a byword and reproach" to the people. The resolutions contrasted the conduct of this man who "posed as a friend of the down-trodden and oppressed" with that of other Union commanders at Pulaski and condemned him "not as a Union soldier but as a marauder and despoiler of the helpless."[42] Though General Weaver denied the charges and produced testimony to refute them, the Democratic press very naturally did not feature this in its discussion of the affair. Democrats could scarcely have found more effective propaganda with which to convince the wavering farmer of the dangers of Populism.

The result of the election of 1892 was not a surprise. Buchanan, supported by the Populists, ran a poor third in the state contest, though he polled some eight thousand votes more than

---

[40] *Knoxville Tribune,* October 25, 1892.

[41] Hicks, *op. cit.,* pp. 250-251.

[42] *Nashville Banner, Nashville American,* October 8, 9, 10, 1892. A cartoon illustrating this attack upon Weaver is reproduced in Hicks, *op. cit.,* p. 252.

the Populist candidate for president. Judge Turney, the Democratic candidate for governor, ran some 10,000 votes behind
Cleveland while Winstead, Republican gubernatorial candidate,
received some 900 votes more than the presidential candidate of
his party.[43] A study of the distribution of Buchanan's vote
shows that he failed to carry a single county and that in only
one did he receive more than 30 per cent of the total vote cast.
It also reveals that his vote was lightest in counties which held
considerable Republican population. This indicates that the
Populist strength in Tennessee, such as it was, lay in Democratic rather than Republican areas.

In the state's congressional elections of that year, Republicans and Populists competed in only two of the ten districts.
In those districts which were normally Democratic, the Repub-

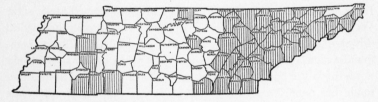

GOVERNOR'S ELECTION 1892
White—Democratic   Vertical—Republican

licans did not enter a candidate. This may or may not indicate
an understanding between the two parties.[44]

[43] *Election Returns,* MS, vol. in the office of the Secretary of state, Nashville, Tennessee.

	Vote for President		Vote for Governor		
Democratic	136,400	....	126,348		
Republican	99,600	....	100,577		
Populist	23,600	Buchanan	31,515		

[44] Election Returns, *op. cit.*

Congressional Dist.	1st	2nd	3rd	4th	5th
Democratic	13,207	7,815	15,984	14,010	13,709
Republican	17,890	18,952	15,035	.....	.....
Populist	.....	698	2,171	11,225	8,062
	6th	7th	8th	9th	10th
Democratic	15,645	12,113	13,038	14,334	12,164
Republican	.....	.....	.....	.....	.....
Populist	9,002	8,480	12,920	10,883	4,785

More study has been given to the two campaigns and administration of Buchanan than either the length of the period involved or the importance of the man in Tennessee political history would seem to justify. Yet it must be remembered that it was with him as a candidate that the agrarian movement reached its high tide in Tennessee. Though he was not a member of the Populist party, that organization polled its greatest vote while supporting him as an Independent. With his defeat in 1892, Populism rapidly died out. True, the party nominated Professor A. L. Mims for governor in 1894 and again in 1896, but in neither campaign was the party or its candidate an important factor.

Buchanan was the first avowed "farmer's" candidate and his nomination in 1890 was indeed a victory for the Farmers' Alliance in the state. Yet it is important not to ignore the Taylor period just preceding. Taylor, it will be remembered, consolidated those elements in the state's population which forced the nomination of Buchanan on an unwilling party leadership. Taylor's victory must be attributed to his personal ability to lead those elements. That of Buchanan represented the power of organization and of an aroused determination on the part of the farmers to right their wrongs by political action. It has been pointed out that Buchanan, to a great degree, continued the administrative policies of the Taylor administrations. The extreme ideas of western Alliance men did not appear in Buchanan's program as governor.

Not only did Governor Buchanan lack the ability to win a large personal following to himself, apart from the organization which he represented, but he also appears to have lacked the ability to harmonize discordant groups and to hold extremists of his party to his policy of moderation. Attention has been called to his inability to relieve an embarrassing situation with a joke, a fiddle, or with Delphic words. The Blair bill and sub-treasury scheme were equally irrelevant to the successful conduct of state affairs and yet both were hotly disputed in gubernatorial campaigns. The ways in which Taylor and Buchanan dealt with the two questions illustrate clearly the difference in their ability to meet such situations. When it is remembered that Taylor, in 1886, assumed the leadership of a party "broken into . . . factions" and "rent with feuds," the words of a Chattanooga editor are all the more significant when he said of Buchanan, Taylor's immediate successor: "He inherited the leadership of the party when it was compact, enthusiastic, confident, in the best trim for years in point of organization. He now lays down that leadership . . . whining that under him, faction has superseded unity, distrust has replaced loyalty. . . ."[45]

The editor's judgment against Buchanan, however, seems unfair in the light of the general political situation of his time. When Taylor placed himself at the head of the rural Democracy of Tennessee, there were only faint rumblings of the coming storm. Buchanan was swept into the lead by the first gusts of that storm which grew in violence until it threatened old political parties in all agricultural areas. In its final stages it swept over him and left him "a man without a party." In justice to Buchanan, one must again call to mind the circumstances of his nomination. It was due to the power of the Alliance and, in a large measure, to the work of McDowell. Renunciation of Alliance principles and the friendship of McDowell, the price of renomination, was repugnant to a man of Buchanan's character. Had he paid the price he would have been subject to a charge of ingratitude and betrayal of friends and principles. In politics, ingratitude and treason are major crimes. Taylor, fortunately for his career as conciliator, owed no such allegiance save to the rural Democrats of the state. He was never faced with the necessity of repudiating them or of renouncing their principles.

Finally, the agrarian revolt ran counter to economic and social conditions in Tennessee. Its program ignored traditional political beliefs in the state. One Democratic editor understood this when he appealed to the voters in these words: "When the farmers of Tennessee realize that they are being robbed of millions every year by an oppressive system of tariff taxation, for which neither the Republican nor the Populist parties offer any relief, they will realize the necessity of voting the Democratic ticket."[46]

---

[45] *Chattanooga Times,* August 1, 1892.
[46] *Knoxville Tribune,* August 11, 1892.

12

CHAPTER VIII

THE RETURN OF TAYLOR

INSTEAD of consolidating the Democracy of Tennessee, Governor Turney failed to inspire unity and enthusiasm to such an extent that his reëlection in 1894 was effected only by an unusual procedure. This failure necessitated the recall of Robert L. Taylor to leadership in 1896. In order to understand the political developments in the state from 1892 to 1896, it is necessary to scan briefly the personality of Governor Turney, together with some of the chief events of his administrations.

Peter Turney was 65 years old when he became governor and was distinctly of the old school. His father, Hopkins L. Turney, was a lawyer and had served as United States senator from Tennessee during the period 1845 to 1851. Peter, born in Franklin County in 1827, began the study of law the year his father entered the senate, was admitted to the bar in 1848, and practiced law in Winchester in partnership with his father upon the latter's retirement from the senate in 1851. Peter Turney, therefore, had been engaged in his law practice some twelve years when the election of 1860 precipitated the secession of the South. In that election Turney was alternate elector on the Breckenridge ticket, and, when the success of Lincoln was known, he became an active advocate of secession. He was a member of the convention which passed the ordinance designed to take Tennessee out of the Union in February, 1861. When the people of the state defeated this ordinance and signified their desire to remain in the Union, Turney was exasperated and led a movement by which the people of Franklin County seceded from Tennessee and sought to attach themselves to Alabama. The county proceeded to raise a company for the Confederate army, of which Turney was captain. Upon the seces-

sion of Tennessee, this company was expanded into the First
Tennessee Infantry, C. S. A., with Turney as its colonel. Colonel Turney served with credit, was wounded at Fredericksburg,
Virginia, and at the close of the war resumed the practice of
law at Winchester. He gained political prominence through his
opposition to the reconstruction measures of Governor Brownlow and when the Democrats gained control of the state in
1870, Turney became a member of the supreme court. He served
on that body continuously from 1870, was made chief justice
in 1886, and held that position until he became governor in
1893.[1]

Turney's activity in favor of secession in 1861 was in line
with the policy of Isham G. Harris, then governor of the state.
They both represented the extreme state's rights school of democracy. Turney, as a member of the supreme court, had little
occasion to take part in the factional fights of his party, but
there can be small doubt of his friendship with the Harris
group. Certainly, he was groomed by that wing for the governorship in 1892, and the papers of that faction supported him
most enthusiastically.[2] The press aligned with the Colyar group
was more restrained in its praise, though all were agreed upon
Judge Turney's honest and upright character.

In spite of Turney's sterling qualities, admitted by all, there
were those who questioned his qualifications as a party leader
during the campaign of 1892. One Middle Tennessee editor
voiced this attitude when he warned that the danger to the
Democratic party did not lie in the number of voters who would
follow McDowell but in the apathy among the rank and file of
the party. He said: "The expectation that Judge Turney's candidacy would reunite the disaffected elements and that he would
go in with a rush has been dissipated."[3] The accuracy of this

---

[1] For a sketch of Governor Turney's life, see Moore and Foster, *op. cit.*,
II, 241, and Allison, *op. cit.*, I, 115-116.

[2] For illustration of this editorial policy, see *Memphis Appeal-Avalanche,*
April 12, 1892 also numerous issues of *Nashville American* and *Knoxville
Tribune* of that year.

[3] *Tullahoma Guardian,* quoted in *Nashville Banner,* June 16, 1892. Somewhat similar views were expressed in *McMinnville New Era* and *Manchester
Times,* quoted in *Nashville Banner,* June 17, 1892.

view was attested by the fact that Turney polled approximately 10,000 fewer votes than the presidential candidate of that year, and 30,000 fewer than Taylor polled in the presidential years of 1888 and 1896. In the off-year election of 1894 Turney's total fell 9,000 below that of Buchanan in 1890, 14,000 below that of Bate in 1882 and 22,000 less than Taylor's vote in 1886.[4] This decrease in Governor Turney's popular vote cannot be attributed to the old factional fight within the party, for not within many years had the leaders of Harris and Colyar factions been in such accord. The explanation seems to lie in his inability to appeal to those elements of the Democracy which had been Taylor's main support and had nominated and elected Buchanan in 1890. The older party leaders had sought to reestablish the rule of the generals, colonels and majors in spite of the young men's movement. The man whom they selected was definitely associated with issues of the past. He was furthermore out of touch with the mass of voters because of his long service on the supreme court where successful political leaders are seldom made.

The first administration of Governor Turney afforded little of the spectacular, though, on the whole, it was regarded as satisfactory. His interest in the judiciary appeared in his first message to the legislature, for his first two recommendations dealt with that branch of the state government. He urged the creation of an intermediate court to relieve the supreme court of excessive labors, and to speed up legal processes so that capital might not be frightened from the state. He further recommended that the salaries of supreme court judges be increased. In addition to these suggestions, he believed that the office of coal oil inspector should be abolished or its fees greatly reduced, that slight changes in the registration law were needed, and that the road law was not satisfactory. He made no specific recommendations on the two latter question. He followed the examples of Taylor and Buchanan in urging a new penitentiary and this was erected during the Turney administrations. As a solution to the problem of competition between convict and free labor in coal mines, which had brought on the violent measures of Buch-

[4] See table, Chapter III, p. 71.

anan's term, he recommended state-owned coal mines where convict labor could be used in producing fuel for state consumption. His one suggestion affecting farmers dealt with the fence question. He believed that there should be some protection against stock running at large for those farmers who were not able to build fences.[5] One editor seems to have expressed the concensus of opinion when he pronounced the message "a plain practical document without flourishes or equivocation."[6]

Later in the legislative session the governor made another suggestion which was not acted upon but which caused considerable discussion. In line with the views of Taylor and Buchanan, Turney believed the state's constitution should be changed. Yet he believed a general revision of the constitution unwise at the time. He therefore suggested that the legislature call a convention which would be limited in its actions to those reforms designated in the call. He justified his position by the clause in the constitution which gave the general assembly power to call a convention to "alter, reform, or abolish" the existing constitution.[7] Needless to say, this proposal met with wide dissent.

In the early months of 1894 rumors became current to the effect that there would be opposition to the renomination of Governor Turney. Though a number of the larger city dailies referred to such rumors "floating around through the columns of the state papers and in political circles,"[8] it is difficult to determine the extent or location of the supposed opposition. A few papers were quoted as favoring the nomination of another, though there was an apparent reluctance on the part of the larger papers supporting the governor to quote or name them.[9] The charge was made that this opposition arose from disap-

---

[5] Governor's Message, *House Journal,* 48th General Assembly, Tennessee, 1893, pp. 172-176.

[6] *Nashville Banner,* January 27, 1893.

[7] Special Message, *House Journal,* 48th General Assembly, 1893, pp. 276-278.

[8] *Nashville American,* January 10, 1894; *Nashville Banner,* January 23, February 3, 4, 5, 1894.

[9] Among those papers mentioned as favoring the nomination of another than Governor Turney were: *Obion News, South Pittsburgh Statesman,* quoted in *Nashville American,* January 16, 20, 1894.

pointed office seekers, many of whom had been among the governor's most ardent supporters in 1892, and the editor of the *Nashville American* was named as the leader of the disgruntled.[10] It is a noticeable fact that many papers which had been moderate in their praise of Turney in 1892 were his staunchest advocates two years later while many of the Harris papers, which had praised him most extravagantly in his first campaign, were more reserved in their commendation.

It became evident early in the year, however, that opposition to Governor Turney's renomination lacked sufficient strength to be effective. The second term tradition was well established and the governor's line of action had given no plausible reason for a failure of the party to endorse his administration. Furthermore, in 1894 the Populist strength in the state was an unknown quantity and Democratic leaders felt the necessity of a candidate who could prevent an open break between the rival factions. The party press, therefore, with varying degrees of enthusiasm endorsed Turney's administration and demanded his renomination.[11] The silver question was becoming an issue in the state and the party was dividing along the old factional lines, with the Harris group favoring silver and the Colyar wing advocating the gold standard. Though Turney announced that he favored a bi-metallic standard as well as an income tax and tariff for revenue only,[12] the industrialist press continued its support on the ground that a governor's views on national

[10] *Nashville Banner*, May 16, 1893, *Athens Post, Clarksville Progress, Dresden Enterprise, Knoxville Journal, McKenzie Herald, Bedford County Times, Obion Democrat, Nashville Sunday Times,* quoted in *Nashville Banner*, May 20, 26, 30, June 7, 1893.

[11] For illustration see *Memphis Commercial*, February 18, 1894, and *Pulaski Citizen* quoted in same issue; *Gibson County Democrat, Giles Democrat, Knoxville Tribune, Shelbyville Gazette, Smithville Review, Clifton Enterprise,* quoted in *Nashville American*, February 2, 3 and April 28, 1894; *Fayetteville Observer, Manchester Times, Dresden Enterprise, Tipton Record, Martin Mail, Franklin County Leader, McMinnville New Era,* quoted in *Nashville Banner*, January 19, February 12, 22, 23, 1894. The independent *Nashville Banner* was one of the strongest advocates of Turney's renomination, insisting that it was certain and deserved since "Old Pete" had made a good and efficient governor and had gained the confidence of the people. The attitude of this paper is of special interest in view of the bitter criticisms later directed at Turney and his official record.

[12] *Memphis Commercial*, May 13, 1894.

issues were of little importance so long as his management of
state affairs was satisfactory.

Such was the situation when the Democratic state convention
met in Nashville on August 15, 1894. Hon. E. W. Carmack,
brilliant editorial spokesman of the Harris followers and ardent
champion of free silver, placed Governor Turney's name before
the convention and the nomination was made by acclamation.
The state platform was silent on the subject of silver, in spite
of the fact that ten of its twelve planks dealt with national
questions.[13] This was evidently a compromise and, as one editor
put it, "absolute harmony prevailed."[14] The prediction was
freely made that a united Democracy would score the greatest
victory in the state's history.

The campaign which followed was lacking in color. Governor
Turney made but one set speech between his nomination and
election day. This rather unusual course was explained later
on the grounds that his friends believed he would "win hands
down" and "thought not to tax his rather feeble physical
strength."[15] Evidently campaign managers accepted at face
value the announcement of one enthusiastic editor that although
the governor was "old and well stricken in years and somewhat
crippled by rheumatism," yet he was able to run "a mighty
swift race."[16] Undoubtedly, over-confidence had seized those
responsible for the conduct of the campaign. In spite of the
fact that the governor made but one speech, the state executive
committee did not announce its list of party speakers until some
two weeks before the election and this list included only sixteen
names, some of which were of no great prominence.[17] A striking
fact with reference to this list was the absence of the name of
Robert L. Taylor. The man who ten years before had caught
the imagination of the public as presidential elector, who had
united the party in 1886 and had further consolidated it two
years later; the man who, in Turney's first campaign, had been

---

[13] *Nashville Banner,* August 16, 1894.

[14] *Memphis Commercial Appeal,* August 16, 1894. The *Commercial* and
Appeal had been consolidated on July 1, 1894.

[15] *Chattanooga Times,* March 24, 1895.

[16] *Fayetteville Observer,* quoted in *Nashville Banner,* January 19, 1894.

[17] *Memphis Commercial Appeal,* October 26, 1894.

placed at the head of the electoral ticket as the only man able to "wean back" the "disgruntled and disaffected," was strangely ignored in the campaign of 1894. This failure to utilize Taylor's devotion to the party and his rare ability to arouse rural Democrats excites curiosity. Was over-confidence the sole cause? Could the fact that Senator Harris was to come up for reëlection a few months later and the further fact that Taylor was known to have ambitions to represent Tennessee in the United States senate have contributed to the latter's omission from the list of speakers? At any rate, Harris Democrats controlled the party machinery. Senator Harris was one of the chief campaign speakers, and "Bob" Taylor was not among Democracy's champions that year.

The Republican candidate for governor in 1894 was H. Clay Evans, a man of substantial business connections. He was a native of Pennsylvania and was accused by the Democrats of being a "carpet-bagger." As a member of congress, he had voted for the so-called force bill and was credited with the statement that the whites of the South should be "disciplined." Disregarding the Democratic attacks upon him, Evans made a vigorous campaign and, in contrast to Turney, spoke in all sections of the state. He confined his discussions to state affairs, again in contrast to Democratic speakers.[18]

When the ballots were finally counted and reported, Democratic leaders were astounded to find that Evans had defeated Governor Turney by 748 votes. The vote stood: Democratic 104,356; Republican 105,104; Populist 23,088.[19] A comparison of this vote with that of the presidential candidates in the state two years earlier reveals that the Populist vote remained practically the same, the Republicans increased about 5,500 and the Democrats lost slightly more than 32,000,[20] It must be remem-

---

[18] *Chattanooga Times,* November 12, 1894.

[19] Election Returns MS. Vol., in the office of the Secretary of State, Nashville, Tennessee.

[20] *Ibid.*

	Presidential Vote 1892	Gubernatorial Vote 1894
Democratic	136,400	104,356
Republican	99,600	105,104
Populist	23,600	23,088

bered that 1892 had been a Democratic year throughout the
country and had marked Cleveland's second victory, while, on
the other hand, a decided reaction had brought heavy Democratic losses nationally in 1894. Without a doubt, the national
tendency was reflected in the Tennessee vote, though editorial
"post mortems" gave slight importance to this. Before election
day keen observers noted the general apathy among the Democratic rank and file, and one declared that "apathy is more to
be dreaded than the Republican party.[21] After the election one
editor expressed the consensus of opinion when he declared:
"There was something in the atmosphere of politics that was
uninspiring to the Democracy, or there was a determined disaffection in the ranks."[22] A Chattanooga paper was more specific and attributed Governor Turney's defeat to his own infirmi-
ties, which prevented an active canvass, to the "spineless"
campaign of the Democrats, who dealt poorly with national

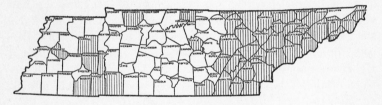

GOVERNOR'S ELECTION 1894
As shown by the returns
White—Democratic   Vertical—Republican

questions while Evans discussed state matters, to the blunders
of the penitentiary commission for which Turney was held
responsible, and to the fact that many congressional candidates
"hurt Judge Turney."[23] Among all the opinions expressed, it
would seem that a Knoxville editor described the situation very
well when he declared: ". . . the younger element are not crying

---

[21] "Progressive Democrat" in *Nashville Banner*, October 31, 1894. See also
Morristown Gazette, quoted in *Nashville American*, November 1, 1894.

[22] *Nashville Banner*, November 12, 1894. See also *Jackson Blade, Knoxville Tribune, Memphis Avalanche*, quoted in *Nashville Banner*, November
9, 10, 1894.

[23] *Chattanooga Times*, November 12, 1894.

at the rebuke given the old worn-out fossils who would lead the people to vote to keep them in office whether school keeps or not."[24]

The closeness of the vote, together with their complete control of the legislature, led certain Democratic leaders to charge fraud and to demand a recount by the general assembly. The delay of certain East Tennessee counties, strongly Republican, in reporting returns gave a plausible excuse for carrying out this plan. Imediately upon the suggestion of such a move, there was an alignment of the city press for and against the proposal very much along the lines of the old Harris-Colyar division. The papers of the latter faction, it will be remembered, had been most outspoken in their support of Governor Turney while those of the Harris group had been temperate. Now the tables were turned. The Colyar press denounced the proposed recount

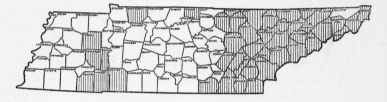

GOVERNOR'S ELECTION 1894
As revised by legislature
White—Democratic   Vertical—Republican

as a "steal" and, while admitting possible fraud by the Republicans in East Tennessee, declared that they were not comparable to those practiced by the Democrats in the middle and western sections of the state.[25] The press of the other faction, under the leadership of the *Memphis Commercial Appeal* and *Nashville American,* professed the desire for a fair investigation by the legislature with justice to both sides and denounced those party papers which assumed that Evans had been elected without fraud.

When the general assembly convened in January, 1895, Governor Turney filed a protest against the count and demanded

[24] *Knoxville Sentinel,* quoted in *Nashville Banner,* November 14, 1890.

[25] *Chattanooga Times, Nashville Banner, Memphis Avalanche, Memphis Scimitar* in numerous editorials during the winter of 1894-95.

that the legislature take corrective action. That body appointed
an investigating committee which spent several weeks taking
evidence and which finally reported in favor of the Turney
claims. On May 3, 1895, a joint convention of the Assembly
voted 70 to 57 that an "honest count" gave the victory to
Turney by a vote of 94,620 to 92,266, or a Democratic majority
of 2,354.[26]

During and after the legislative contest many Democratic
papers, aside from the ones already indicated, denounced the
proceedings. "Rank party animus" was said to direct the whole
affair and such terms as "the steal," "a count-out villainy,"
"shame and outrage" clearly show the attitude of many party
editors. One of these referred to the affair as "a great crime"
second only to the Tilden theft.[27] A Middle Tennessee editor
expressed the view of a large section of the party press when
he declared: "If any man actively connected with the counting-in
board is nominated for governor, it will be 'Katie, bar the door'
to the Tennessee Democracy in '96."[28]

Thus it was that Governor Turney began his second administration handicapped by the opposition of that section of the
party which had included his strongest supporters in the preceding campaign. A series of events intensified this opposition.
The amount of time devoted to the gubernatorial contest during
the regular session of the assembly necessitated the calling
of a special session almost immediately to deal with appropriation and revenue bills and other important matters.[29] Governor

---

[26] Election Returns, MS, Vol. *op. cit.* For a complete report of the
whole proceedings, see: *Contest for Governor of Tennessee, Complete Proceedings of the Joint Convention and the Investigating Committee, the
Evidence in Full and Arguments of Counsel.* The vote in convention is
found in "Report of the Committee on Governor's Election to the Joint
Convention," II, 268.

[27] *Athens Athenian, Hollow Rock Times, McMinnville Standard, Bolivar
Bulletin, Murfreesboro Independent Banner, Lebanon Tribune, Tullahoma
Guardian, Tracy City News, Chattanooga Press, Marshall County Sentinel,
Covington Leader, Manchester Times, Giles County Record, Bristol Cou-
rier, Brownsville States-Democrat,* quoted in *Nashville Banner,* April
27, 30, May 13, 15, 20, 1895.

[28] *Lebanon Tribune,* quoted in *ibid.,* May 18, 1895.

[29] Governor's Message, *House Journal, 49th General Assembly, Tennessee,*
Extraordinary Session, 1895, pp. 3-4.

Turney's failure to include in the call the matter of appropriations for the approaching Tennessee Centennial Exposition caused wide criticism. The revenue bill, passed by the extra session, carried a radical reduction of 33 1/3% in many privilege taxes as well as in the advalorem tax and the rate on railroads. There had been a surplus in the state treasury when this action was taken, but a nation-wide decrease in property values had reduced the state revenues by more than a half million dollars at a time when the expenses of the state had increased.[30] It was claimed that much of this expense was inexcusable, and the so-called "Paste Pot" affair furnished an effective illustration of this charge. According to this, two members of the legislature received a total compensation of $3,000 per year to paste coupons on cancelled bonds. It was pointed out that, under Taylor's administration, practically the same work had been done by one man and an assistant in five weeks time at a total cost of $150.[31] Faced by a large deficit, Governor Turney had found it necessary to call a second extra session of the legislature in September of 1896 to provide more revenue. This added to the criticisms already being directed at the governor. When the legislature failed to make adequate provisions to strengthen the state's finances, discontent with the administration became all the greater. In addition to the troubles mentioned, irregularities were revealed among certain state appointees, one of whom was a relative of the governor. Though there was no breath of suspicion attached to Governor Turney and though he promptly dismissed all officials concerned, the incident certainly added no prestige to the administration. Then too, in 1895 Turney had undertaken to see that the railroads of the state were assessed at their true value but had gone no further than to investigate the subject.[32] It is probable that this attempt had aided the industrialist press to discover the shortcomings of his administration and had sharpened its desire to give them wide publicity. In a word, it was evident to all, by the opening months of 1896, that the Turney administration

---

[30] Governor's Message, *Senate Journal, 49th General Assembly, Tennessee,* 2nd Extraordinary Session, 1896, pp. 4-6.

[31] *Nashville Banner,* January 14, 1896.

[32] See Chapter V, p. 123.

would pass "unwept, unhonored, and unsung." The importance
of this fact at this point lies in its bearings upon the political
situation and upon the state campaign of 1896.

This situation had many striking similarities with that of
1886. A mass of Democratic voters had expressed dissatisfaction
with the old régime by not voting two years before, and at the
same time there was an open breach between the leaders of the
two old factions which had been occasioned by the "count-in"
and widened by other events. In 1886 the Blair bill and tariff
were national issues around which the state factions waged
warfare against each other. By 1896 the Blair bill was dead
and there was little discussion of the tariff, but the silver question had become acute. The fierceness of the fight between the
"silverites" and "gold bugs" is too well known to require description here. It is only necessary to say that Tennessee Democrats were divided on the subject and this followed, in a general
way, the lines of the old Colyar-Harris division. The industrialists supported the gold standard, while the old state's rights
Democrats favored free coinage of silver.[33] So pronounced were
the differences on this subject that there was much serious
discussion of a proposal to hold two state conventions, for,
said one editor, should party leaders unwisely try to hold a
single one there would be "an inevitable clash between the free
silver and sound money Democrats."[34]

Indeed, Democratic prospects in Tennessee were so discourag-
ing in the spring of 1896 that a nomination for governor by
that party had little attraction. As one paper remarked, the
leaders had placed the party in such "uglyness" that considering the money issue, the "steal," and the unified strength of
the Republicans, no aspiring Democrat wished to risk "having
his boat swamped upon troublous seas." It added that only an
unusually strong man could win under the circumstances.[35]
Under such conditions, Benton McMillin was prominently men-

---

[33] Hon. Josiah Patterson of Memphis was a notable exception. He had
long been closely identified with the Harris forces but as a member of
Congress had supported Cleveland and, in the campaign of '96, actively
opposed free coinage of silver. Of course, there were other exceptions.

[34] *Nashville Banner*, January 13, 1896.

[35] *Memphis Sunday Herald*, quoted in *ibid.*, February 18, 1896.

tioned as the logical man to lead the party. McMillin was a member of congress where, as head of the ways and means committee, he had gained a wide and favorable reputation. His ambition to be governor was no secret, and party leaders had long regarded him as a "coming man." In January of 1896 McMillin spent some time in the state looking over the situation. By the 3rd of February he had announced his determination not to seek the nomination, in spite of his belief that the Democrats could easily win. One rural editor designated this optimistic portion of McMillin's statement as mere "idle twaddle" for, he declared, victory was only possible if the party could be unified, and that remained to be done.[36] The *Nashville Banner*, commenting upon McMillin's withdrawal from the race, called attention to his many excellent qualifications as a gubernatorial candidate and pronounced him an "experienced, energetic, and forceful leader." It believed that his withdrawal, after looking over "the lay of the ground," indicated that the party was not turning to him. Whoever gets the nomination, it declared, will be faced with "exceptional difficulties and embarrassments," and it added further that even McMillin, "good strong fighter" that he was, must have announced his decision "with a sigh of relief."[37] The prominence of McMillin, together with the wide interest in the Tennessee situation, gave his decision a national significance. Particularly did Republican papers outside the state comment upon it with the general agreement that Mc-Millin held to the old adage about "a bird in the hand. . . ."[38] These Republican editors interpreted McMillin's action to mean that "the Solid South is melting and these be solemn times for bourbon statesmen." Though time proved their optimism to be excessive, there can be no doubt that McMillin's action did indicate "solemn times" for Tennessee Democrats.

If the statement of a West Tennessee editor was correct when he declared in February of 1896 that gubernatorial candidates

---

[36] *McMinnville Standard*, quoted in *ibid.*, January 28, 1896.

[37] *Nashville Banner*, February 3, 1896.

[38] *Troy (N. Y.) News Banner, Albany (N. Y.) Journal, St. Louis (Mo.) Globe Democrat*, quoted in *ibid.*, February 10, March 7, 1896.

were "coming to the surface like suckers in a mill pond,"[39] he
might very well have continued his comparison by adding that,
unlike suckers, they easily took fright. As a matter of fact,
there were remarkably few candidates mentioned for the place,
and fewer still announced their willingness to accept the nomination. Almost no one was making an avowed canvass. One
disgusted editor was moved to remark that after McMillin's
withdrawal there was "nothing left except Jimmie Harris and
a few dried apples,"[40] and the Populist organ at Nashville
asserted that "none of the old party hacks or pop suckers" were
willing to take the Democratic nomination for governor.[41] Some
of the names suggested at this time were Hon. E. W. Carmack,
Chancellor T. M. McConnell of Chattanooga, Hon. Albert T.
McNeal, Hon. Ernest Pillow and Comptroller James A. Harris.[42]
Of these, Carmack and Pillow apparently never entertained
an idea of entering the contest, while McConnell and McNeal
definitely removed themselves from consideration before the end
of February.[43] Comptroller Harris alone, of the group mentioned, declared his candidacy and made an active canvass. One
paper set forth his qualifications as follows: A splendid organizer,
sound in state issues, willing to accept the party platform,
thoroughly imbued with reform ideas, and a young man with
a very fine record. As detracting from his availability, it pointed
out that he was the "ruler of the hierarchy of taxeaters" and
had been too closely connected with the contest beween Turney
and Evans.[44] In spite of the fact that Comptroller Harris was

[39] *Ripley Enterprise,* quoted in *Memphis Commercial Appeal,* February
15, 1896.

[40] *Bristol Courier,* quoted in *Nashville Banner,* February 10, 1896.

[41] *Nashville Current Voice,* quoted in *ibid.,* April 8, 1896.

[42] *Memphis Commerical Appeal,* February 9, 1896 and quoted in same
issue *Lebanon Tribune, Franklin Review Appeal, Columbia Herald, Ripley Enterprise.* See also *Nashville Banner,* January 13, 14 and *Murfreesboro News, Knoxville Sentinel, McMinnville Standard, Bristol Courier,
Hartsville Vidette, Clarksville Times,* quoted in *Nashville Banner,* January
10, 22, February 10, 1896. Comptroller James A. Harris must not be confused with Senator Isham G. Harris, so often mentioned in these pages as
the leader of the Harris wing of the party.

[43] *Nashville Banner,* February 22, 26, 1896.

[44] *Knoxville Sentinel,* quoted in *ibid.,* January 22, 1896.

believed to be in "dead earnest" and proposed to fight for the nomination[45] and in spite of one declaration that the majority of the party press supported him,[46] his candidacy aroused little enthusiasm. After a canvass of some two months he announced his withdrawal.[47]

If aspiring statesmen sensed the coming storm and sought cover, if wise old editors could see no hopeful signs on the horizon, if party leaders were perplexed and confused, no such doubts or misgivings worried the rank and file of Tennessee's Democracy. From hills and valleys, from the small farm and shop and cross-roads store came the clear call for one who had led the party ten years before and had led it to victory. One Middle Tennessee editor heard the call and announced it by the middle of February. The people are demanding "Bob," he declared; "they have called him from the mountains to the western border."[48] A neighboring paper expressed the same view in these words: ". . . the people are for 'Our Bob,' and when we say the people we mean the every day people. Not the so-called leaders of the party, but the rank and file, the men who vote. They are determined to have him and no one else."[49] In the early days of March there came from Cookeville the declaration that the drift of public sentiment indicated a "well-nigh unanimous" demand for Taylor,[50] and from Sparta came the prediction that county after county would instruct for "Bob" and that he would be nominated on the first ballot.[51] A month earlier, a Shelbyville paper had declared that Taylor could have the nomination for the asking and offered to wager that the party would nominate him whether he asked or not,[52] and another at McMinnville asserted that Taylor could "pull more votes" than any man the Democrats could name.[53] These and similar expressions from

[45] *Ibid.*, January 13, 1896.

[46] *Mountain City Tomahawk*, quoted in *ibid.*, February 18, 1896.

[47] *Chattanooga Times, Memphis Commerical Appeal*, April 1, 1896.

[48] *Springfield Herald*, quoted in *Nashville Banner*, February 18, 1896.

[49] *Lebanon Tribune*, quoted in *ibid.*, April 4, 1896.

[50] *Cookeville Press*, quoted in *ibid.*, March 7, 1896.

[51] *Sparta Expositor*, quoted in *ibid.*, March 2, 1896.

[52] *Shelbyville Gazette*, quoted in *ibid.*, February 7, 1896.

[53] *McMinnville Standard*, quoted in *Chattanooga Times*, January 28, 1896.

the small town papers in widely separated sections of the state left no doubt as to the will of the common people.

Not only did the rural press realize the attitude of the people, but the city dailies soon became aware of it and acknowledged it, generally against their will. "Bob Taylor is the most popular man mentioned," declared one, and another saw in the movement for Taylor "a popular ground swell." One announced that "instead of a Democratic party in the field, we have a Taylor party," and still another predicted that if the counties went "galloping" after him as they threatened to do, "Robert" would be unable to get out of the way.[54]

The demand for Taylor's nomination was certainly not of his own making. It was an open secret that he aspired to the United States senate and only awaited a favorable opportunity to seek that office. In the meantime, he was very much in demand as a lecturer in all parts of the country. The lecture platform was proving to be both a pleasant and lucrative substitute for politics and, for the first time in his life, he was succeeding financially. Under such circumstances it was only natural that he should refuse to seek an honor which he had twice enjoyed previously, and which, in the then distracted state of his party, might easily lessen if not destroy his prestige. When his name became prominently mentioned for the nomination in the early months of 1896, he made it clear that he was not a candidate and would not enter a "scramble" for the nomination.[55] As late as March, he announced that he was "in no sense a candidate for the nomination and would prefer to keep out of the race."[56] His close friends, however, let it be known that "Governor Taylor's great desire is to save the Democratic party and not himself," though they stated positively that "he would not enter a scramble for the nomination" and that if he should be placed

---

[54] *Knoxville Tribune, Chattanooga News,* quoted in *Nashville American,* April 2, 4, 1896; *Nashville Current Voice, Bristol Courier,* quoted in *Nashville Banner,* April 2, 8, 1896. See also *Nashville Banner,* January 14, 1896.

[55] *Springfield Herald,* quoted in *Nashville Banner,* February 18, 1896, *Chattanooga Times,* February 18, 29, April 1, 1896.

[56] *Chattanooga News,* quoted in *Memphis Commercial Appeal,* March 5, 1896.

13

at the head of the party, it would be by the action of the Democracy and not by his own efforts.[57] There were not lacking skeptics, however, who refused to take the ex-governor's declarations at face value. One of them noted that while "Bob Taylor doesn't say much, he keeps adding rosin to his bow,"[58] and another was of the opinion that "If the gubernatorial lightning doesn't want to strike something soft, it should not be fooling around Bob Taylor's inclinations."[59] With all respect to the opinions of such skeptics, there can be little doubt that Taylor was not eager for the nomination and that he had good reasons for that attitude.

From the beginning, it was evident to keen observers that only a very popular candidate could compete with the passive candidacy of Taylor, and this fact, in addition to the rather poor prospects of party success, no doubt influenced the early and rapid withdrawals from the contest. Particularly was Taylor's strength evident when county conventions began to instruct their delegates. These conventions met earlier than usual that year in spite of some protest from influential groups,[60] and the unanimity of their action was impressive. In the first week of March one West Tennessee editor noted that "several counties held conventions Monday . . . and all but one instructed for Bob Taylor."[61] By the 22nd of March Taylor's delegates numbered 371 while those instructed for Comptroller Harris totaled 54.[62] It is probable that this state of affairs had some weight with Harris when he withdrew from the canvass on April first. As convention time approached, the very unusual situation developed that there was no avowed candidate for the gubernatorial nomination of the majority party, although it was universally conceded that Taylor would be named by acclamation. As one paper put it: "The Democracy of Tennessee, in Bob Taylor's case, has done a thing unprecedented in its

[57] *Chattanooga Times*, February 18, 29, 1896.
[58] *Nashville Times*, quoted in *Nasville Banner*, February 18, 1896.
[59] *Chattanooga News*, quoted in *ibid.*, February 7, 1896.
[60] *Memphis Commerical Appeal*, April 1, 1896.
[61] *Jackson Sun*, quoted in *Nashville Banner*, March 6, 1896.
[62] *Chattanooga Times*, March 22, 1896.

history. It has nominated a man who is not a candidate, nearly sixty days before the convention."[63]

It must not be supposed that Robert L. Taylor had no opposition within the party simply because other candidates were lacking in the contest. There did exist decided opposition, particularly among the party leaders. One East Tennessee observer noted this fact while making a trip through the middle and western portions of the state. While there was a very strong sentiment for Taylor, he asserted, yet there was an "influential element" decidedly opposed to him.[64] Some light is thrown on this "influential element" by a West Tennessee paper which declared that the business men as well as other conservative and thinking people opposed Taylor and held that it was "nonsense to talk of popular demand for him."[65] Sedate editors sought to belittle Taylor's availability by referring to his methods of canvassing as a "jigety-jig entertainment" which might appeal to the "hurrah crowd" but which failed to inspire confidence among the thinking people. One held that the majority of the press opposed Taylor's nomination, while another thought the party in a "sorry plight" if "Bob" was the only man with which it could win.[66] Not all admitted that the party could win with Taylor and one went so far as to declare that his nomination would "set the Democracy back ten years."[67] Some of the more influential party papers chose to ignore Taylor altogether and his name rarely appeared in their columns.[68] Perhaps they foresaw the results and desired to maintain their party regularity with the least possible embarrassment. At any rate, it was not to the leading papers of the party, either of

[63] *Dyersburg Herald,* quoted in *Nashville Banner,* April 6, 1896.

[64] *Knoxville Tribune,* quoted in *Nashville Banner,* February 20, 1896.

[65] *Brownville States-Democrat,* quoted in *ibid.,* February 28, 1896. Similar views were quoted in the same issue from the *Knoxville Sentinel.*

[66] *Knoxville Sentinel, Murfreesboro Home Journal, Dyersburg Advocate, Mountain City Tomahawk,* quoted in *Nashville Banner* from February 14 to March 6, 1896. See also numerous editorials in the *Nashville Banner* during this period.

[67] *Knoxville Sentinel,* quoted in *ibid.,* February 6, 1896 and *Murfreesboro Home Journal,* quoted in *ibid.,* March 6, 1896.

[68] See *Memphis Commerical Appeal* and *Nashville American* for the winter and spring of 1896.

the Harris or Colyar faction, that "Bob" Taylor owed his nomination in 1896.

Governor Taylor's indifference to the nomination and, perhaps, the certainty of his receiving it, led him to maintain silence on the issues of the day. As has been stated, he never announced his candidacy nor did he enter upon any political discussions. The Populist organ was disgusted that he should be nominated "without a single utterance of his opinions on any of the great issues involved in the coming canvass."[69] While many of the party papers insisted that he express his views on the various issues, others ridiculed the idea that he had any views to express. It was said that perhaps a few Democrats, "one here and there," might want to know "Bob" Taylor's views but "most of them don't care about it for they know he hasn't any."[70] Taylor's strength consisted simply in his being Bob Taylor, declared a West Tennessee editor, who added: "Nobody seems to ask or care what Bob thinks on public questions. He might be for or against the Blair educational bill; be for protection or free trade; or be sound money or silverite; but most Democrats think he is good bait to catch the other fellow."[71]

While such criticisms and witticisms were being leveled at him, Governor Taylor went about his lecture engagements, saying or doing nothing that suggested his desire for the nomination or that would tend to widen the breach in the party. The similarity of his course at this time with that of 1886 commands attention. At both times the gubernatorial nomination and election meant financial sacrifice. In both years party solidarity seemed to be threatened by national issues toward which Taylor maintained complete silence until after the nomination was made; and then, he stood on his platform. Another similarity between the two campaigns suggests itself. In neither year did powerful opposition to Taylor make any impression on the public mind. Apparently, at both times it was agreed as to the man it wanted, regardless of issues or of his views on them. One editor saw

[69] *Nashville Current Voice*, quoted in *Nashville Banner*, April 8, 1896.

[70] *Knoxville Journal, Knoxville Tribune, Clarksville Times*, quoted in *ibid.*, April 5, 29, 1896 and in *Nashville American*, April 24, 1896.

[71] *Jackson Whig*, quoted in *Nashville Banner*, February 11, 1896.

this and summed it up when he said: "Bob Taylor is a platform all by himself."[72]

When the Democratic convention met in Nashville on May 6, the nomination of Taylor was a foregone conclusion, and he was given the honor by acclamation.[73] Hardly less certain was the fact that the convention would declare for free silver. The "gold bugs" and "silverites" had watched the actions of the various counties closely and knew how delegates were instructed. The one question about which there was doubt was whether or not the convention would censure the Cleveland administration. Here moderation prevailed and a compromise resulted in the omission of any reference to the Democratic president. Many party leaders were disturbed by the fear that the convention would make overtures to the Populist party, but they were relieved of this fear when the body "avoided several ugly entangling alliances."[74] Yet in spite of this indifference toward the "Populites," the Democratic platform clearly showed the influence of the agrarian agitation and contained several planks which smacked of Populism. Among such measures were: free and unlimited coinage of silver and the use of both metals for legal tender, and opposition to issuance of interest bearing bonds. It not only opposed the federal tax on the issue of state banks but demanded the abolishment of national banks. It declared for an income tax and insisted that laborers be paid in money rather than in scrip.[75] The *Nashville Banner* thought that the document lacked a "ring of sincerity," that its framers had at heart neither the best interests of the party nor of the people, and that it was "built on expediency props."[76] Another severe newspaper critic resorted to the measuring process. It pointed out that the platform occupied fifteen inches in its column of which only four inches were devoted to state matters. Three of these four, it declared, were used to express meaningless generalizations so that only one inch, or one-fifteenth of the platform, touched on the real issues of the state campaign. As to the candidate, it be-

---

[72] *Nashville American,* May 8, 1896.
[73] *Idem.*   [74] *Idem.*   [75] *Idem.*
[76] *Nashville Banner,* May 8, 1896.

lieved that Democrats could ignore the platform and elect Taylor on his record.[77] On the other hand, the *Nashville American*, which favored the gold standard but which was always loyal to the party, was relieved because the platform "read no one out of the party" and was so framed that it allowed every Democrat who earnestly desired to preserve Democratic supremacy "to turn out and work for Governor Taylor." Its view of the situation was that "regardless of financial questions, the people demanded Bob Taylor and regardless of financial questions, they will elect him."[78]

The facts, as they appear, do not indicate that Robert L. Taylor influenced the party to declare for free silver. Prior to his nomination he had not expressed himself on any issue and, it will be remembered, the county conventions which instructed for him also instructed their delegates on the silver question. On the other hand, the moderation of the convention which enabled "sound money" papers to support him while they opposed Bryan might be regarded as the result of Taylor's influence. This attitude was certainly in line with his acceptance speech. In this he came out flatly in favor of free coinage of silver, but, in the best Taylor manner, added that in such distressing times Democrats must "reason together." They must not deal in "intolerance and denunciation."[79] Thus spoke the man who, ten years before, had united the Democracy of Tennessee when the Blair bill and tariff issues threatened its disruption. Called again to the leadership of a distracted party, his task in 1896 seemed difficult if not, indeed, hopeless.

From the nomination of Bryan by the national Democratic convention at Chicago in the early part of July, 1896, throughout the greater part of the campaign, the state contest in Tennessee was entirely overshadowed by the struggle between Bryan and McKinley. As has been pointed out, the Democracy of the state was divided on the money question. As was natural, those favoring free silver supported the national ticket. Those favoring the gold standard, on the other hand, were not united in their

---

[77] *Chattanooga Times,* May 9, 1896.

[78] *Nashville American,* May 8, 1896.

[79] *Nashville Banner,* May 8, 1896.

attitude. Many, under the leadership of the *Nashville American* and Colonel Colyar, supported the ticket in spite of their disagreement with the platform and candidate on the money question. Others supported the ticket of the National or "gold" Democrats,[80] while the more independent favored the Republican candidates.[81] The national campaign developed along the same general lines in Tennessee as it did elsewhere, which fact makes a detailed presentation of it unnecessary here. Of much greater significance to this study are the developments in the state campaign, particularly those of the closing weeks.

As has been suggested, the gubernatorial contest attracted little attention at first. The Republicans of the state, like the Democrats, had declared for free silver and had named Hon. George N. Tillman as their candidate. Tillman was described as a man of "recognized ability and of personal worth and integrity, . . . a conservative and useful citizen, a careful observer and thinker and an earnest and positive advocate." One of his chief qualifications, it was declared, was the fact that he was not a professional politician.[82] It is worthy of note that throughout the campaign Democrats showed no disposition to attack Tillman's record, character, or ability. He made his appeal almost entirely on state issues. Taylor, unlike his Republican opponent, devoted the greater part of his attention to the national situation, arguing strongly for increased currency and lower tariffs.[83] When pressed to declare his attitude toward the gubernatorial "steal" of 1895, he made a reply which was so characteristic that it is worth noting here. "I was away out West when that count was made," he declared, "and do not know whether he [Evans] was counted out or not, but until I have proof to the contrary, I shall believe that a majority of the House voted as it thought right."[84] Thus his opponents failed to force him either to condemn or to approve the action of 1895, either of which would probably have caused his defeat.

Taylor's failure to discuss state issues, together with his old

---

[80] Notably the *Chattanooga Times*.

[81] Chief in this group was the *Nashville Banner*.

[82] *Ibid.*, August 13, 1896.

[83] For illustration, see speech at Maryville, *ibid.*, September 7, 1896.

[84] *Idem.*

campaign method of entertaining his audiences, furnished the opposition press with ammunition for its spirited attack upon him. One editorial is typical of the many that appeared in the few Democratic papers which opposed him openly. It called attention to Tillman's efforts to get people to think and contrasted them with Taylor's attempt to make them laugh. "The cap and bells" do not become the Republican candidate, it asserted, and declared that "Bob" was making the greatest mistake of his life in assuming that he could win with stale jokes.[85]

Though Taylor lacked the active support of any large city daily during the pre-nomination days, this was not the case during the campaign itself. Yet, strangely enough, the two papers which actively championed his cause were advocates of the gold standard and one of them bitterly opposed Bryan.[86] In spite of Taylor's decided stand with the "silverites," this group held that Democrats should support him. In the first place, they held it would be disastrous to turn the state over to the Republicans, especially since Taylor's currency views had nothing to do with running the state government. Secondly, they held that the sound money Democrats had not only helped to nominate him but many of them had been instrumental in inducing him to enter the canvass against his wishes. They held that Taylor's money views were known at the time he was nominated and that if they were such as to justify defeating him for governor, hard money Democrats should have opposed him before and at the convention. They believed that since that body represented all factions and since its action was the compromise agreed to, all gold Democrats were "honor-bound" not only to support the nominee but to work actively for him.[87]

---

[85] *Memphis Scimitar,* quoted in *Nashville Banner,* October 14, 1896. See also *Athens Athenian,* quoted in *ibid.,* October 26 as well as numerous of the *Banner's* own editorials of October and early November 1896.

[86] These papers were the *Nashville American* and *Chattanooga Times.* It appears that the *American* at this time was again under the control of the Colyar group and its policy was in line with that of Colonel Colyar's personal attitude.

[87] *Chattanooga Times,* August 14, and especially October 29, 31, November 1, 1896. The *Nashville Amercian* became active in Taylor's behalf around the middle of October and continued so to the date of election.

The attitude of the leaders in the Harris wing of the party
toward Taylor was such as not only to perplex the student of
today but to give rise to charges of treachery during the campaign. In spite of the fact that the nominee stood squarely
with them on both the money and tariff issues, they appeared
to ignore him or else to damn him with faint praise. The course
of the leading Harris organ at Memphis is illustrative.[88] The
paper supported Comptroller Harris for the nomination until
his withdrawal from the canvass. From that time until the convention it ignored Taylor. In its first issue after the convention
its leading editorial reviewed the work of that body and approved
specifically the plank on free silver as well as that on the gubernatorial "contest" of 1894 but strangely enough, it failed to
mention the party's nominee for governor who had been chosen
by acclamation. Four days later it did mention Taylor as the
best candidate "under the circumstances" and predicted that
"Bob" would make an old fashioned campaign "full of fun, frolic
and fusillade" and would have every Democrat in a good humor.[89]
Though the convention met on May 8, it failed to put Taylor's
name at the head of its editorial page until June 30 and, between
those dates, mentioned his name editorially but once or twice.
By the latter part of August, it was able to predict that Bryan
would receive the largest vote ever polled in Tennessee and
that "Bob Taylor ought not to fall very much behind him."
It stated that Taylor was making a great fight for the Democracy of Tennessee, that he was reviving old-time enthusiasm,
that on him depended the size of the Democratic majority,
and that he should have the coöperation of all tried and true
Democrats.[90] From that time an occasional editorial mentioned
the party nominee for governor. One that appeared on October
29th may be cited as typical. It declared that although the
Republican candidate was a good man, the people had nothing
to gain by electing him, that Taylor was also a good man, and
there was no reason why Democrats should not vote for him.

This practically coincided with the period during which the *Nashville
Banner* was making its bitter attack upon him.

[88] *Memphis Commerical Appeal.*

[89] *Ibid.*, May 8, 12, 1896.

[90] *Ibid.*, August 27, 1896.

On the day before election, it reminded its readers that Taylor had given up the lecture platform, which had been paying from $10,000 to $20,000 per year, to answer his party's call though he had no political ambitions.[91] After the election, however, when it became certain that the Democratic nominee had been successful, it contained no word of congratulation or comment. For nearly two weeks the silence continued, until a report gained circulation that Taylor would resume his lectures and continue them until time to take office. This elicited criticism of a strong character. It offended the paper's sense of propriety that the governor-elect of the great state of Tennessee should appear in the rôle of "a public entertainer going about the country making himself ridiculous for the amusement of such as desire to pay the price of admission." It was offended that the office of governor should be used as "an advertisement of a minstrel performance."[92]

It appears that the policy of this paper was in accord with the course of Senator Harris himself and of Senator Bate, both of whom were rebuked by one party editor for being too "sick" to aid in the state campaign.[93] In fact, the charge was repeatedly made that the "machine," synonymous with the Harris organization, was preparing to "knife" Taylor and that it had entered into a "deal" with the Populists whereby he was to be sacrificed for the presidential and certain congressional candidates.[94] This "treachery" would appear incredible, it was declared, "if it was not well known that the popularity of Bob Taylor had been a thorn in the side of a few old fossils who have fed on the party for years and who have burdened it with their insatiable greed for office."[95]

Whether or not there was any truth to the charge of a "deal" with the Populists, the fact was that 7,000 more votes were cast for that party's nominee for governor than for its presi-

[91] *Ibid.,* November 2, 1896.
[92] *Ibid.,* November 13, 1896.
[93] *Obion Democrat,* quoted in *Chattanooga Times,* October 25, 1896.
[94] *Chattanooga Times,* October 23, 24, 27, 28, 1896; *Bristol Courier, Obion Democrat, Murfreesboro Free Press,* quoted in *Chattanooga Times,* October 24, 25, 1896.
[95] *Obion Democrat,* quoted *op. cit.*

dential candidate. It was apparent on the morning after the
election that Bryan had carried the state, but it also appeared
likely that Taylor had lost. For two days the issue remained
in doubt, and it was only after the complete returns from the
rural counties were received that Taylor's election was assured.[96]
Although he had defeated his Republican opponent by only
6,854 votes and had run 7,423 behind Bryan, his total vote was
greater than had been cast for any other candidate for governor
within twenty-five years.[97]

In an analysis of the results, one editor pointed out the
obstacles against which Taylor had contended. They included
a united Republican party filled with the hope of victory and
possessing an abundance of money; the open or secret oppo-

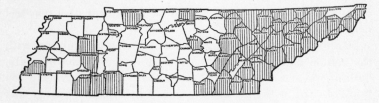

GOVERNOR'S ELECTION 1896
White—Democratic　Vertical—Republican

sition of so-called Democratic newspapers; active efforts to
widen the breach in the party. In the face of these, the editor
declared, Taylor had carried his cause to the people and the
result had been "the most glorious victory ever won by Tennessee Democrats."[98] A rural paper put it this way: "Mr. Taylor

---

[96] *Nashville Banner, Nashville American, Memphis Commerical Appeal,
Chattanooga Times,* November 4, 5, 6, 1896.

[97] *Election Returns,* MS, Vol. in the office of the secretary of state,
Nashville, Tennessee.

	National Election	State Election
Democrats	164,000	156,228
Republicans	149,000	149,374
Populists	4,600	11,971
Gold Democrats	2,000	

(Note: The count on the national election is approximate for the reason that the various electors did not receive the same vote.)

[98] *Nashville American,* November 7, 1896.

may feel a pardonable pride in the knowledge that he is the only man in the state who could have saved Tennessee from Republicanism."[99] After making full allowance for partisan ardor, one must admit that the editors had some ground for their assertions. Certainly, Taylor was called to the leadership of a party that had seemed hopelessly divided, he had fought a trying battle for the sake of his beloved Democracy, he had gone before the rural voters of Tennessee without the active aid of party leaders and had won. He had brought to a fitting climax his career as conciliator in Tennessee politics.

[99] *Gallatin Examiner,* quoted and endorsed in *Chattanooga Times,* November 9, 1896.

CHAPTER IX

TAYLOR'S CONTRIBUTION IN TENNESSEE POLITICS

A PROPER interpretation of the events recorded in the foregoing pages must take into consideration the decade in which
they happened, the political trends of the time as well as the
peculiar conditions in the state of Tennessee, and, finally, the
significance of Robert L. Taylor, around whom so many of those
events centered. Frequently these factors are so closely inter-
woven as to be almost indistinguishable. Yet a study of Tennessee politics during the period 1886 to 1896 leaves the impression that all three played a part in shaping political history
in the state.

The decade 1886-1896 marked the final overthrow of agricultural America as a controlling factor in the national life.
By its close the United States had definitely entered upon that
stage of its development in which industry and finance were to
have the dominant voice in its affairs. It must not be supposed
that this was a sudden change or one which took place within
the decade named. It was a long process which might be said
to have entered its first stages of success when the agricultural
South and West divided on the issues growing out of slavery.
It assumed tangible form when the agricultural West and industrial East compromised on Lincoln and the protective tariff.
It was definitely launched when the policies of Lincoln, then
sponsored by Andrew Johnson, were discarded as a result of
the elections of 1866. This has been aptly called the "critical
year."[1] The process continued throughout the seventies and

---

[1] Howard K. Beale, *The Critical Year, A Study of Andrew Johnson and
Reconstruction*, pp. 1-9, 225. In his introductory chapter Professor Beale
describes admirably the significance of the campaign of 1866 in the struggle
between industrialism and agrarianism in the United States. The full import

eighties. Acute agricultural distress through much of that time, together with the labor troubles which grew to a head in the famous Haymarket affair in 1886, were but symptoms of its growth. Although the labor troubles showed a tendency to subside after 1886, the former did not. The subordination of agriculture, so long dominant in the nation's life, required a longer time. The Farmers' Alliance and its political successor, the Populist party, were yet to do battle for the cause of the farmers. They were to try unsuccessfully to enlist labor in the fight and finally, in 1896, they were to suffer crushing defeat. Though the struggle continued after that year, the issue was settled.

Tennessee could not escape the effects of this change in the national life or of the contest by which it was brought about. The state was primarily agricultural and remained so in spite of results elsewhere. Yet industry had made its appearance and soon became a force that had to be reckoned with. Railroads, mines and manufactures grew in importance and many leaders in Tennessee, as elsewhere in the South, envisioned a new economic and social order like that of the North. They thought to attract capital and labor in order to hasten this proposed development and favored making conditions as attractive as possible, especially for outside capital. They believed that instead of fighting against the trend of the times, Tennessee should fall in step with the new America.

Nor did Tennessee escape the agricultural distress incident to the transition. Yet the broad basis of diversification upon which the state's agriculture rested, together with its comparative nearness to the markets, tended to lessen the intensity of that distress. Its farmers were not so burdened with mortgages, incident to over-expansion, as were those of the newer

---

of "revolution" in America is strikingly stated by Claude G. Bowers when he says, "A new order had been established, built upon the ruins of the old. The Jeffersonian Republic that came in with the revolution of 1800 gave way to the Hamiltonian Republic brought in by the counter-revolution of 1865-76. The tables had been turned." Claude G. Bowers, *The Tragic Era, The Revolution After Lincoln,* p. 538. For the same idea expressed a little differently but as interestingly, see James Truslow Adams, *The Epic of America,* pp. 273-274, 302-306, 310.

West. The crop lien system, so deadening to the initiative of small farmers in the lower South, had not become common in large sections of the state. The large number of small but independent farmers who had neither known great wealth nor suffered extreme poverty tended to stabilize the state's economic as well as its social and political life and to temper the results of the changing order. The absence of a large alien population as well as the numerical superiority of whites over the blacks, except in restricted areas, simplified the social problems of the transitional period.

It was inevitable that the change from an agricultural to an industrial nation should have its reactions upon the politics of the times. These were not so apparent during the seventies and early eighties, for the people still did their political thinking in terms of the great conflict through which they had passed. At both the North and the South, generals, colonels, and majors waved the "bloody shirt" with such effect that the minds of the voters were distracted from the problems of the present or the future. The force of their appeal held them in power long beyond the normal span of their generation. Because of this extraneous issue the politics of that period are chaotic and confusing. Seldom did one party control all branches of the national government. The national platforms of the two major parties were usually vague and subject to varied interpretation when dealing with such important subjects as the tariff and currency. When action became necessary it was full of contradictions. By the late eighties the Republicans could pass the McKinley tariff only through large concessions on the silver issue to western members of their party. In the early nineties a Democratic congress labored and brought forth the Wilson-Gorman tariff which a Democratic president refused to sign. Senator Sherman, Republican stalwart, fathered a silver purchase act which added immeasurably to the difficulties of President Cleveland in maintaining the gold standard. In the senate, protectionists of New England sought to fortify their system by granting large sums to Southern education and were supported in this by representatives of the lower South. By 1886, however, the dominance of the generals, colonels and majors was beginning to be challenged. A new generation was demanding its right to leadership. During the next ten years economic and social changes forced many to discount the "bloody shirt" as a campaign issue, and by 1896 political lines had been drawn on more modern issues. In that year the primacy of industry in determining national policies of government became an established fact. Though the agrarian revolt had cleared the way for many reforms in the future, it had failed to reëstablish the dominance of agriculture at Washington.

The factors which contributed to the political situation, as it existed in Tennessee in 1886, included some that were not peculiar to that state. The "damned Brigadiers," to use Andrew Johnson's favorite term, were still in the saddle everywhere, but in all sections their appeal to war memories was losing its power. The young man's movement was a natural reaction against the rule of the brigadiers. Rural unrest was a result that was to be expected from the policies of industrialism. Neither was confined to one state or section.

In Tennessee, agricultural dissatisfaction first became apparent among the small-farmer Democrats who had been largely without a spokesman in party councils since Andrew Johnson's death. This had found expression in 1884 when the "wool-hat boys" had "gone fishing" on election day and had thereby endangered Democratic control. That this dissatisfaction was an early expression of the agricultural unrest which later threatened the party by more direct action seems likely. By 1890 it had developed into the Farmers' Alliance and, under the leadership of Buchanan and McDowell, had dictated the policy of the Democrats. With the reaction against its influence under the Turney régime, large groups of the disaffected had followed the third party, while others resorted to the "fishing" tactics, with the result that Turney was defeated in 1894, at least on the face of the returns. In 1886, 1888, and again in 1896 the "wool-hat boys" had forced the nomination of Robert L. Taylor, under whose leadership they expressed their allegiance to the Democratic party.

No true picture of the political situation in Tennessee during the decade 1886-1896 can fail to show the factional rivalries of the state's rights and industrialist groups within the Democratic party. Whether these factions be designated as the Harris and Colyar wings, the survivors of the Calhoun school and old-line Whigs, or the "Bourbons" and "Mugwumps," they had existed within the party since the days when the question of white supremacy had dictated an alignment that was both artificial and difficult to maintain. The struggles of these factions over policies, prestige, and patronage had played a large part in Democratic as well as in state politics. Their rivalry was a factor in the situation at the beginning of the period under study and continued so throughout the decade. The presence of these two groups, together with the successors of the old Jackson-Johnson Democracy, created a diversity within the party which required the hand of a master conciliator if disruption were to be avoided. The decade 1886-1896 was a period of adjustment in which these three groups compromised their differences and adapted themselves to the changing order in the state's and nation's life.

The presence of a comparatively strong white Republican party within the state was another factor in the political history of this period that must be kept constantly in mind. Though it was never able to challenge successfully a united and alert Democracy, it was a very real threat at any time the Democrats allowed discord or indifference to weaken them. Undoubtedly, it had a decided influence upon the course of events. It tended to make Democratic factionalists more amenable to reason. All realized that unrestrained factional warfare, such as marked the period in one-party states, would have meant Republican supremacy.

At the beginning of this decade of rapid transition, within which the order of American institutions definitely changed and within which the people of Tennessee determined the character of their political life for perhaps half a century to come, Robert L. Taylor appeared for the first time upon the stage of action in Tennessee with a major part to play. For the ten years under study and, indeed, until the end of his life, he was to be a leading character in the politics of his state. For that matter, after death the story of him quickly became one of the traditions of the people among whom he lived. Necessarily, a study of this

14

period in Tennessee political history must accord him much space, and it would be incomplete without an evaluation of him and his influence upon affairs.

An estimate of this kind must begin by distinguishing between Robert L. Taylor, the governor, and "Bob" Taylor, the candidate and popular figure. Governor Taylor has been largely obscured by Candidate Taylor. In the former capacity, however, he showed many qualities which do much to explain the confidence reposed in him by the people. His state papers were pronounced concise and clear by those who had opposed him. In them he was said to have presented positive recommendations "firmly and squarely."[2] A study of those papers, as they were delivered to three different general assemblies over a period of ten years, leads to the conclusion that Robert L. Taylor presented important matters with clarity and treated them in a manner which showed an understanding of state problems. Not only that, but they convince one that he was progressive in his attitude and was determined to keep Tennessee abreast of the more advanced states, so far as its financial condition would permit and its legislature decree. In all his messages he showed a concern for the financial stability of the state and no less a determination that the burdens of taxation be equitably distributed among all the people. In the matter of taxation he at no time demanded special consideration for the classes which had elected him, but he constantly asserted that taxation of all property at its full and fair value would relieve those classes of the unjust burdens which they then carried. He recognized the difficulties involved in a satisfactory settlement of this problem and never hesitated to point out wherein measures adopted under his administrations fell short of the ideal he had in mind.

At all times Governor Taylor was solicitous that the policies of government encourage the development of all the state's resources. Though he had been elected by the agricultural elements and showed a concern for their welfare that was natural, he constantly urged the development of railroads, mines and manufactures. Perhaps his East Tennessee origin influenced him in this. These were not to be fostered through special favors from

---

[2] *Nashville Banner, Knoxville Tribune,* February 11, 1887.

the state to a privileged class. On the contrary, this form of wealth was to be encouraged in order that, by assuming its just share of public expense, it might aid the state in maintaining and developing its institutions. Revenue from this added wealth would lighten the burden of the already over-taxed owners of small real estate holdings.

Taylor's suggestions on the subject of public education are interesting. Whether one agrees with them or not, they certainly indicate that he and his advisers were acquainted with a trend in education which was then getting under way and which has since gained wide acceptance.

When his ideas were not acted upon by the legislature, Governor Taylor showed a spirit of toleration that was to have been expected from the man. Only in one matter did he show a determination to carry his point, one way or another. The confinement of children in the penitentiary along with hardened criminals excited his indignation, and when the legislature ignored his appeals for a reform school, he announced and executed his policy of pardoning the youngsters as rapidly as they were sentenced. This policy, no doubt, accounts in part for that large increase in pardons during his administrations which was the object of criticism by his foes and which earned him the reputation of being the pardoning governor. A brief review of penal conditions in the state at that time has indicated that Taylor's pardon record may have been an expression of the growing public consciousness of obligations to its criminal wards. The fact that succeeding governors went beyond Taylor in the number of pardons granted would lend strength to this view.

Whatever may be said of Governor Robert L. Taylor and his administrations, it is "Bob" Taylor, the popular leader, who holds the chief interest in a study of this kind. Indeed, it seems likely that it was in this capacity that he left his most lasting impression on the public life of Tennessee. Other governors could and did administer the affairs of state as well as he, but it is difficult to imagine another so fitted to meet the exigencies inherent in the political situations of the time. One must, therefore, inquire into the significance of "Bob" Taylor if he is to understand properly Tennessee political history of period 1886-1896.

With regard to Taylor and his part in the politics of his time, three facts stand out in bold relief and must be borne in mind when reaching a conclusion as to the significance of the man and as to his influence. The most obvious of these is his immense popularity with the common people. To them he had an appeal that was recognized by friend and foe alike. In strong contrast to this fact is that of his unpopularity with party leaders and with those who were so burdened with the seriousness of life as to be offended by his manners before the public. Finally, "Bob" Taylor was preëminently a conciliator and, as such, probably made his greatest contribution to the political history of his state.

Aside from everything else, the vote cast for Taylor in each of the campaigns he made as head of the state Democratic ticket demonstrates his popularity with the masses.[3] His vote in the two presidential years of 1888 and 1896 was, in each case, greater by nearly 30,000 than that given a Democratic candidate for governor in a presidential year within the previous quarter of a century. In the off-year election of 1886 he polled nearly 8,000 more than the most popular candidate had been able to do in any off-year between 1870 and 1894. When it is remembered that in two instances when he headed the ticket, Democratic prospects had been very poor, the size of his vote is all the more significant. When it is further remembered that in 1886 and again in 1896 he received the nomination without any active effort on his part and in the face of opposition by influential groups, the popularity of Taylor with the masses is beyond doubt. His admirers may have been contemptuously referred to as the "certain classes," the "hurrah crowd," the ignorant, the unthinking, or just the plain common people, yet they formed the voting strength of Tennessee's Democracy. They had supported Andrew Jackson, they had made Andrew Johnson, and later, they were loyal to Robert L. Taylor. They included the young men, eager to follow a young man. While they respected

[3] See Chapter 3, p. 71.

the old leaders, they themselves would solve the problems of the
new day.

Undoubtedly, Taylor's methods of campaigning and his ability as an entertainer had much to do with bringing about his
popularity with the great body of the people. Yet one feels that
this does not entirely explain it and certainly does not account
for the long continued confidence reposed in him. A study of his
views on public matters, expressed both as candidate and as governor, leads to the conclusion that he generally spoke the attitudes of the common man in Tennessee, particularly him of the
small farm, country store and blacksmith shop. His conduct of
affairs as chief executive of the state was such as to convince this
class that their confidence had not been misplaced. It is clear,
however, that Taylor's popularity as a candidate did not extend
to all classes of the people. Many of the more educated and
serious-minded could see him only as a shallow entertainer. In
their view, the "cap and bells" sat more becomingly upon him
than did public honors. They usually regarded him as incapable
of having a worthwhile opinion on issues of state if, indeed, he
had any opinions at all. They tended, however, to regard him as
a harmless rather than a dangerous variety of "fool."

What seems to be one of the most striking facts revealed by
this study is the lukewarmness if not actual hostility with which
party leaders and the city press regarded Taylor throughout
the period under discussion. It is true that, with few exceptions,
they gave him at least nominal support as party nominee but it
is equally true that he was never their choice for that position.
The explanation of this is a matter for conjecture since frequently, in politics, real reasons are obscured. In the first place,
it appears that he was never aligned with either faction of his
party. Though at times he would lean toward one or the other in
his positions, he was apparently never committed entirely to
either. He was never accepted by them as one of their own. He
did not "trot" with either of them.

The attitude of the Harris faction toward him affords an interesting study, particularly so since it prided itself upon its
regularity and usually held control of the party machinery.
Clearly, his nomination in 1886 was not of its choosing, though

its press did not oppose him openly as did many of the Colyar faction. During the "War of Roses" it was the Harris wing which was most active in his behalf, while the Colyar support was lacking in any semblance of enthusiasm. Their positions were reversed, however, when Taylor announced his Blair bill views to the legislature in 1887. At that time the attacks of the Harris wing became virulent and continued so through the convention of 1888. While these attacks were being directed against him, the Colyar faction came to his rescue, but everything indicates that this defense arose from a desire to combat a hostile group rather than from admiration for Taylor. In the campaign of 1894 party machinery and control was completely in the hands of the Harris people and it is significant that Taylor did not appear as one of the campaign speakers for that year. The failure to use the party's most popular campaigner at this time stirs curiosity, particularly since apathy among the masses had been manifest and all but resulted in the defeat of the Democratic nominee. Again, in the doubtful contest of 1896 when it appeared that even the popularity of "Our Bob" could not save the party from defeat, Senator Harris and his ally, Senator Bate, were both too "sick" to come to the rescue of the state ticket. It is important to remember that during this campaign the charge was openly made that Taylor was to be sacrificed by the organization in order to insure the success in the state of the national ticket and of certain congressional candidates.

Indeed, the coldness of Senator Harris and his close friends toward Taylor was ill-concealed—a fact which raises the question as to its cause. There seems to have been some justification for the frequent assertion on the part of Taylor's friends that his known ambition to be a United States senator did not fit in with the plans of either Senator Harris or Senator Bate. It will be remembered that in the senatorial contest of 1885 Taylor had approached near success and, in each contest thereafter, his name was always mentioned. It is possible that there may have been some basis for the assertion that opposition to Taylor was not unconnected with the "significant fact" that he might "become a lion in Senator Harris' path."[4] Whatever may have been the

---

[4] *Clarksville Tobacco Leaf,* quoted in *Nashville Banner,* March 3, 1887.

reasons, it is an obvious fact that Robert L. Taylor was never the favorite of party leaders of either faction within the time limits of this study.

As has been suggested, it was probably in the rôle of conciliator or harmonizer that Robert L. Taylor played his most significant part in Tennessee politics, and there can be little doubt that he was preëminently fitted for such a rôle. In fact, he seems to have been "to the manner born." One side of his house had been prominent in the Union, the other in the Confederate cause. He was eleven years old when hostilities began and was only sixteen when they ended. Prevented by youth from taking part in the great conflict, he had inherited the traditions of both sides in Tennessee. It would have been difficult for him to have entertained bitter thoughts toward either. Who could have been better suited to head the young men of his state in a time when they chafed at the over-long leadership of generals, colonels and majors? In all his appeals to youth, he never offended the passing generation. He would forget only the animosities of the late struggle. He would cherish and hallow the memories of those who had been brave and devoted to the cause they had espoused.

Not only was Taylor "to the manner born" to unite Unionist and Confederate in Tenessee, but his very nature and talent seemed designed to harmonize. His jovial disposition could harbor or arouse no bitterness. His political enemies always spoke of him kindly, almost affectionately, when he was not a candidate. His anecdotes excited mirth among his admirers but they left no sting among those who opposed him. His trusty fiddle may have offended the dignity of the more austere but even they, no doubt, often found their feet patting to the rhythm of "Rack Back Davy," and it is difficult to pat the foot and think bitter thoughts at the same time. Some contemptuously termed it the "mob" which gathered around Taylor and later voted for him. Perhaps so, but it was a laughing, singing, cheering mob, and there was nothing of the sullen about it.

If breeding and personality fitted Taylor for the part of conciliator, his political faith was an additional qualification. He was, above everything else, a Democrat. Grounded in the traditions if not the philosophy of Jefferson, he sprang from the same section, the same people and the same environment that had produced Andrew Jackson and Andrew Johnson. Forced from an early age to defend his political beliefs against the attacks of his brothers and other Republican neighbors, he developed a devotion to his party that was an outstanding trait of his character. The party was above faction and above the individual. If it demanded that he make personal sacrifice, he would do so; if it required him to modify his individual views to conform to its platform, he found it natural to comply. As the party nominee he could not think of departing from the platform. If it was positive, he was positive; if it was ambiguous, he was ambiguous; if it was silent, all the jibes or fulminations of interested factionalists could not force him to speak. To him the solution of all issues lay in the application of the principles of progressive Jeffersonian Democracy. These he defined as "free thought, free action, free labor, a free ballot, justice, law, order, the education of the masses, the autonomy of the state, constitutional government, one flag and a reunited Republic."[5] These principles could not be applied, he believed, when the Democracy was divided. As compared to these principles, the "isms" and "cisms" of the moment were unimportant and could be ignored.

Such was the man who, in 1886, was called by the common people of Tennessee to the leadership of a party threatened by factional strife between the old state's rights Democrats and the new Whig-industrialist group. His own popularity was such that he was not compelled to trade with either faction. His personality and views were such that he would force neither faction to actual rebellion. When a decided stand on an irrelevant issue would have divided the party, he "straddled." When it was necessary to take a stand, he did so with a tolerance that was calculated to mollify the opposition. One editor pointed this out by declaring: "Our Bob tells the truth but knows how to make it palatable."[6] Under his leadership, the Democracy banished factionalism and presented a solid front to the enemy. When others took command and dissension or indifference again threatened the party, he again responded to the call and won what seemed an impossible victory.

[5] *Nashville American,* September 10, 1886.
[6] *Memphis Commercial,* May 29, 1894.

Such was the man who rose to guide the small farmers of Tennessee in the earliest stages of the great agrarian revolt. In the states to the south there arose such agrarian leaders as Ben Tillman of South Carolina, Tom Watson of Georgia and Reuben F. Kolb of Alabama. All were apostles of bitterness, and the fights they waged resulted in political extermination of one faction or the other. In those states, however, the Republican party was impotent and Democrats could fight among themselves with little danger to white supremacy. Such was not the case in Tennessee as was demonstrated by the election of 1894, when only legislative interference kept the Democrats in control of the governorship. Such was not the case in North Carolina, which state Tennessee resembles as a daughter does a mother. Between these two there exists the strongest similarity, geographically, economically, socially, and politically. What happened in that state is suggestive of what could easily have happened in Tennessee had there been no "Bob" Taylor to assuage animosities and conciliate Democrats. In 1896 when Taylor was reuniting the Democracy, North Carolina fell into the hands of a Republican-Populist combination where it remained until 1900. "The period of misrule" which resulted from this combination, says one authority, "revived memories of reconstruction. . . ."[7] By this "costly and unfortunate experiment," he declares, North Carolina drove from power "the ruling caste of elderly politician whose conservatism had for years thwarted every progressive or forward-looking movement" and out of this experiment grew a rehabilitated Democracy with eyes turned to the future and not to the past.[8]

Happily for Tennessee, the transfer of the Democratic party from the old to the young resulted in nothing more bloody than the "War of the Roses." The agrarian revolt began thus mildly in Tennessee. It got out of hand when Taylor was succeeded by Buchanan and Turney and came near to producing results similar to those in North Carolina. This seemed a certainty in 1896, until the Jackson-Johnson Democrats from the rural areas of

---

[7] John D. Hicks, "Farmers' Alliance in North Carolina," *The North Carolina Historical Review*, II (1925), 162-187. For a description of this period in North Carolina, see also Samuel A'Court Ashe, *History of North Carolina*, II, 1202-1215.

[8] Hicks, *op. cit.*

Tennessee called "Our Bob" once more to lead them. Again the fiddle and the bow and "Rack Back Davy," again the droll anecdote and laughter, again good will replaced hatreds. Democratic unity succeeded factionalism.

Thus it was that Robert L. Taylor completed his task as conciliator in Tennessee politics. During his final administration as governor, America definitely entered upon its new order as an industrial nation and Tennessee adjusted itself to the change. During this administration the political control of the state passed definitely into the hands of the younger generation. The generals, colonels and majors yielded the power they had held so long. During this administration Tennessee celebrated its hundredth anniversary with a centennial exposition at Nashville. Delegations of visitors came from far and near and were welcomed by the state's "centennial governor," Robert L. Taylor. In these addresses of welcome he paid tender tribute to the Tennessee that was, but his favorite theme was the glories of the Tennessee that was to be. It was at this time that the state passed through its "era of good feeling."

It would do violence to sound historical or political judgment to ascribe to Robert L. Taylor those qualities which distinguish a statesman of the first order, for no great program is associated with his name. He did, however, save his party from disunion and, if North Carolina be an example, he saved his state from bitter experiences. He was preëminently the conciliator and remained so to the end of his life. In 1907 he at last realized his ambition to represent Tennessee in the United States senate, but three years later his party was again divided—this time on prohibition. It appeared certain that a Republican governor would be elected. Taylor was called from his seat in the senate to make the hopeless race for governor. Again the young men of the party were in revolt, but "Bob" Taylor was an old man. In 1910 he was, for the first time in his life, the favorite of party leaders and organization and, for the first time in his life, the people failed to respond to his appeals. But he had again shown his willingness to make personal sacrifices for his threatened party. In spirit he was still Robert Love Taylor, conciliator in Tennessee politics.

SELECTED BIBLIOGRAPHY

SOURCE MATERIAL

MANUSCRIPTS

Election Returns, MS. Vol., in the office of the secretary of state, Nashville, Tennessee.

Private Papers of Honorable L. C. Houk, in the Lawson-McGhee Library, Knoxville, Tennessee.

OFFICIAL DOCUMENTS

United States Government

 Census Reports, 12th Census, 1900, V, Agriculture, Part 1.

 Congressional Record

   Vol. IX, 46th Congress, 1st Sess., 1879-1880.

   Vol. X, 46th Congress, 2nd Sess., 1880-1881.

   Vol. XIII, 47th Congress, 1st Sess., 1881-1882.

   Vol. XV, 48th Congress, 1st Sess., 1883-1884.

   Vol. XVII, 49th Congress, 1st Sess., 1885-1886.

   Vol. XIX, 50th Congress, 1st Sess., 1887-1888.

State of Tennessee

 Acts

   45th General Assembly, 1887.

   46th General Assembly, 1889.

   47th General Assembly, 1891.

   50th General Assembly, 1897.

 Appendix to the House Journal

   45th General Assembly, 1887.

   46th General Assembly, 1889.

   47th General Assembly, 1891.

   50th General Assembly, 1897.

   51st General Assembly, 1899.

Appendix to the House and Senate Journal
    51st General Assembly, 1899.
Appendix to the Senate Journal
    45th General Assembly, 1887.

House Journal
        45th General Assembly, 1887.
        47th General Assembly, 1891.
        48th General Assembly, 1893.
        49th General Assembly, Extraordinary Sess., 1895.

Senate Journal
        .... General Assembly, Regular Sess., 1865-1866.
        42nd General Assembly, 1881.
        45th General Assembly, 1887.
        46th General Assembly, 1889.
        49th General Assembly, 2nd Extraordinary Sess., 1897.

Contest for Governor of Tennessee, Complete Proceedings of the Joint Convention and the Investigating Committee, the Evidence in Full and Arguments of Counsel, 2 vols., Nashville, 1895.

COLLECTIONS AND COMPILATIONS

Annual Cyclopaedia, 42 vols., New York, 1861-1901.

Bassett, John Spencer (Ed.), *Correspondence of Andrew Jackson,* 5 vols., Washington, 1926-1931.

Brownlow, W. G., *Sketches of the Rise, Progress and Decline of Secession, With a Narrative of Personal Adventures Among the Rebels,* Philadelphia, 1862.

Miller, Charles A. (Comp.), *Official Manual of Tennessee,* Nashville, 1890.

Porter, Kirk H. (Comp.), *National Party Platforms,* New York, 1924.

Rice, DeLong (Comp.), *Lectures and Best Literary Productions of Bob Taylor,* Nashville, 1912.

Richardson, James D. (Comp.), *A Compilation of the Messages and Papers of the Presidents,* 10 vols., Washington, 1896-1899.

NEWSPAPERS

Chattanooga Times, 1890-1896.
Johnson City Comet, 1884-1892.

Knoxville Daily Chronicle, 1886.

Knoxville Daily Journal, 1886-1892.

Knoxville Sentinel, 1892.

Knoxville Tribune, 1887, 1891.

Memphis Appeal, 1888-1890.

Memphis Avalanche, 1886-1890.

Memphis Appeal-Avalanche, 1891-1894.

Memphis Commercial, 1893-1894.

Memphis Commercial Appeal, 1895-1896.

Nashville American, 1884-1896.

Nashville Banner, 1884-1896.

Nashville Union, 1886-1887.

New York Nation, 1884-1888.

Weekly Toiler (Nashville), 1889-1890.

SECONDARY REFERENCES

Books

Adams, James Truslow, *The Epic of America,* Boston, 1931.

Abernethy, Thomas Perkins, *From Frontier to Plantation in Tennessee,* Chapel Hill, N. C., 1932.

Allison, John (ed.), *Notable Men of Tennessee,* 2 vols., Atlanta, 1905.

Arnett, A. M., *The Populist Movement in Georgia* (Columbia University Studies in History, Economics, and Public Law, CIV, No. 1), New York, 1922.

Ashe, Samuel A'Court, *History of North Carolina,* 2 vols.; vol. I, Greensboro, 1908; vol. II, Raleigh, 1925.

Augsburg, Paul Deresco, *Bob and Alf Taylor,* Morristown, Tennessee, 1925.

Baker, Ray Stannard, *Woodrow Wilson, Life and Letters,* 4 vols., Garden City, New York, 1927-1931.

Beale, Howard K., *The Critical Year,* New York, 1930.

Bowers, Claude G., *The Tragic Era,* New York, 1929.

Bradford, Gamaliel, *Lee the American,* Boston and New York, 1929.

Brooks, R. P., *Agrarian Revolution in Georgia,* Madison, Wisconsin, 1914.

Brown, W. G., *The Lower South in American History*, New York, 1902.

Buck, Solon Justus, *The Agrarian Crusade*, New Haven, 1920.

——, *The Granger Movement*, Cambridge, 1913.

Caldwell, Joshua W., *Sketches of the Bench and Bar of Tennessee*, Knoxville, 1898.

Cole, Arthur Charles, *The Whig Party in the South*, Washington, 1913.

Driver, Carl S., *John Sevier, A Pioneer of the Old Southwest*, Chapel Hill, N. C., 1932.

Dromgoole, Will Allen, *The Heart of Old Hickory and Other Stories of Tennessee*, Boston, 1895.

Fertig, James Walter, *The Secession and Reconstruction of Tennessee*, Chicago, 1898.

Fine, Nathan, *Labor and Farmer Parties in the United States*, New York, 1928.

Fleming, Walter Lynwood, *The Sequel of Appomattox*, New Haven, 1919.

Garrett, William Robertson, and Goodpasture, Albert Vergil, *History of Tennessee, Its People and Its Institutions*, Nashville, 1900.

Gettell, Raymond G., *History of Political Thought*, New York, 1924.

Hall, Clifton R., *Andrew Johnson, Military Governor of Tennessee*, Princeton, 1916.

Hicks, John D., *The Populist Revolt*, Minneapolis, 1931.

Jennings, W. W., *A History of Economic Progress in the United States*, New York, 1926.

Jones, Ira P., "Reconstruction in Tennessee," in *Why the Solid South?*, Baltimore, 1890.

Lee, [Captain] Robert E., *Recollections and Letters of General Robert E. Lee*, New York, 1904, 1924.

Lytle, Andrew, *Bedford Forrest and His Critter Company*, New York, 1931.

McCormac, Eugene Irving, *James K. Polk, A Political Biography*, Berkeley, 1922.

McGee, Gentry R. and Ijam, C. B., *A History of Tennessee from 1863 to 1930*, New York, 1930.

McVey, Frank L., *The Populist Movement*, New York, 1896.

Marshall, Park, *A Life of William B. Bate,* Nashville, 1908.

Merriam, Charles Edward, *American Political Theories,* New York, 1924.

Milton, George Fort, *The Age of Hate,* New York, 1930.

Mitchell, Broadus, and Mitchell, George Sinclair, *The Industrial Revolution in the South,* Baltimore, 1930.

Moore, John Trotwood, and Foster, Austin P., *Tennessee, the Volunteer State, 1769-1923,* 4 vols., Chicago and Nashville, 1923.

Neal, John R., *Disunion and Restoration in Tennessee,* privately printed and not dated.

Oberholtzer, Ellis Paxson, *A History of the United States Since the Civil War,* 4 vols., New York, 1917-1931.

Parrington, Vernon Louis, *Main Currents in American Thought,* 3 vols., New York, 1927-1931.

Pitts, John A., *Personal and Professional Recollections of an Old Lawyer,* Kingsport, Tennessee, 1930.

Rhodes, James Ford, *History of the United States from the Compromise of 1850 to the McKinley-Bryan Campaign of 1896,* 8 vols., New York, 1892-1919.

Rice, DeLong, *Old Limber or the Tale of the Taylors,* Nashville, 1921.

Schlesinger, Arthur Meier, *New Viewpoints in American History,* New York, 1922.

———and Fox, Dixon Ryan, *A History of American Life,* 12 vols., New York, 1927.

Simkins, Francis B., *The Tillman Movement in South Carolina,* Durham, N. C., 1926.

Speer, W. S., *Sketches of Prominent Tennesseans,* Nashville, 1888.

Stryker, Lloyd Paul, *Andrew Johnson,* New York, 1930.

Taussig, F. W., *The Tariff History of the United States,* fifth edition, New York, 1903.

Taylor, James P., Alf A. and Hugh L., *Life and Career of Senator Robert Love Taylor,* Nashville, 1913.

Thompson, Holland, *The New South,* New Haven, 1919.

White, Robert Hiram, *Development of the Tennessee State Educational Organization, 1796-1929,* Nashville, 1929.

Winston, Robert W., *Andrew Johnson,* New York, 1928.

PERIODICAL MATERIAL

Abernethy, Thomas P., "Origins of the Whig Party in Tennessee," *Mississippi Valley Historical Review*, XII (1925-1926), 504-22.

———, "The Political Geography of Southern Jacksonism," *East Tennessee Historical Society's Publications*, No. 3 (1931), 35-41.

Brockway, Z. R., "Beginning of Prison Reform in America," *Charities*, XIII (1905), 437-44.

Caldwell, Joshua W., "John Bell of Tennessee," *American Historical Review*, IV (1898-1899), 652-64.

Cooper, Waller Raymond, "Parson Brownlow, A Study of Reconstruction in Tennessee," *Southwestern Bulletin*, XIX, No. 1 (1931).

Folk, Reau E., Treasurer of Tennessee, "Tennessee's Bonded Indebtedness, Retrospective and Prospective," *An Address Before the Tennessee Bankers' Association*, Nashville, 1908.

Hamer, Marguerite, "The Presidential Campaign of 1860 in Tennessee," *The East Tennessee Historical Society's Publications*, No. 3 (1931), 3-22.

Hesseltine, W. B., "Tennessee's Invitation to Carpet-Baggers," *The East Tennessee Historical Society's Publications*, No. 4 (1932), 67-101.

Hicks, John D., "Farmers' Alliance in North Carolina," *The North Carolina Historical Review*, II (1925), 162-87.

Moore, Powell, "The Political Background of the Revolt Against Jackson in Tennessee," *The East Tennessee Historical Society's Publications*, No. 4 (1932), 45-66.

Nixon, Herman C., "The Populist Movement in Iowa," *Iowa Journal of History and Politics*, XXIV, 3-107.

Sharp, J. A., "The Downfall of the Radicals in Tennessee," *The East Tennessee Historical Society's Publications*, No. 5 (1933), 105-24.

White, Melvin Johnson, "Populism in Louisiana During the Nineties," *Mississippi Valley Historical Review*, V (1918-1919), 3-19.

Unpublished Studies

Hargis, Robert Loren, *The Know Nothing Party in Tennessee,* M. A. Thesis, Vanderbilt University, 1931.

Mahoney, John Hascue, *Apportionments and Gerrymandering in Tennessee Since 1870,* M. A. Thesis, George Peabody College for Teachers, 1930.

Robertson, Mary Emely, *Tennessee's Attitude Toward Secession,* M. A. Thesis, Vanderbilt University, 1929.

Sharp, Joseph A., *The Farmers' Alliance and Tennessee Politics, 1890-1892,* M. A. Thesis, University of Tennessee, 1931.

Summersell, Charles Grayson, *A Life of Reuben F. Kolb,* M. A. Thesis, University of Alabama, 1930.

Westphal, Corinne, *The Farmers' Alliance in Tennessee,* M. A. Thesis, Vanderbilt University, 1929.

INDEX

titude on contested election, 186;
opposes Turney, 188; significance
in state politics, 209, 216

(2) Harris (referred to also as
the Calhoun school, state's rights
wing, "machine crowd," and Bourbons) formation of, 8; favors secession, 9; post-war views of, 14-15;
revolt against, 32; in senatorial
contests, 1, 16, 56; opposes Blair
bill, 83 ff.; various attitudes toward
Taylor, 88 ff., 195-96, 201-3, 213-15;
views on tariff, 97 ff.; supports
Josiah Patterson, 139-40, 143-44;
sponors Turney, 165, 179-80; as-
sumes leadership, 170, 183; opposes
McDowell, 161; cools toward Turney, 182; views on currency issue,
182, 189; attitude toward contested
election, 186; purported "deal"
with Populists, 202-3; sginificance
in state politics, 209, 216

(3) Rural Democrats (referred to
also as the small-farmer group, the
old Jackson-Johnson Democracy,
"wool hat boys," and Jackson's
followers)
Jackson's followers, 1; views of, 2,
3; dominance broken, 4; led by Polk
and Johnson, 6-8; views on secession, 9; post-war views of, 15 apa-
thetic, 23; becomes articulate, 32;
supports Taylor, 32, 34, 42 ff., 65-66,
212-13, 217-18; Taylor's appeal to,
69; elects Taylor, 72; Taylor represents 103; influence on agrarian
revolt, 156-57, 163; Taylor con-
solidates, 176; nominates Buchanan, 176; Turney fails to inspire,
180; dissatisfaction among; 208;
significance in state politics, 209,
212

Democractic party, factional rivalries
in, 23, 38, 47, 68, 140, 143-44, 182,
208-9, 216; disruption threatened,
23-24; harmony program, 25 ff.,
104; gubernatorial candidates in
1886, 34 ff.; convention of 1886, 45
ff.; platform of 1886, 59-60; vic-
torious, 70-72, 95-96, 148, 175,
184 ff., 203; national platform on
Blair bill, 76-77, 87; state platform on Blair bill, 83, 87; factional
fight on Blair bill, 83 ff.; state platform of 1888, 94; national divisions

on tariff, 96-97, 207; state divisions
on tariff, 97 ff.; power of conservatives in, 132-33; agrarians seek
control of, 132-34, 138; Republican
strength modifies factional fight in,
134; convention and platform of
1890, 143-45; agrarians opposed by
Southern leaders of, 162-63; adopts
Populist principles in South, 162-
63; factions consolidate, 164-66;
convention and platform of 1892,
170; Turney fails to unify, 178;
convention and platform of 1894,
183; apparent defeat of, 184-86;
"counted in," 186-87; desperate
situation of, 189 ff.; convention and
platform of 1896, 197-98; influence
of Populism on, 197; divisions on
currency issue, 198-99; 207; defeat
of 1910, 218. See also Cleveland,
Grover; Currency; Corporations.

Dibrell, George B., industrialist, 19;
gubernatorial candidacy of, 34 n.,
36-37, 45-47. See also Democratic
factions, Colyar

Diversification, economic effect on
agrarian movement, 134

East, Edward H., gubernatorial
possibility, 58 n

Education, public, party platforms
on, 59-60; as state issue, 68; Blair
bill's provisions for, 76; in South,
79; federal aid to, discussed, 79 ff.;
Georgia legislature on, 81-82; Taylor's views on federal aid to, 84 ff.,
88-89; Taylor urges better system
of, 105; during Bate's administration, 115; Taylor's views and recommendations on, 115-17, 211;
Public School Officers Association
formed, 116; Democratic-Alliance
policies toward, 138, 145; Buch-
anans views on, 149, 171

Educational test. See Election laws

Election contests, that of 1896, 127;
that of 1894, 186-87, 191, 199

Election laws, party platforms on,
60; educational test opposed by
Taylor and Buchanan, 126, 154;
Taylor's recommendations on and
acts passed, 126-28; attitude on
Force bill, 149-50, 183; Buchanan's
suggestions on, 154; Populist plat-

form on, 167; Republican-Populist "deal" contemplates change in, 173; Turney's views on, 180

Election results, for 1886, 70-72; from 1876 to 1894, 71; for 1888, 95-96; for 1878, 1880, 1882, 136; for 1890, 148; for 1892, 174-75, 180; for 1894, 184 ff.; for 1896, 203

Enloe, B. A., gubernatorial possibility, 34 n

Evans, H. Clay, Republican gubernatorial candidate, 58 n., 183, 185; supports Force bill, 183; elected on face of returns, 183-84; "counted out," 186-87

Farmers' Alliance. See Alliance.

Federal dollars, matching, principle introduced, 74-76; Isham G. Harris opposes, 81

Fee system. See Courts

Felton, William H., Agrarian leader in Georgia, 133

Fence law, Turney's views on, 181

Florida, education in, 79; Populist principles in, 163

Foster, Ephraim H., anti-Jackson leader, 4

Franklin, Taylor's debate at, 61, 64

Franklin County, Turney born in, 178; secedes from state, 178

Fraternal campaign. See War of the Roses

Frierson, R. P., gubernatorial possibility, 34 n

Frontier, political views of, 3

Futures, Populists oppose dealing in, 167

Gates, Robert, gubernatorial possibility, 34 n

George Peabody College for Teachers, Taylor's suggestion regarding, 117-18

Georgia, Indian controversy, 3; education in, 79, 81-82; Populist principles in, 163. See also Brown, Joseph E.; Colquitt, Alfred H.; Felton, William H.; Gordon, John B.; Watson, Tom

Gibson, Henry R., gubernatorial possibility, 58 n

Gordon, John B., in Georgia politics, 18, 33

Granger movement, anti-railroad sentiment, 29; strength in state, 135

Grant University. See Athens University

Greenback party, strength in state, 135-36

Hamilton, T. A., gubernatorial possibility, 58 n

Hampton, Wade, views on Blair bill, 80

Happy Valley, Taylor born in, 52

Harris, Isham G., represents cotton influence, 8; favors secession, 9; returns to leadership, 15-16; on state debt issue, 20-21; leads Democratic faction, 21, 170; discusses Blair bill, 81-82; leadership challenged, 83; Turney adherent of, 179; attitudes toward Taylor, 91, 184, 202-3, 214-15. See also Democratic factions, Harris; Federal dollars, matching

Harris, James A., gubernatorial aspirant, 191-92, 194, 201

Harrison, Benjamin, relation to national surplus, 82; presidential campaigns, 95, 172

Hawkins, Alvin, elected governor, 20; fails to settle state debt issue, 20; defeated, 21; Republican gubernatorial possibility, 58 n.; pardons granted by, 108

Hayes, Rutherford B., vote in state, 24

Haymarket affair, 206

Haynes, David, Taylor's grandfather, 51

Haynes, Landon C., Taylor's uncle, 51; Confederate senator, 51, 66; influence on Taylor, 53; florid orator, 62

Health, Board of, Taylor recommends, 129; Buchanan endorses, 150

Henderson, C. C., reminisces on break between Buchanan and Democratic papers, 160-61 n

Henderson, W. A., gubernatorial aspirant, 34 n; sectional support of, 45-47

126830